CHICAGO POLICE DEPARTMENT

Pictorial History

TURNER PUBLISHING COMPANY
Paducah, Kentucky

Table of Contents

TURNER PUBLISHING COMPANY
Publishers of America's History
412 Broadway • P.O. Box 3101
Paducah, Kentucky 42002-3101
(270) 443-0121

Publishing Consultant: Keith R. Steele
Project Editor: Charlotte Harris
Designer: Susan L. Harwood

Library of Congress Control No. 2001107857
ISBN: 1-56311-815-7

Printed in the United States of America.
Additional copies may be purchased directly from the publisher.
Limited Edition

CHICAGO POLICE DEPARTMENT
MISSION STATEMENT

THE CHICAGO POLICE DEPARTMENT, AS PART OF, AND EMPOWERED BY THE COMMUNITY, IS COMMITTED TO PROTECT THE LIVES, PROPERTY AND RIGHTS OF ALL PEOPLE, TO MAINTAIN ORDER, AND TO ENFORCE THE LAW IMPARTIALLY.

WE WILL PROVIDE QUALITY POLICE SERVICES IN PARTNERSHIP WITH OTHER MEMBERS OF THE COMMUNITY.

TO FULFILL OUR MISSION, WE WILL STRIVE TO ATTAIN THE HIGHEST DEGREE OF ETHICAL BEHAVIOR AND PROFESSIONAL CONDUCT AT ALL TIMES.

PUBLISHERS' MESSAGE

Dave Turner, Founder (left) and Keith Steele, Publishing Consultant

In keeping with our commitment to preserve America's history, Turner Publishing Company is proud to be the publisher of this volume on the Chicago Police. We extend our sincere appreciation to Mark Donahue, Bill Nolan, and the Chicago Fraternal Order of Police for their cooperation in producing this book. A special thank-you is also extended to the individuals who submitted photographs and additional materials for the book, creating an outstanding tribute to the Chicago Police.

A police officer's life is filled with hardship and danger. Sacrifices made by police officers not only for the profession but for the people they serve are too many to detail, and rewards often come at a price. Turner Publishing is proud to salute those individuals who daily choose to serve their country, risking their lives in the process. We admire your commitment to the safety of America. Let us never forget their courage and bravery.

Dave Turner, Founder
Turner Publishing Company

Keith Steele, Publishing Consultant
Turner Publishing Company

A Part of America Died

Somebody killed a police officer today and

A part of America died.

A piece of our country he swore to protect

Will be buried with him at his side.

The suspect who shot him will stand up in court,

With counsel demanding his rights,

While a young widowed mother must work for her kids

And spend many long, lonely nights.

The beat that he walked was a battlefield too,

Just as if he'd gone off to war.

Though the flag of our nation won't fly half-mast,

To his name, they will add a gold star.

Yes, somebody killed a police officer today,

It happened in your town or mine.

While we slept in comfort behind our locked doors,

A cop put his life on the line.

Now his ghost walks a beat on a dark city street,

And he stands at each new rookie's side.

He answered the call, and gave us his all,

And A Part of America Died.

~ Author Unknown ~

Dad Retires; Son to Wear Police Star

Policeman Frank J. Fitzgerald has retired, but his star and star number will still be active.

They will be worn by his son, Albert, a Woodlawn policeman with 12 years on the force.

Fitzgerald, 59, joined the force in 1929. He spent 20 years at Woodlawn station and the last seven years at the Detective Bureau.

He earned seven creditable mentions and com-...

'56 RETIREMENTS — CHICAGO POLICE DEPARTMENT

NAME	RANK	DIST.	DATE OF RETIREMENT
...eremiah	Sgt.		June 5
...ohn J.	Ptlmn.		June 7
...nk E.	Ptlmn.		...e 10
...rd J.	Ptlmn.		
...amin G.	Ptlmn.		
...Frank A.	Ptlmn.		
...E.	Ptlmn.		
...k J.	Ptlmn.		
...B.	Ca...		
...w W.	Pt...		
	P...		
	C...		
...as H.	I...		
...F.			
...liam E.			
...ael			
...as J.			
...ward			
	R.		
	...am F.		
	...s J.		
	...J.		
...F.			

STATION 9 NOTES

EAST SIDE

Capt. John T. McAvoy
Commanding

THE crime fighting man power of the 9th district has been enhanced by the addition of seven probationary patrolmen from the police training school. We extend to them the best wishes of a long successful career in the finest Police Department in the world.

Stanley "Bahoo" Szymanski is on the medical roll suffering from an infection of his trigger finger.

The 9th District has been assigned a brand new Sergeant's patrol car. Sgts. Sevick, Smith and Mullaney are well pleased and take pride in keeping the turquoise upholstery neat and clean.

We of the figthing 9th take great pride in the fact that Ptlmn. Allen Jacobson of this command, detailed to the Chief of the Uniformed Division Emergency Squad, has received two creditable mentions in a month's time. It is men of this catagory that comprise the Fighting 9th District.

STATION 41 N...

ROGERS PARK

Captain Martin Mu...
Commanding

WELCOME to the far... where the air is fres... think is quiet and peacefu... ary Patrolmen: Patrick C... Dettmer, Howard Jachim... mour Karoff, Wm. Kouve... Quagliano, and Robt. Simo...

Ptlmn. James Cumm... to the fold after 3 mo... pastures; he finally fou... lice Dept. was the best, a...

Ptlmn. John Cleary of... has a very bright son... who won national honors... college level.

We now have three C... dors in the persons of B'... and Kouvelis. Sergts. ... row took off recently... loughs for different po...

Hoban and family... parts of California ... card showing "Alcat... Having a wonderful... were here."

"Snug" Powers ar... quietly for parts un... will drop his furlou... fore long.

Geo. Gannon of "Ryan's Raide... FOUR creditable mentions in 3 months time. Very good for a Junior Patrolman ... one year's service.

Here are the Curtins, six stalwarts of Chicago's police and fire forces. Seated are (left to right) Police Lts. Thomas, Michael and James Curtin. Standing are (left to right) Fire Lts. Joseph and David Curtin, and Police Sgt. William Curtin.

SPECIAL STORIES

2 BROTHERS HELD IN 7 KILLINGS

by John O'Brien

Once fought duel with police. One year before their arrest for seven killings, two alleged members of a black gang fought a karate duel with Chicago policemen posing as drunks on a West Side elevated train platform on the night of Oct. 3, 1971.

Subdued and later brought to court, a judge reasoned that because Reuben Taylor, 22, and his brother, Donald, 21, had no record of criminal behavior then they were eligible for probation.

Charged in 9 Slayings...

Thus, the Taylor brothers were serving a one-year probation period due to expire next month when arrested Oct. 13 and charged along with eight other alleged gang members with nine slayings this year. All of the victims were white. They were slain between May 3 and Sept. 3.

Recalls Attack...

The assault victim a year ago was an undercover patrolman, James Davern, a member of the police transit authority decoy unit, whose job is to catch robbers who prey on CTA patrons.

Although Davern has participated in scores of such arrests since then in his role as a drunk or a sleepy white businessman, he hasn't forgotten the Taylors.

"They came on strong and knocked me senseless, but ignored my wallet and wristwatch," he recalled yesterday in describing the brawl at the Lake Street-Cicero Avenue elevated station.

"It was the only time we ever had a 'hit' [attempted jackroll of an undercover policeman] that didn't involve robbery. It seemed that they just wanted to punch me."

Davern said he was on the platform only a few minutes when a west-bound train stopped, the Taylor brothers got off, and Reuben struck him in the face with a karate chop as the two brothers passed him. He said the blow nearly toppled him into Lake Street 30 feet below.

Doesn't Blame Judge...

Davern's partner, Patrolman Sam Summer, was struck with a karate kick in the groin when he intervened, and it took three other policemen to subdue the brothers, said Lt. Donald Kelley, decoy unit commander.

Davern said he has no quarrel with the decision by Judge John Crowley in North Boys Court placing the brothers on probation.

"I can't blame him really because they had no [police] backgrounds. Nobody can predict the future." (Copied)

3RD DISTRICT, 31 DEC '73

To: Watch Commander, 3rd Dist. 1st Watch
From: Patrolman James Davern, 2475, S.O.G. Mass Transit Unit
Subject: Injury to reporting officer after arrest:

1. Reporting officer, along with Patrolman W. Smith #14314 and Ptlmn. #10290, Mass Transit Unit while working on Beat L:762 on the first watch, arrested one (Smith, Johnny M/N 1941) at 63rd and Stoney Island "L" station.

2. Reporting officer handcuffed arrestee and waited for the arrival of a wagon to transport him.

3. When the wagon arrived, we took the prisoner down the stairs and began to remove our cuffs. When we had removed one of the cuffs, the prisoner jumped at R/O and the cuffed hand, striking R/O below left eye inflicting two inch laceration.

4. The above incident was witnessed by the wagon crew (Officers Bell, #13438 and Valkenburg #13360, Beat 371).

5. R/O transported to Jackson Park Hospital by Beat 309 and was treated and released by Dr. David.

6. After release from hospital R/O was transported into Third District by Beat 309 where we completed case report, charging offender with battery.

Patrolman James Davern, #2475

$3 MILLION CIVIL RIGHTS SUIT ACCUSES 20 COPS

Wednesday, Sept. 17, 1958
Chicago Daily News

Twenty Chicago policemen were sued for a total of $3 million Wednesday in a civil rights case.

A Federal Court suit accused the policemen of assaulting, beating and illegally detaining 13 Puerto Rican men. All were locked up in Racine Ave. station on the night of August 9, according to the suit.

Sgt. Thomas Owens of Racine Ave. station, one of the defendants, asserted arrests were made that night because of street disturbances.

The Puerto Ricans were rounded up near Chicago and Ada, according to the charges.

The suit charged indiscriminate arrests "without cause."

All the arrested men were beaten at the police station, held until the following night and falsely accused of crimes, the suit contended.

"At no time were the plaintiffs permitted to make any phone calls, contact lawyers or relatives, nor were they permitted to make bail ... or brought before a magistrate as required by law," it was charged.

Attorneys Charles Pressman, Ernest Liebman and Donald Page Moore filed the suit. Its three counts charged a denial of civil rights and a conspiracy under the U.S. civil rights statute.

Fourteen of the accused policemen were listed attached to Racine Ave. station. *Submitted by Ted Louis Sparrow.*

8 'L' STATIONS GET 24-HOUR POLICE PATROLS

by Philip Wattley

A new crackdown on criminals who prey on Chicago Transit Authority passengers was announced yesterday by Police Supt. James M. Rochford.

Police officials cited statistics that show crimes against CTA riders — especially robberies — are increasing and they said they intend to put a stop to the increasing crime rate.

He said eight elevated stations will have 24-hour police patrols. The stations, which were not identified, will be in addition to the department's 24-hour patrols of Loop subway stations.

"One of the most important responsibilities that the Chicago Police Department has is to insure safety for all citizens using the rapid transit system," Rochford said at a press conference at police headquarters, 1121 S. State St.

"We are going to locate offenders who wander and wait at platforms and in stations for victims, and we are going to arrest and remove them to increase security."

The elevated stations were not identified to prevent alerting potential criminals where police surveillance is being increased, officials said.

Rochford also said he was adding more policewomen to the mass transit detail. He said they will dress in street clothes, serving as decoys on trains and at stations.

He would not disclose the size of the department's mass transit detail for security reasons, but noted 3,168 policemen are assigned to riding New York City's mass transit vehicles. It is known that Chicago's mass transit detail is not nearly that large.

The crackdown also includes a new aggressive attitude toward persons loitering on CTA station platforms, he said. Any person who allows two or more trains to pass while standing on a platform will be questioned if a policeman is present, he added.

Walter Vallee, deputy chief of special operations in charge of the mass transit detail, said 653 persons were robbed on CTA property in 1973. In the first six months of this year, 445 major crimes were committed in CTA trains and stations.

Police assigned to the CTA made 29,100 arrests last year, Vallee said. But most of those arrests were for misdemeanors—17,000 for truancy, 4,500 for curfew violations, 5,000 for disorderly conduct, and other minor violations. (*Copied*)

21 ARRESTED, 3 COPS HURT IN N.W. SIDE VIOLENCE

A prolonged wave of disturbances, minor assaults and vandalism in a Northwest Side area resulted in the arrest of 21 men and minor injuries to three policemen Saturday night.

It was the third straight night in which carloads of juveniles, teenagers and men in their early 20s had swept through the area bounded by Grand, Chicago, Ashland and Racine.

Police Get Aid...

Twelve persons were arrested Thursday but charges against them were dismissed Friday in Boys Court. Action against six persons arrested Friday is still pending.

With the number of outbreaks of assaults and property damage swiftly mounting by Saturday night, Racine Avenue Station police received aid from neighboring districts which provided 15 additional three-wheel motorcycles and squad cars to quell the disturbances.

Police confiscated an assortment of weapons, including two guns, knives, pipes, a 1-1/2 foot linked chain, baseball bats and other clubs from the troublemakers.

Injured during the course of arrests were policemen Henry Kramer, who suffered a split lip when one youth hit him in the mouth with a handcuff; Theodore Sparrow, bitten on the finger by another, and Fred Dimitri, who injured his wrist unloading prisoners from a squadrol.

Called For Help...

The trouble began Saturday night when one policeman called for help trying to break up a crowd of rowdies near Chicago and Noble.

The area was reported under control by midnight Saturday.

27 POLICEMEN ARE HURT IN FIGHTING SDS

by Ronald Koziol and William Jones
Chicago Tribune

Oct. 12, 1969, National Guard is released. A Loop march by 300 revolutionary Students for a Democratic Society ended in a bloody battle with police yesterday.

The demonstrators, using tire chains, clubs, railroad flares and their fists, smashed windows and fought a running battle with police in Madison Street in the three-block area from La Salle street to State Street.

The battle surged around buses, taxicabs and autos.

Injured Toll Rises...

Before it was over 105 demonstrators had been arrested, 27 policemen had been injured, and two as-

Policeman subdues rioter in Loop after revolutionaries hurled railroad flares and fought police with fists and chains. (Tribune Staff Photo by Walter Kale)

sistant corporation counsels had been hurt, one of them seriously. More than 250 demonstrators have been arrested and more than 50 policemen have been injured since Wednesday.

After police cleared the Loop, 300 Illinois National Guardsmen were called into the area to help police guard against further outbreaks of violence. At 7:00 p.m., Gov. Ogilvie said it appeared there would be no more trouble and released all 2,600 guardsmen who had been ordered into the city on Thursday.

The marchers, who had been expected to continue south on La Salle Street to Jackson Boulevard before turning east to their destination in Grant Park, broke ranks on signal at La Salle and Madison streets.

Policemen Bowled Over...

They bowled over the thin line of policemen flanking the route of march and ran east, knocking aside pedestrians, as they smashed windows in 15 buildings.

With police in pursuit, other patrols fought the demonstrators at the intersections of Madison and Clark streets, Dearborn and Madison streets, and State and Madison streets.

As the demonstrators ran, they drew weapons which had been hidden in their clothing. They used the sharp metal points of the railroad flares to stab at and slash policemen.

Richard Elrod, assistant corporation counsel, was struck in the head by a lead pipe.

Elrod was taken to Illinois Research hospital where doctors said he is paralyzed from the neck down.

"Continue To Fight"...

Before the marchers headed east on Randolph Street to La Salle Street, two speakers told them, "We must continue to fight."

After the battle along Madison Street, 100 marchers gathered in Grant Park and shouted obscenities at police who stood guard nearby. Two more men were arrested, one for carrying a knife. The second was accused of mob action on the near north side Wednesday night.

Police Lieutenant Hurt...

Police Lieutenant Joseph Healy of the criminal intelligence unit was struck in the head with a tire chain. Lawrence Chambers and Terrence Corsentino, two other assistant corporation counsels, also were injured.

Some of the marchers threw cherry bomb firecrackers at police.

Four marchers were arrested in Haymarket Square before the protest parade began. Police identified them as among those who ran wild on the near north side Wednesday night, assaulting pedestrians and breaking windows of buildings and automobiles.

In Separate Actions Here...

Identified as Members of the SDS. Police arrested 15 persons in separate incidents throughout the city yesterday and Friday night, all of whom were identified as members of the Students for a Democratic Society or their sympathizers."

Four members of the SDS were arrested yesterday near Balbo Drive and State Street as they carried bottles of gasoline. Lt. Stanley Bazarek said a citizen notified police that he smelled an odor of gas from a cardboard box the men had with them as they rode into the Loop on an Illinois Central commuter train.

Make $500 Bonds...

Gary Ferguson, 20, James Goodman, 21, and Charles Chapman, 24, were charged with unlawful use of a weapon. Ferguson and Goodman were identified by police as students at the university and Chapman as a truck driver. All made $500 bonds and were scheduled to appear in North Boys court October 21.

Damen Avenue youth officer Donald Heefron said he stopped the trio because of a loud muffler on their car and noticed two shotgun shells on the back seat. He then ordered them to open the trunk where he found the weapons. The trio told police they were going duck hunting.

Police battle revolutionary rioters during confrontation in Loop. (Tribune Staff Photo by Walter Kale)

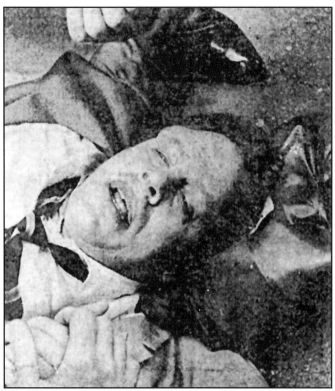

Richard Elrod, assistant city corporation consul, lies on sidewalk after being seriously injured by S.D.S. mob. (Tribune Staff Photo by Walter Kale)

Police arrest Brian Flanagan in attack on Richard Elrod, assistant city corporation counsel. (Tribune Staff Photo)

Five others were arrested Friday night as they carried sticks and clubs in the 2700 block of Wilson Street. Held on $5,000 bonds for mob action and unlawful use of a weapon were Richard Ochs, 31, of College Park, MD; Robert Duggan, 30, of Venice, CA; Gregory Dunkel, 29, of Adelphi, MD; Charles Swett, 19, of 681 N. Ridge Ave., Lombard; and Michael Braun, 19, of Appleton, WI, who said he was a University of Wisconsin student.

Finds Four Bottles...

Patrolman Harvey Cohan stopped them and found the four bottles in a cardboard box. The four, who said they are students at Purdue University, are Lee Hettema, 21, of New York City; Lee Gloster, 21, and George Ogden, 21, of Lafayette, IN; and Stanford Terry, 19, of Gary.

Bazarek said they told him they planned to set fire to the Standard Oil Company building, 910 S. Michigan Ave. All were charged with possession of incendiary devices and were scheduled to appear in violence court October 22.

Three Ann Arbor, MI men, all members of the University of Michigan SDS chapter, were arrested at 1628 Clybourn Ave. when police discovered two 12 guage shotguns in the trunk of their car after stopping them for a traffic violation.

Three Are Arrested...

A raid Friday night on the apartment of a University of Chicago student, whom police identified as an SDS member, resulted in the seizure of 15 pounds of marijuana and three arrests.

Acting on a search warrant issued by a judge in South Chicago court, Grand Crossing detectives entered the apartment of Eugene Vogel, 23, of 7205 Yates Ave., and arrested him and two others, Joseph Tokar, 19, of 5945 Hyde Park Blvd., and Deborah Newell, 21, of 6750 Chappell Ave.

Vogel was charged with possession of narcotics and being the keeper of a disorderly house. Tokar was charged with being an inmate of a disorderly house and Miss Newell with possession of narcotics.

Elrod Is Slugged In Riot, Paralyzed...

Richard J. Elrod, (pictured above) assistant corporation counsel who was hit on the head by a pipe-swinging demonstrator in a Loop fracas yesterday, was paralyzed from the neck down as the result of a broken neck, University of Illinois hospital spokesmen said last night.

Elrod, 35, was attacked by a group of revolutionaries in front of 64 W. Madison St. during a violent foray. (Article by Richard Phillips)

Suspect, 22, Is Arrested...

Arrested and charged with attempted murder in the incident was Brian D. Flanagan, 22, a Columbia University student from New York City and Southampton, NY. Flanagan also was charged with aggravated battery, felonious mob action and resisting arrest.

Bond was set at $100,000 for Flanagan last night by Magistrate Russell DeBow of Bond court, after state's attorneys asked for a bond of $75,000 and Flanagan's defense attorney requested a lower figure.

He Tells Why...

"I am setting the bond at $100,000 because I understand Mr. Elrod's condition is serious, and I want to wait for further results of his condition," DeBow said.

Flanagan was identified by Policeman Kenneth Sarcerano of criminal intelligence as having hit Elrod in the face and then kicked him several times in the neck, back and thigh after Elrod fell to the street.

Another policeman and Stephen Zucker, an assistant corporation counsel, said it appeared Elrod's assailant used a pipe. Zucker, who also was injured, was seen walking with a limp after the fracas.

Mayor Rushes to Hospital...

Flanagan was subdued and arrested by policemen at the scene.

Elrod's wife, Marilyn, his parents, and Mayor Daley were among those who rushed to the hospital after Elrod was admitted to the neurology section. He was reported in serious condition.

Elrod, whose duties include negotiations with protesters during demonstrations, has been slightly injured at least three times in the last year and a half in anti-war demonstrations. Last month, he was hit on the head by a demonstrator outside the federal building.

1969 Demonstration...

During the 1969 demonstration in downtown Chicago, police officer William Jaconetti restrains Bernadine Dorhn. Ms. Dorhn later was arrested and went underground for 10 years as a wanted fugitive.

Police restrain woman revolutionary demonstrator during Loop clash. (Tribune Staff Photo

She turned herself in after being on the run and living in another state. The radical revolutionary group called the Students for a Democratic Society (SDS) organized the march. During the battle in the streets prominent assistant corporation council lawyer, Richard Elrod, was paralyzed.

100 Attend Services for Slain Policeman

June 5, 1968. Friends, relatives and fellow policemen paid their final respects yesterday to Patrolman Henry Peeler, 28, killed in a gun fight last Wednesday as he and his partner patrolled the streets of the Englewood police district.

More than 100 persons attended the funeral services in the Open Door Baptist Church, 1301 S. Sawyer Ave., the same church in which Peeler was baptized in 1952.

In his eulogy, the Rev. L.B. Little, pastor of the church, called upon all men to respect law and order.

"Men have become bitter, one against the other," he said. "Man's heart must change and instead of hate must be filled with love.

"Patrolman Peeler laid down his life to make the streets safe and to protect all citizens. He had love and respect for the church and now he has gone on to a world where everyday will be Sunday."

As the Rev. Mr. Little spoke, Peeler's wife of seven years, Julia, leaned across to comfort their two

Henry Peeler

children, Keeley, 6, and Sherry, 4.

The flag-draped casket was carried into the church by six of Peeler's fellow policemen from the Englewood District. His police hat was atop the casket.

Peeler was killed when he and his partner, Ronald Lillwitz, 30, stopped their patrol car to question three men sitting in front of a building at 57th and Morgan streets. The three had been sought in connection with the killing of an East St. Louis railroad detective and the wounding of a policeman there.

Peeler was killed after he chased Lyon Herbert, 21, of East St. Louis, into a gangway. Herbert was shot and killed moments later by Lillwitz, who was shot in the right arm and left hand and is in good condition in Englewood Hospital.

Comdr. Harold L. Miles of the Englewood District said that Lillwitz wanted to attend yesterday's services, but doctors would not allow it.

Peeler was a graduate of Farragut High School, and after serving in the Army, joined the police department in October 1966.

1942 COMPLAINTS OR "BEEFS" ABOUT OFFICERS

Complaints ("beefs") about Officers Coru #2336 and Ed Delso #7127 existed back then and absurd accusations are not just a modern day problem — i.e. "How the bitten finger couldn't possibly have been done by one of the drunken boys — but the officers had to be at fault!!"

August 4, 1942

After seeing your brutal attack on the Babb twins Friday evening, it made me think of the book I read "Out of the night." Surely your talents are being wasted in these United States, as why not go to Germany and take charge of one of Hitler's Concentration Camps?

As for the finger you claim was bitten by one of the boys — probably you did it when you struck him in the mouth.

It is a shame I couldn't have testified in court this morning like I had planned — as I wanted all of Chi-cago to read about it in the papers. Two police officers beating two defenseless and unarmed 19-year-old boys that were drunk.

I have lived 26 years in this city and 18 years of these I have been in politics, but I can truthfully say — I have never seen anything as brutal as this affair.

This is America and we are fighting to keep this country free, so our children can grow up to be good citizens and live like our forefathers.

Marion J. Hanna

THE 1996 DEMOCRATIC CONVENTION

by Detective Linda Flores, CPD

In my 15 years as a Chicago police officer my most memorable experience was the assignment to Post #114 - the front podium at the 1996 Democratic National Convention. For four unbelievable days I was able to represent the Chicago Police Department and watch our country's political system at work.

The last day is the one I remember the most. On the last day of the convention, the United Center had a full house. I was joined at the front podium by several other detectives and secret service agents. After the nomination process was finalized, balloons and confetti began raining down. With music filling the arena we looked out at the standing crowd in utter amazement. We were literally buried up to our knees in the balloons and confetti and it was impossible to speak to each other because we couldn't hear anything but the crowd. They were clapping, screaming, and singing. Electricity filled the air. It was an awesome sight.

I will always be thankful to Commander Tom Cronin and Superintendent Terry Hillard for allowing me the opportunity to stand in front of that podium.

ALERT POLICEMAN FOILS TWO BANDITS IN JEWEL ROBERY

Chicago Sun-Times

Dec. 18, 1962. An alert policeman foiled an attempt Monday by two men to rob a north side jewelry store of jewels and cash totaling more than $10,000.

Otto Zeitz, 66, proprietor of Zeitz Bros. Jewelers, 3941 N. Lincoln, said two armed men entered his store and bound and gagged him and an employee, Harvey Reeves, 66.

The two men put $219 and jewelry valued at more than $10,000 in a shopping bag, Zeitz said. As the robbers were about to leave, three policemen challenged them.

Policeman Mel Itter had seen the two men enter the store and became suspicious. A call from Itter brought Town Hall District policemen, Jerry Patterson and George Pocius. The three policemen disarmed the bandits after firing a warning shot.

The two robbers were identified as Harry F. Jones, 39, of 2100 W. Warren Blvd. and Thomas H. Casey, 25, of 1100 N. Ridgeland, Oak Park. They were held for questioning by robbery detectives.

A POLICE SLAYER CAPTURED– ROUTED BY TEAR GAS, HEAVY GUNFIRE

Desperado held family captive, August 19, 1955. The gun-crazy killer of a detective has been subdued and captured by tear gas, gunfire and the physical brawn of the slain man's comrades on the force.

Richard Carpenter, 26, was seized by police Thursday night in a third-floor apartment at 2042 W. Potomac.

For the preceding 23 hours, ever since he wounded a patrolman in a movie theater gun battle, he had held a family captive in a next-door apartment at 2040 W. Potomac.

When he was taken into custody, it was disclosed that Carpenter had been shot in the right thigh Wednesday night by Patrolman Clarence Kerr, the officer he wounded.

Identified By Wounded Policeman...

Later, Carpenter was taken from Bridewell Hospital to St. Mary of Nazareth Hospital, where Kerr identified him as his assailant in the gunfight.

He also was identified by a man whose auto was commandeered after the fatal shooting of Det. William J. Murphy on Monday in the Roosevelt Road subway station.

Carpenter confessed to the Murphy slaying early Friday, suddenly breaking after answering police questions evasively for hours, said Harry Glos, chief investigator for the coroner's office.

Glos said Carpenter made the confession when the captive was taken early Friday under heavy police guard back to the W. Potomac apartment where he had intruded.

At the apartment, Carpenter showed police where he had concealed his gun—in a pipe leading from an oil stove. The recovered gun, investigators determined, was stolen by Carpenter from a policeman during a robbery.

The gun battle with Kerr occurred in the crowded Biltmore Theater at 2046 W. Division, two blocks from the scene of Carpenter's capture.

In the meantime, *The Sun-Times* had posted a $5,000 reward for information leading to the apprehension of the fugitive.

Phone Call Tipped off Police...

The dramatic end of one of the City's most intensive man-hunts was touched off at 9:01 p.m., Thursday when Leonard Powell phoned Lt. Frank O'Sullivan, acting deputy chief of detectives, to report:

"A woman and two children are being held at bay at 2040 Potomac."

Four squads of police, armed with submachine guns, rifles and tear gas, sped to that address.

It later developed that Powell, 30, a truck driver, was the head of the captive household. He had slipped out of his home on the pretext of going to a drugstore. Then he phoned O'Sullivan.

Carpenter had forced his way into the Powell apartment after the movie gun battle, terrorizing Powell, his wife and their two children, Diane, 3, and Robert, 7.

By the time police arrived at the Powell apartment, Carpenter had kicked his way out of a second floor window.

He entered an opposite second floor window in the apartment of Stanley Sciblo at 2042 Potomac.

As he emerged into the bedroom of Sciblo's wife Stella, 31, he told her: "Don't worry, nothing's going to happen."

She said he appeared calm and was limping. Sciblo and his family saw Carpenter pass through the dining room to the kitchen, where he attempted unsuccessfully to leave by a rear window.

He retraced his steps through the Sciblo apartment and went to the third floor apartment of Alfons Krolikowski.

Krolikowski and his wife ran to the street. By that time police had arrived. They tossed tear gas bombs into the apartment, yelling to Carpenter to drop his gun and come out with his hand up.

Carpenter, 26, said he would, but he didn't. The police then fired machine-gun and rifle bullets along with more tear gas into the apartment, as hundreds of spectators gathered at the scene.

Kick Down Door...

After the barrage, Sgt. Herbert Rothstein and patrolmen Theodore Sparrow, Bernard Krusicki and John Kennedy, all of North Ave. Station, kicked down the door. Although he had returned fire at the earlier barrage, Carpenter evidently was out of ammunition when the officers entered.

Nevertheless he put up a vicious physical struggle. He was subdued and hand-cuffed and led to a patrol wagon.

Crowds Shout Angrily...

As he passed through the crowd, there were angry shouts of: "Kill him! Kill him!" He was taken first to the North Ave. Station, then to the Bridewell Hospital for treatment.

Answers Query...

Only 16 minutes elapsed between the time Deputy Chief O'Sullivan received the phone call and the time at which Carpenter was subdued.

As he was carried into the hospital on a stretcher, Carpenter was a ragged, dirty object. His nose was bleeding and he needed a shave. He wore a ragged T-shirt and undershorts.

"Why didn't you put up more of a struggle?" a *Sun-Times* reporter asked him.

"They would have killed me," replied the two-gun bandit who is accused in federal and state warrants of murdering Det. William J. Murphy, Monday night.

Since the gun battle with Patrolman Kerr 24 hours before his capture, Carpenter had dodged a manhunt that included use of a helicopter.

The aircraft hovered over the jungle of alleys, buildings and railroad tracks in the area in which the fugitive eventually was found.

From the Bridewell Hospital, handcuffed and clad only in a white nightgown, Carpenter was taken to Kerr's room at St. Mary of Nazareth.

There Kerr positively identified Carpenter as his opponent in the movie shooting.

Next, Carpenter was confronted at Police Headquarters by Charles A. Koerper, 67, of 1816 N. Clark, whose auto was commandeered by the fleeing slayer of Det. Murphy.

Koerper said Carpenter was the man.

Meanwhile, Patrolman Kerr, 26, rallied somewhat in St. Mary of Nazareth Hospital after nine blood transfusions. He was shot near the heart.

A hospital spokesman said Policeman Kerr was "progressing satisfactorily," but that did not mean he was out of danger.

Kerr, of 1759 Erie, had attended a double feature at the theater with his wife, Marion, 24.

Upon leaving, he spotted a man resembling photographs of the hunted gunman, dozing in a chair.

The young policeman put his wife in their car after telling her, "I think I saw Carpenter. I'll have to go back and get him."

Failing to heed her appeal to get help, he went back in the movie house and sat next to the dozing man. Kerr later told Capt. Phillip Breitzke, deputy police commissioner.

"I showed the man my star, drew my gun and said, "Come with me. You're under arrest."

"The man said, 'OK. I give up.'"

As they approached the street door, the prisoner began shooting. The policeman fell and the man dashed out a fire door near the front of the theater.

Four .38 caliber revolver slugs recovered from the theater were useless for ballistics identification, police said. The pellets were mashed and out of shape.

Kerr, a policeman for less than a year, was assigned to the Hudson Ave. District. Kerr has two children, Karen, 5, and Edward, 3.

Funeral services for Det. Murphy will be conducted at 10 a.m. Friday at Our Lady of Help Christians Church, 832 N. Leclaire.

Murphy, of 7824 W. Summerville, was shot to death in the Roosevelt-State subway station Monday night.

ARREST AND CAPTURE OF RICHARD CARPENTER

by Theodore L. Sparrow

While assigned to Sq. #107 with Richard Ryan, we heard and responded to a call in regards to Richard Carpenter being in a building at 2040 W. Potomac Street.

Upon our arrival on the scene I ran around the back of 2040 W. Potomac into the yard. I then noticed a man jump from the second floor of 2040 Potomac to 2042 W. Potomac. A short time after, I saw him appear at the third floor porch window, where he ran from the second floor. He then put one leg over the window sill. He appeared like he wanted to climb up to the roof of the building.

I fired a shot and he ducked back into the porch area which was enclosed. We then called out asking him if he was Carpenter. He replied that he was. We then told him to throw out his guns. When he failed to reply, we opened fire into the location he was last seen.

Officer's Krusike and Adam and myself then broke the glass window of the door leading to the porch stairs, and proceeded to go up the stairs. We called out to the officers on the out-   side to stop their firing, but the firing continued. We then crawled up the stairs to keep from being hit. Reaching the third floor we went in and proceeded to work our way to the front of the building. We then noticed Carpenter at the doorway leading to the front stairway, we then apprehended him and pushed him out into the hallway. He reached for my gun

Theodore L. Sparrow

and I struck him with my flashlight. We then subdued him and took him downstairs.

I then accompanied the prisoner to the 30th District Station and afterwards to the Bridewell Hospital where he was treated for lacerations caused while attempting to resist arrest.

THE CAPTURE OF KILLER CARPENTER

Chicago Daily Sun-Times

August 20, 1955. Some of our readers have expressed cynical surprise that Richard Carpenter was captured alive. It is assumed that when the police corner a policeman killer he never lives to die in the electric chair.

If the policemen who cornered Carpenter wanted to kill him it could easily have been arranged. They advanced under fusillade of bullets, any one of which conveniently could have saved the state the expense of a trial. But they took him alive and disposed of the canard, at least in this case, that the police always set themselves up as judge and executioner of policeman killers.

Carpenter's captors had to subdue him. Patrolman Theodore Sparrow did it with a flashlight on Carpenter's head, not a police .38. They did this at the risk of their own lives; the tricky Carpenter might have killed them as he did Det. William Murphy last Monday night.

The capture was police professionalism and teamwork at its best. Policemen are not supposed to have personal feelings about the criminals they handle. The capture of Carpenter alive serves as an example for those trigger-happy members of the force who shoot first and ask questions afterward, and sometimes find out they've shot not a criminal but an honest taxpayer. Our compliments to Sgt. Emil Smicklas, who directed the capture, and the rest of his team.

Another aspect of the case involves Carpenter's history of crime. Society had plenty of warning about him.

Carpenter had been a juvenile delinquent. When he was 15, he was picked up as a robbery suspect. When he was 19, he was up on a disorderly conduct charge and fined $10. In 1950 he shot his mother— accidentally, she said. Then in 1951 he was captured just after he had stuck up a cab-driver and was waiting to rob another.

Police charged him with robbery, and if the charge had stuck he could have been sent to the penitentiary for one year to life. There, he might have learned a trade and been rehabilitated.

penitentiary. But 434, like Carpenter, were found guilty of lesser offenses and presumably sent to the county jail. There may be another Carpenter among them.

DID COPS USE BRUTALITY ON KILLER?

by Ray Brennan
Chicago Sun-Times

Aug. 25, 1955. Published photographs of Richard Carpenter, his face bloody, have aroused a blistering debate among Chicagoans.

There have been angry charges of police brutality, as against enthusiastic praise for the arresting officers.

What really happened when the law grabbed Carpenter in a West Side apartment where he had terrorized a family for 23 hours?

Was he beaten and kicked with outrageous police brutality at that time or any time afterward?

Protecting Own Lives?...

Or were the police merely protecting their own lives from a crazed, viciously fighting killer?

How much was he hurt by a milling mob which screamed: "Kill him! Kill him!?

How badly did he injure himself in jumping through a screen window in trying to escape?

Sun-Times staff members have investigated every possible angle to get the answers to those vital questions - the true, unbiased answers.

Documented Findings...

Their documented findings add up to the following points:

1) The police used only the force and violence necessary to subdue Carpenter, known killer of a detective.

2) Not one witness, and there were dozens, including news reporters, has told of seeing an unnecessary blow struck on Carpenter.

3) A medical report at Bridewell Hospital shows Carpenter suffered only superficial injuries.

4) At the hospital almost immediately after his capture, Carpenter talked lucidly, showing no signs of shock or intense pain.

"The public clamor over alleged brutality definitely is based on misunderstanding and misinformation," Gutknecht said.

He said his office would go ahead with prosecution of Carpenter for murder in the killing of Detec-

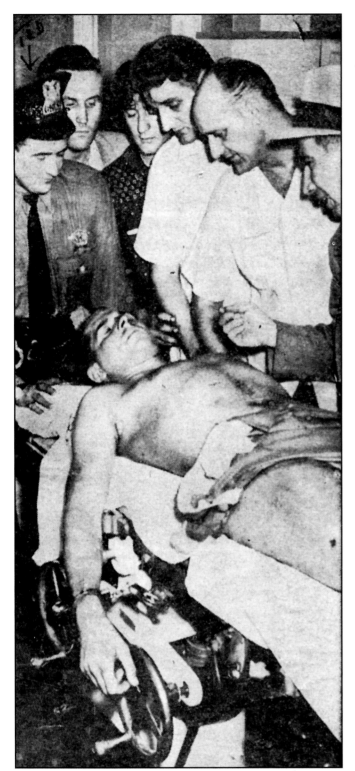

Ted Sparrow (in uniform) guards "Cop Killer" Carpenter while he is being treated at Bridewell Hospital.

Instead, it developed that the cab driver's identification of Carpenter was weak. In Municipal Court, the charge of robbery was knocked down to carrying a concealed weapon, a misdemeanor. Carpenter spent a year in the overcrowded county jail, where there is little else to do but sit and brood. They had to let him out after a year and he came out a murderer.

The police have a good record for getting their men alive. Last year they charged 1,700 with robbery. Of these 1,130 were convicted and presumably sent to the

tive William J. Murphy and for assault to kill in the wounding of Policeman Clarence Kerr.

Denied by O'Connor...

Police Commander Timothy J. O'Connor denied vigorously that his men used any force more than necessary to subdue Carpenter, saying: "I am proud of the work the police did. I believe they did a fine job."

Capt. John W. Ryan, commanding the North Ave. District, pointed out that Carpenter was rushed to the Bridewell as soon as possible.

Carpenter talked freely with three newspaper reporters at the Criminal Courts Building for an hour on the day after his capture. At no time did he complain of police brutality, but said instead: "I'm lucky. I'm

Officer Sparrow testifies that he struck Richard Carpenter on his head when the outlaw reached for gun at time of arrest.

lucky I didn't get killed in that apartment. One bullet went past my nose so close I could feel the heat."

Crashed Through Screen...

Among the witnesses who saw Carpenter before the police reached him was Mrs. Stella Sciblo, into whose apartment the fugitive crashed through the screen.

"There was blood on his shirt," she said definitely.

Another witness, Michael Pass, 1301 N. Hoyne, told of seeing Carpenter being led from the apartment by police through a hostile mob. "He was kicking and squirming," Pass said.

Among the many policemen interviewed were Sgt. Herbert Rothstein and Patrolmen John Kennedy and Theodore Sparrow.

They crawled into the besieged apartment on hands and knees to escape barrages of tear gas and machine-gun fire, risking their lives.

Lunged for Gun...

Sparrow conceded frankly that he struck Carpenter on the head with a flashlight, adding: "Other officers were trying to put handcuffs on him. He lunged for my revolver. I had my revolver extended in my right hand, with the flashlight in the other. I withdrew the revolver and struck him the head with the flash.

"The glass in the flash did not break. I hit him with the other end. It was a light, two-cell flashlight and it would have broken if I had hit him hard." (The flashlight, showing as a weapon in some of the news photos, was responsible for many of the charges of police brutality.) Sgt. Rothstein and Patrolman Kennedy, interviewed separately, confirmed Sparrow's statement in all details.

Fought Violently...

The three officers and others added that Carpenter fought violently at the police station and had to be pinned on the floor. The prisoner kicked viciously and smashed about with his handcuffed wrists, they said.

Harry Glos, assistant chief deputy coroner, denied there was any unnecessary force in capturing Carpenter or getting a confession. "People in the mob outside the apartment were striking at the prisoner with sticks," he said. "That's how he got some of his injuries." Glos said he was present during the questioning of Carpenter at the detective bureau from 11:00 p.m. until he confessed at 2:20 a.m.

BANDIT'S LIFE CAN BE FRUSTRATING

by Lynn Taylor

A 60-year-old mother of two policemen and a watch that didn't work were the undoing of two robbers, and two suspects were in custody yesterday.

One victim, Mrs. Helen Rogers, chased, pounded, and eventually nabbed a 19-year-old youth she said had snatched her purse.

Police charged the youth, Hank Williams of 2112 N. Karlov Ave., with theft and battery after Mrs. Rogers chased him into the arms of two police patrolling the 4300 block of West Fullerton Avenue.

Mrs. Rogers said that after a robber grabbed her purse, she struggled with him, then screamed as she chased him. The commotion attracted two pedestrians who helped her pursue Williams until police caught him.

After the incident, Mrs. Rogers said her sons called her "gutsy" but "bawled me out for taking chances."

In another incident, Donald Jones, 20, of 6037 S. Hermitage Ave., was charged with theft after he allegedly took a watch from a man lying on the platform of the elevated train station at 63rd Street and Ashland Avenue yesterday morning.

After his watch was taken, the "victim," who had acted drunk, stood up, and announced he was James Davern, an undercover policeman, and that Jones was under arrest.

Davern later told the surprised Jones that the watch didn't even run.

****

Four of the 22 alleged robbers who were fooled by the drunken masquerading of Patrolman James Davern of the Chicago Police CTA Decoy Unit were sentenced to jail terms or probation today by North Felony Court Judge Robert J. Sulski.

Davern, 38, "retired" from his role as the unit's most successful decoy on September 24, after making 22 arrests during a span of only 36 days.

He will continue as a back up man in the unit which has combined to nab more than 100 persons since its inception last June.

Davern stood as the complaintant through six consecutive cases before Judge Sulski, who finally asked in amazement, "Mr. Davern, did you make all these arrests posing as a decoy?"

Davern answered that he had. The judge suggested, "Maybe you'd better forget about being a policeman and go out to Hollywood."

Judge Sulski had heard the same account of every arrest: Davern posing as an inebriated businessman, was accosted by one or more robbers who took either his "famous gold watch" or currency, but before the bandits could escape the platform, they were arrested by the five or six backup patrolmen who remained hidden until the robbery actually occured.

THE BATTLE OF CHICAGO

The Chicago Police Officer Quarterly
by PO Mike Haas, Unit 124

Cultural/Class Conflict in Chicago during the 1968 Democratic National Convention at street level. Shortly before court resumed for the afternoon session, the mayor entered and took his seat. Abbie Hoffman entered next, saw the mayor, and in a mock swagger walked to within a few feet of him and said, with a shake of his shaggy head, "Why don't we just settle this right here?" The mayor laughed aloud and settled back into his chair."—Jason Epstein, *The Great Conspiracy Trial*, 361.

Chicago's 1968 Democratic Convention...

Chicago's 1968 Democratic Convention ranks not only as the most controversial, if not infamous, convention in American political history, but as one of the defining moments of the turbulent decade that was the 1960s. It was here that two conflicting views of American consciousness, divided by class orientation, confronted the other. With the "whole world watching" both sides "let it all hang out" on the streets of Chicago that week, allowing America to decide for itself the righteousness of each other's actions. The street fighting which ensued not only earned for this

Mike Haas, 19th District CPD.

convention historical notoriety, but societal scars that have yet to heal. As the action in the amphitheater exposed the internal, political dissension within the Democratic Party itself, the drama on the streets also revealed a cultural and class divide in an America that was beside itself in coming to grips with not only the war in Vietnam but other societal questions that erupted during the 60s as well—the Civil Rights Movement, the sexual revolution and the ever increasing use of illegal, mind altering drugs by their youth. The '68 DNC also marks the origins of a larger cultural war that continues to this day.

Part I: Prelude To A Rumble

An Offer the DNC Could Not Refuse...

Though what transpired at the DNC in Chicago in 1968 quite possibly could have taken place in any other American city the Democrats might have chosen that year, given the volatile nature of 1968, it was Chicago's mayor, Richard J. Daley, who insisted the DNC be hosted by and in his town.

His mind was made up; it was going to be held in a place known as Daley's Chicago. The man himself was even more specific about where the nation's Democrats would meet, when he said, "I would say that it is an important sign of faith to the American people for this national convention to be held here, not in some resort center, but in the very heart of a great city, where people live and work and raise their families, and in one of the biggest neighborhoods in Chicago—my neighborhood!" Other cities had wanted it when the choice was being made late in 1967, but few cities had a mayor or who, with a hundred or so delegates in his pocket, could go straight to the White House and make his pitch.[1]

This was a pitch loaded with political capital that had been amassed through the years, especially since the presidential election of 1960 when JFK personally credited Daley with delivering him the presidency. RFK acknowledged as much when he remarked, "Daley's the whole ball game," in appraising his own chances for the 1968 nomination. LBJ "personally advertised his esteem for the Mayor by informing the White House switchboard that all calls from Daley were to be put through to him, personally and promptly."[2]

Because Chicago had managed to avoid the rioting that had plagued several other cities across the United States in 1965, 66 and 67, it also appeared to LBJ that, aside from Daley's political clout within the Democratic Party, Daley was in firm control of his city. In March of 1968, however, Daley's infamous "shoot to kill" order, issued during the rioting on the city's west side in the wake of Dr. King's assassination, only served to embarrass him and the city as well. When it was learned that anti-war groups were making plans to stage demonstrations and marches in Chicago during Convention Week, speculation surfaced the DNC would relocate elsewhere. Daley, however, would not stand for it, stating, "By God, you gave it to us and by God, we're going to keep it."[3] To do so Daley felt compelled to calm the fears of his fellow party members as well as those of the city's citizenry. "As long as I am mayor," he vowed, over and over again, "There will be law and order in Chicago. Nobody is going to take over this city."[4]

The Yippies Weigh In...

Although rallies, marches, and other protest actions surely would have been planned no matter where the convention was held, once the DNC's site became known, the Yippie tag team of Abbie Hoffman and Jerry Rubin were quick to weigh-in with a "On to Chicago" campaign.

(Both) had been civil-rights workers in the South—an experience they found, if not stale and flat, largely unprofitable. Yet they were still revolutionaries, in the sense of wanting to refashion a society they despised. The basic revolutionary text of Hoffman and his friends, however, was not Karl Marx but Marshall McLuhan. And with the creation of YIPPIE, they developed a new revolutionary premise for the electronic era; when the might of a society cannot be challenged, strike at its myths. In the process of blasting off Hoffman's triple barreled shotgun (charisma, myth and put-on), they would clearly incur the contempt of much of society, but this was to be expected. It would be worthwhile if, in the process, the society they were at odds with could be made to look stupid or brutal.[5]

To Hoffman the future of America belonged to what he later described in terms of the "Woodstock Nation."

Hoffman concluded that the Woodstock people foreshadowed a climactic break not only with conventional American decorum—which he despised—but with puritanism itself and thus with the Protestant habit of self restraint, deferred gratification for the sake of future gain. Thus Hoffman extrapolated from the Oedipus complex the political imperative that children should kill their parents; that the new generation should break abruptly—even violently—with the old, and that the family, as the fundamental social institution, should be destroyed.[6]

Harboring no real hopes of actually influencing the nomination, but extremely cognizant of the positive effect live television coverage had in advertising their "movement" as well as in swelling the ranks of their numbers, Hoffman and Rubin, "talked about the possibility of having a demonstration at the Democratic National Convention in Chicago. Jerry said that it would be a good idea to call it a festival of life in contrast to the convention of death and to have it in some kind of public park or something in Chicago."[7]

The New Left Joins In...

There was also the more staid umbrella group known as MOBE, National Mobilization Committee to End the War in Vietnam. Among its lieutenants included longtime Quaker Pacifist David Dellinger and two SDS (Students for a Democratic society) leaders, Tom Hayden and Rennie Davis. The SDS was far more politically oriented than the Yippies, and "suspicious of Yippie Hedonism." They were also firmly convinced that by provoking the police into confrontation in Chicago, it would somehow demonstrate to the nation that, if Vietnam wasn't proof enough, America was a violent and sick society:

Davis felt that he understood the mayor and his police force; he had, in his earlier work in the City (SDS/ERAP community action projects in an Appalachian white neighborhood in Uptown), experienced a running battle of mutual harassment with police at the Foster Street station. He had, a few years before, been involved in a march of 300 people on that very police post. At close quarters, he began to realize that policemen, no matter how restrained or professional, could be drawn across an invisible line into the territory of overreaction. Davis was convinced that authority would back up on itself in Chicago, that if the protesters played it right, the police, and Daley with them, could be drawn into perpetrating the very violence they were pledged to prevent.[8]

In light of their successful, 50,000 man, peace march and rally on the Pentagon in October 1967, the same month Chicago was awarded the convention, MOBE decided that again utilizing this "creative synthesis of Ghandi (New Left) and guerrilla (Yippies)," a "gigantic demonstration of antiwar, anti-establishment, anti-Johnson and anti-racist sentiment" could be harnessed, displayed, and broadcast before the entire nation in Chicago the following August. "The word was that it would make the Washington march (the Peace Movement's largest to date) look like a Sunday school outing."[9]

More easily said than done, however, for although they originally envisioned "500,000" like-minded spirits to join them, no matter how many came, of primary importance was, where would/could they stage their operations and overnight it during that week. This was crucial because, unlike previous anti-war protests, which had been over in a day, this one was to last four days.

At Ringside...

The national news media though, especially the television networks, which had also provided coverage for the Republican National Convention in Miami Beach earlier that August, were none too pleased with the DNC's choice of Chicago as its location. Not only were the telephone and television lines already laid in Miami Beach, meaning that they could have saved millions in the cost of transport dollars, but also in Chicago at the time was an existing telephone strike as well as the possibility of a taxi and bus strike. In fact:

The TV networks applied massive pressure to shift the convention. In Chicago, because of the strictures of the strike, their cameras would be limited to the hotels and to the amphitheater—they would not be able to take their portable generators out to the street and run lines to their color cameras. That would not be permitted. They were restricted to movie cameras, which would make them a half a day late in reporting action or interviews in the streets. How they must have focused their pressure on Daley and Johnson. It is to the mayor's curious credit that he was strong enough to withstand them. Any such man would have known the powers of retaliation which resided in the mass media. One did not make an enemy of a television network for nothing; they could repay injury with no more than a chronic slur in the announcer's voice every time your deadly name was mentioned over the next 12 months or next 12 years.[10]

This early situation, no doubt, colored the media's perceptions about "Boss" Daley and not only led to disparaging descriptions of him and his city as feudal anachronisms in modern times, but to a generalized media bias that would later be revealed in the outright hostility displayed toward Daley and his police department on the eve of the convention itself:

Although the day to day building of tensions by the news media had gone on for almost four months, nothing that had taken place prepared the mayor or the police for the torrent of national media criticism which was to become intensified on Sunday, August 25, the day before the convention opened. The anti-

Chicago, anti-police, verbal assault began on NBC with Frank McGee's commentary followed by Chet Huntley and David Brinkley, and on CBS, by Walter Cronkite. The latter told his national television audience there was no other way to describe Chicago except as a "police state."[11]

Chicago Won't "Play the Fool" ...

Of course, Daley didn't want them, and he was not about to accommodate them in any way. Politically they were of no value to him, and, as the host of the convention, he was well aware of their aims to disrupt it.

Daley had heard all about the Yippies' plans for a "Festival of Life" to be held in Lincoln Park on the near north side of the city. Rock bands would play as thousands of young people would arrive to live out the alternate lifestyle of the counterculture while the Democrats held a "Convention of Death" on the south side. The leaders of the various movement factions, often at odds with each other, represented the changes in attitude, values and behavior that produced revulsion and outrage in the blood of Mayor Daley. Promising great disruptive crowds—had they not marched successfully on the Pentagon just the previous October, making the troops and their bayonets look ridiculous as they defended the building against unarmed protesters?—these leaders knew exactly what they wanted: through their "politics of absurdity," they would transform Chicago into a metaphor for their interpretation of America. They would celebrate a free culture of blaring music, drugs and lovemaking in Chicago parks while they forced the Democratic Party to nominate a presidential candidate under heavy guard in an old fashioned arena next to the stockyards.[12]

Stare-down ...

Nevertheless, Daley was not going to be the one to blink first. If these "outsiders" thought they were going to push his red button and make a fool of him in his own town, he'd show them just who was going to be pushing whose buttons. Besides the "shoot to kill" order in March, in late April his police had roughed up a peace march in the Loop that was sponsored by the local Chicago Peace Council. In the face of a privately funded commission's criticism over his police department's actions, Daley merely remarked, "Much of it is not true. I had a long conversation with Superintendent Conlisk and I know it isn't."[13] Members of Chicago's counterculture were becoming increasingly nervous and annoyed as Hoffman and Rubin's well-publicized, obscene and irreverent, pre-convention put-ons were adding more police pressure on their local scene:

They were, in fact, in a most unhippie like condition: uptight. Early in August the Chicago group circulated a letter, picked up by all the underground newspapers, to the effect that the festival of life could turn into a "festival of blood." It advised pacifically inclined out-of-town brethren to stay put. "The cops will riot," the letter warned. The word has gone down— Brutality be damned.[14] Then, a few days before the convention commenced, it was revealed that the city's 12,000 man police department would be put on 12 hour shifts; 6,000 Illinois National Guardsmen would also pull convention duty, and if need be there were 6,000 regular Army troops also available for deployment.

Trespassing, Not Permitted! ...

Though Daley's pre-convention security tactics definitely spooked the more pacific minded in the anti-war movement from coming to Chicago, it was the city's/Daley's refusal to grant permits for marches and rallies (except for August 29 in Grant Park—nomination day for the Convention) as well as their refusal to waive the 11:00 p.m. curfew in Lincoln and Grant Parks throughout the week that cast a decisive chill in persuading yet even the more hardier types not to come. If it was going to be illegal to overnight it in the parks and march on city streets anywhere in close proximity of the amphitheater, then doing so anyway certainly might provoke a police response many of them would rather not experience.

This relationship between permits and violence was acknowledged by Abbie Hoffman in the *Realist* that summer:

"All of (our) plans are contingent on our getting a permit, and it is toward that goal that we have been working. A permit is a definite contradiction in philosophy since we do not recognize the authority of the old order, but tactically it is a necessity. We are negotiating with the Chicago city government, a six-day treaty. All of the Chicago newspapers as well as various pressure groups have urged the City of Chicago to grant the permit. They recognize full well the huge social problem they face if we are forced to use the streets of Chicago for our action. The possibility of violence will be greatly reduced. There is no guarantee that it will be entirely eliminated. This is the United States, 1968, remember. If you are afraid of violence you shouldn't have crossed the border. This matter of a permit is a cat and mouse game. The Chicago authorities do not wish to grant it too early, knowing this would increase the number of people that descend on the city."[15]

As noted by Hoffman, the media was putting pressure on the city to grant the permits, in fact, their coverage suggested that "The city was a powder keg about to explode," because of the stubbornness on the part of Daley in refusing to grant the permits. Thus the media was doing their part in stoking the public's expectation of violence.

The police department turned down media requests to have the police demonstrate on television the use of mace and to discuss the possible acquisition of armored vehicles to be used in crowd control. Requests came to me (Frank Sullivan, Daley's press secretary) from network owned television stations to permit the filming of police target practice, to arrange for interviews with members of the police anti-sniper teams, and to set up demonstrations of any police training to combat rioting. Much of the media worked to develop the thesis that the police planned to have a confrontation with the demonstrators. The truth was that confrontation was the National Mobilization Committee's goal and the police hoped to avoid it. Everything connected with the police was given a sinister connotation.[16]

In fact, for the New Leftists and the Yippies, the role of the media was turning out even better than had been expected.

There were already signs that Daley's heavy handed tactics had alienated the mass media. On Sunday (August 25), the leaders of the National Mobilization Committee met in a mood of near euphoria. Some of them had just finished watching a correspondent on NBC News conclude that democracy was being impaled on the barbed wire around the convention site... "The most chilling sight of the decade." "One hundred percent victory in propaganda," exulted Hayden.[17]

"Now to do More with Less"...

By varied accounts, by showtime on August 25, MOBE and the Yippies had drawn no more than two to three thousand protesters from out of town and perhaps three to five thousand from the Chicago environs, figures far lower than they had originally expected or at least hoped for. Though resolved, Hayden argued that the numbers didn't really matter, now to do more with less, "Relations grew strained within the Mobilization."

Dave Dellinger no longer trusted Davis and Hayden's declared commitment to tactical non-violence. "Both of them," as Dellinger later described his worries, "were strongly committed to the idea that in the long run the movement would have to move to violent resistance and armed struggle. They couldn't totally resist the temptation to prepare for the future by making occasional contemptuous remarks about pacifists and bourgeois liberals who refused to face up to the necessity of violence."[18]

Indeed, on the eve of the convention, "Hayden's rhetoric rose to a new, feverish pitch of violence." We are coming to Chicago to vomit on the 'politics of joy to expose the secret decisions, upset the night club orgies, and face the Democratic Party with its illegitimacy and criminality. The American reality is being stripped to its essentials. Our victory lies in progressively de-mystifying a false democracy, showing the organized violence underneath reformism and manipulation." Chicago would be a showdown between a police state and a people's movement. The protesters would reassert the sovereignty of the people; they would covertly strike through small guerrilla surprise acts and make their numbers visible in mass demonstrations. "Democracy is in the streets" blared the headline in one of Hayden's pre-convention manifestos. Hayden himself quoted Chairman Mao: "Dare to struggle, dare to win."[19]

But while the general strategy was acceptable and coherent enough for all concerned, the actual tactics encountered much disagreement. The basic issue now was in how far should they go in confronting, provoking, or in acquiescing the police with whom they would shortly be in contact with for much of the week. While some argued that they were there simply to bear witness in a militant but nonviolent manner, others felt that Daley's refusal to grant the protesters permits and the threat of police violence had left the demonstrators no choice but to "turn the convention upside down."

In fact, Hayden stridently called for "a stronger sense of moral resolve." "People have to be faced with the existential question of giving their lives, forced into a moral squeeze and asked what they are willing to do to stop the war."[20]

NOTES

[1] Mike Royko, Boss, (New York, E.P. Dutton & Co.) 1971), 172.

[2] Lewis Chester, Godfrey Hodgson and Bruce Page, *An American Melodrama, The Presidential Campaign of 1968* (New York Viking Press, 1969) 504.

[3] Len O'Connor, *Clout, Mayor Daley and His City* (Chicago, Henry Regnery Co., 1975), 204.

[4] Royko, *Boss, 173.*

[5] Chester, Hodgson, Page, *An American Melodrama,* 514, 515.

[6] Jason Epstein, *The Great Conspiracy Trial* (New York, Random House, 1971), 121.

[7] Eugene Kennedy, *Himself! The Life and Times of Mayor Richard F. Daley* (New York, Viking Press, 1978) 228.

[8] Ibid., 225.

[9] Norman Mailer, *Miami and the Siege of Chicago,* an informal history of the Republican and Democratic Conventions of *1968* (New York, World Publishing Co., 1968), 103, 104.

[10.] Frank Sullivan, Legend, *The only inside story about Mayor Richard F. Daley* (Chicago, Bonus Books, 1989), 40.

[11] Jason Epstein, *The Great Conspiracy Trial,* 337.

[12] Eugene Kennedy, *Himself, The Life and Times of Richard F. Daley,* 223, 224.

[13] Ibid, 223.

[14] Chester/Hodgson/Page, *An American Melodrama,* 519.

[15] Norman Mailer, *Miami and the Siege of Chicago,* 136.

[16] Frank Sullivan, *Legend, The Only Inside Story About Mayor Richard F. Daley,* 37, 38.

[17] James Miller, *Democracy is in the Streets, From Port Huron to the Siege of Chicago* (New York, Simon and Schuster, 1987), 299.

[18] Ibid, 296.

[19] Ibid, 297, 298.

[20] Ibid, 299.

Part II: Let's Get It On!

With the stage now set, the curtain raised and the media's psychological buildup of the past few months at its peak, events were now set into motion that would generate for this convention the controversy that has surrounded it ever since.

Who Provoked Whom?...

Essentially, the controversy rests upon the physical confrontations between the police and the New Left and Yippie protesters that took place in and around Lincoln and Grant Parks early in the week, and that which occurred in front of the Hilton (where most of the Democratic Party's delegates were housed) on Michigan at Balbo on Wednesday evening, August 28. A substantial part of the controversy pertains to the question of provocation—who provoked whom! Did the city/police administration itself provoke their own police by issuing them controversial orders to clear Lincoln Park every night after 11:00 p.m. when perhaps it wasn't really necessary? Did the protesters provoke the police by refusing to leave the parks until forced to do so, by taunting them as "pigs" and other such derogatory epithets and by hurling rocks, bottles and other such projectiles at them? Did the police themselves provoke further unruly action and civil disobedience by the protesters in the heavy handed treatment they administered once they got their hands on many of them? To what extent did the media provoke any of the actions perpetrated by either the police or protesters that week? And ultimately, what level of police response is appropriate given the degree of provocation—is a club on the head a legally justified response to being called a "mother f!#@ fascist pig?"

The Actual Confrontations...

The nature of the physical confrontations when broken down, by and large, basically consisted of policemen clubbing down protesters with their batons (resulting in many instances of people having their heads split open) after being ordered to clear the parks and streets throughout the week, and of protesters pelting the police with whatever objects they could lay their hands on. Much of it early in the week occurred at night, especially in and around Lincoln Park where the Yippie's Festival of Life was being held. After the first night, it became a ritual. The police loudly and clearly announce their intentions to enforce the 11:00 p.m. park curfew and order the crowd assembled there to leave. While some of the protesters leave, hundreds defiantly remain.

Then the police skirmish line, three deep, came through the park. The cop bullhorn bellowed that anyone in the park, including newsmen, were in violation of the law. Nobody moved. The newsmen did not believe that they were marked men; they thought it was just a way for the cops to emphasize their point. The media lights were turned on for the confrontation, Near the Stockton Drive embankment, the line of police came up to the Yippies and the two lines stood there, a few steps apart, in a moment of meeting that was almost formal. The kids (protesters) were yelling: "Parks belong to the people! Pig! Pig! Oink! Oink!" It is legend by now that the final insult that caused the first wedge of cops to break loose upon the Yippies was "Your mother sucks dirty cock!" The kids wouldn't go away and then the cops began shoving them hard up the Stockton Drive embankment and hitting them with their clubs.[21]

This is the scenario that repeats itself throughout the week whether in Lincoln Park, Grant Park, or in front of the Hilton the night "the whole world was watching." Tear gas and mace were also widely employed by the police and the National Guard, and they proved highly, though not completely, effective as dispersal agents.

Media Outrage...

Reporters and cameramen covering the convention at street level frequently became entangled in the melees between the police and the protesters. I thought I would try it just once and I said, "I'm a reporter, officer." "That's nice," he said, shoving me hard again in the back and rapping the back of my head... It was because reporters and photographers felt, in their naive arrogance, that they possessed special rights and asserted them they were beaten so badly. You take a picture of a cop wrecking a kid's ball with his club, and you expect to walk away and publish the picture. Now that is silly. You expect the cop to respect you and say "Sir" to you and protect you and let you walk away and write things that he himself will feel to be disparaging. Very silly. No, sir, all groups in our sectarian, pluralistic society have ways of protecting their own, and police are no different.[22]

When they realized they were at risk, the media's outrage directed toward police conduct markedly intensified and when editors demanded from Daley an accounting, he appeared insensitive:

During the day, the mayor's office had asked the newspapers and the TV media why they were so upset, saying that there were 6,000 newsmen Chicago for Convention Week and that only 17 had been beaten in Lincoln Park Sunday night.[23]

Daley also emphasized that newsmen were not to be afforded special rights, and if they were in areas where city ordinances or police orders were in effect, they were expected to obey the law or suffer the consequences. An order, however, was drafted by Frank Sullivan, Daley's press secretary as well as a former reporter for the *Chicago Sun-Times*. Issued by Superintendent Conlisk, the order directed the police to cooperate with newsmen "despite any personal feelings," and that "specific officers be assigned to the various trouble areas to make certain the rights of the media were not violated."[24] As in the case of the media, however, "innocent bystanders" (non protesters, citizens of the Lincoln Park neighborhood, passers-by, tourists, etc.,) were also not spared if they happened to find themselves within the reach of a frenzied cop swinging a nightstick.

The Yippie/New Left Profile...

Objective answers to the above mentioned questions pertaining to provocation, confrontation and legally justified response, however, have been hard to come by because at the very heart of the controversy, then and today, lies a conflict of cultural and class values. Generally speaking, each side represented two different stratums of American society. The New Leftists and the Yippies were generally, though not exclusively, middle to upper middle class in economic and social orientation. Many of their parents were liberal or socialistic in political orientation. Many of the leaders had been "red diaper babies," whose parents were "Old Leftists." (The Old Left was primarily comprised of socialists (including former communists) who had gone underground during the McCarthy Era of the early 50s and after Khrushchev's striking admissions at the Twentieth Party Congress in Moscow in 1956.)

Reared in an age of "permissiveness," their parents had followed the principles, spare the rod and spoil the child, laid out by the famous 1950s baby doctor, Benjamin Spock, who himself would later play a leading role in the anti-draft resistance movement. This was a generation of middle to upper class youth in which the word no was considered harmful to their self-esteem. This led to a "crisis in authority" that would render many parents helpless for it placed their children on the same level of the family pecking order as the parents themselves:

With children well armed, the negotiations between the generations helped transform many homes into war zones, where, as one minister who specialized in inter-generation counseling wrote, fighting "continued until each has become so defensive and battle scarred" that meaningful communication essentially stopped. Though no doubt painful, such combat was more honorable than the alternatives. Some parents avoided war simply through surrender, which rendered family relationships meaningless; others ignored the fight altogether and refused to compromise. Middle class children were far more likely to suffer from "alienation" than were working class kids. Kenniston's young radicals were all of the middle or upper class. At least in urban and suburban areas, Coleman found, middle class families were more willing to "release" their children into "the adolescent culture." One consequence of this "release" was an estimated 500,000 to one million children who ran away from home annually by 1972, the majority of whom were "middle class dropouts." One such youngster told author Christine Chapman that she ran away because: "I hate living in the suburbs. There isn't anything to do and no one to talk to. My brother is away and my parents and I never talk. I'll probable end up with a psychiatrist again."[25]

For many there was no want, no hardship, too much taken for granted, to such a degree that life itself didn't seem real. Although their parents, having experienced both the Depression and WWII, had perhaps struggled mightily to achieve for themselves and for their children the life they could now afford to enjoy, their children were unable to tangibly appreciate what had been done for them.

In Growing Up Absurb (1960), Paul Goodman wondered why young people growing up in the United States could be anything but estranged. In past societies, Goodman claimed, young people were brought up to maturity through established rites of passage against which they tested their mettle. There being nothing worthwhile in modern America to test themselves against, young men were at a loss to direct their energy to constructive pursuits. Instead they grew "alienated."[26]

It was on university campuses where many of this middle class generation found avenues (via) such radical student organizations as the Students for a Democratic Society and the Free Speech Movement) such radical student organizations as the Students for a Democratic Society and the Free Speech Movement) in which to channel their alienation and discontent into radical politics. It was also on the campuses that many student radicals began their search for "authenticity," for something that was real and not plastic, not disposable and not synthetic. These were all terms that they themselves applied to the well insulated, pre-fabricated, highly mobile if not rootless, sterile, suburban world their well intentioned parents had raised them up into in order to shield them from the "real world."

This also accounts for their experimentation with mind altering drugs: marijuana, LSD and Heroin and eastern religions: Zen Buddhism and Transcendental Meditation, all attempts to experience different kinds of "reality." The war, however, presented this middle class generation with a reality of life they found difficult, if not ill equipped, to come to terms with an early and violent potential death in a rice paddy in a far off land called Vietnam.

Student Rebellion...

The students rebelled. In a society inviting rebellion against authority, this particular generation of students was uniquely suited to oblige. Many of them had grown up with parents who had only recently achieved middle class status and who had responded by giving their children all the benefits of affluence. Moreover, the war touched them as it did no other group. Students and other members of their age group were being asked to fight, and even with easy deferments the war was behind a great many personal decisions and narrowed many options.[27]

The war was also a manifestation of what they perceived to be the inherent violence within the liberal corporate establishment. This, in the words of Carl Ogelsby, an SDS leader present in Chicago in 1968, was a "system that molded together the capitalist search for profit, anti-communism, and imperialism," and one that not only had raised them, but one in which they had come to deplore. It followed then, according to New Left theorists, that rebellion brought liberation, and if peace demonstrations, the burning of draft cards and other protest actions were not enough to stop the war in Vietnam, then "revolution" was not only justifiable but inevitable. However, in spite of this fevered condition, revolution was objectively impossible. Middle-class America was manifestly content with the comforts of consumer capitalism. When radicals tried to organize in working class high schools, they were often chased out and occasionally beaten up. The claims about an imminent were grand in inverse proportion to how distant they were in fact. Unmoored from political reality, the New Left turned extreme, both in theory and in action as it imagined a reality all its own. Increasingly self-contained, having traded politics for the liberating virtues of violence, there was no one to check them but themselves.[28]

Though incapable of "checking themselves," they found a force on the other side of the barricades in the parks and on the streets of Chicago at the Democratic National Convention that was ready and primed to do just that.

Chicago 1968: A Blue Collar Town...

Chicago policemen, like most policemen, reflect blue collar values. Most of them live in the city's bungalow belt because they are required by law to live in the city, so they share the community feelings toward the suburban liberal who wants them to integrate, while the suburbs remain white. Many policemen are veterans and in a quasi-military job, so they dislike peace groups. To the police, the peace marchers were part of the (Red) menace.[29]

Chicago was a blue collar town. Being multi-faceted industrially, it was home to more unions than any other of in America. As Mayor Daley, whose father was a union sheet metal worker, represented the blue collar/working class values of Chicago's citizenry, so did his police department. Thus in their encounters and subsequent confrontations with the radicalized New Leftists and Yippies, they reacted and viewed their actions only according to the dictates of the class value system. Here is one police officer's observation of the confrontations:

We toured the Lincoln Park area, where the hordes of troublemakers were meandering about. There were several thousand unshaven, shabbily dressed, dirty mopes, just spoiling for trouble. They had no cause to champion, just an excuse to flaunt the law—en masse. Anticipation of violence filled the air with the electricity of excitement. The weather was beautiful and the mopes were sprawled all over the place, some drunk, some appearing to be high on drugs. Some who were conned into thinking it would be a peaceful demonstration, were singing and dancing to the music of tape recorders and potable radios. This gaiety would turn to hatred when darkness cloaked the park. National Guard units started to arrive and I for one was happy to see them. We heard reports that the mob was tearing park benches apart to burn along with tree limbs for bon fires. By now, the mood was escalating towards violence.

The police loudspeaker blared, "The park is closed, you will be arrested if you remain!" This announcement was answered with a chorus of four-letter words from the half crazed crowd which was now over 10,000. The search lights were turned on as about 70 policemen, now wearing gas masks, formed two ranks and marched towards the missile throwing crowd. The blue helmeted policemen and the mob were toe to toe. Sporadic incidents were igniting everywhere. In Old Town, just west of the park, windows were being smashed. People were running and screaming. There were fights everywhere. News media personnel were everywhere. Flash bulbs were popping all over. News media cameramen were taking hundreds of feet of film. As usual, the news media cameras recorded the policemen repelling physical attacks, but rarely the attack itself. Whether by coincidence, or editing of film, the police were made to look like the aggressors. In reality, they were doing their job, enforcing the law, meeting force with legal, overwhelming force. God, they did a magnificent job! Not one shot was fired, or a life lost in the madness. I was active at several other disturbances and fortunately not hurt—just ashamed that our society had reached a new low. For their valiant, superb handling of these riots, the police were to be maligned, criticized and actually accused of creating some disturbances. This is probably the biggest injustice of all.[30]

This view is far removed from most media accounts in which the police were depicted as sadistic, psycho-pathic perpetrators of "gestapo tactics." Indeed, it also indicates a clash of cultural values and one in which those of working class cops and those of middle and upper class protesters were diametrically opposed.

Part III: America Decides

Who Did the Fighting/Who Did the Dying...

Vietnam was just one issue among many, but it did not go unnoticed that those who fought the war were overwhelmingly working class and for one primary reason—the class biased mechanism of college deferments. Thus:

A powerful sense of class grievance also infused the way the average American understood the war. Working class parents sent their sons away because establishment liberals had called them to defend the nation. But that same establishment did not call its own children, who all too often responded by joining anti-war protests. "I've got one son, my youngest in Vietnam," a woman explained to Brendan and Patricia Sexton. "He couldn't get out of it by going to college. We can't understand how all those rich kids, the kids with the beads from the fancy suburbs, how they get off when my son has to go over there and maybe get his head shot off." It was possible to wonder whether the government tolerated the protests precisely because "those privileged kids" were the ones "carrying Viet Cong flags around, saying they want the enemy to win," another parent mused. "If my son was doing that, instead of kids whose papas have a lot of pull, he'd be locked up fast." *The cause of the antiwar movement was probably damaged far more by the gap between the protesters and the people fighting the war than by its hippie image.* They had good reason to believe that they were being made saps, forced to fight a war that the children of affluence could safely turn up their noses. "I'm against this war," one woman whose son was killed in Vietnam explained with simple eloquence, the way a mother is, whose sons are in the army, who has lost a son fighting in it. The world hears those demonstrators making their noise. The world doesn't hear me."[31]

As these working class sentiments imply, it was not merely a question of being for or against the war, it was more along the lines of fulfilling one's duty as a citizen to their country. The middle and upper classes were getting rewarded for shirking their responsibilities while the working class was having to pay the price—economically, educationally, psychologically, and physically—in casualties, dead or wounded—for what they perceived to be their patriotic duty, what they owed a land they were proud to live in.

"A Father Who Spares the Rod Hates His Son"…

Proverbs: Ch. 13, V. 24. Chicago policemen were also representative of every ethnic/racial neighborhood in the city. While certainly not the sum total of their existence, ethnic consciousness did provide for a sense of rootedness and an identity that had proven relatively resilient to the mass homogenization process that had taken place in suburbia. As part of their psychological make-up, it had allowed them to maintain many of the time tested and passed down values, faith, family, patriotism, that middle class children, via their parents, had consciously or unconsciously shed as square, uptight and repressive. The ethnic cultures from which Chicago policemen were drawn, more often than not, represented a working class upbringing that contrasted sharply with the ones of those whom they confronted on the streets of Chicago at the DNC.

As pointed out by David Steigerwald and others in regards to the general norms of working class culture:

By nearly all accounts, the working class family was both laggard in accepting the new values and less influenced by mass culture. With regard to child rearing practices—even when controlled for ethnicity and religious affiliation. "working class parents lagged behind" the middle class in embracing permissive techniques. They were more likely to use corporal punishment and to insist on strict obedience to adult authority of any kind, not caring about the child's motives for misbehavior. The working class, Mirra Komarovsky wrote, "retained a pre-Freudian innocence about human behavior," where misbehavior was taken as a sign of insufficient discipline, and the goals of childbearing were "expressed in moral terms." Beyond that, working class Americans were simply more conservative; having achieved some measure of economic comfort, they no longer saw external authority as a class enemy. They "are willing to accord respect to authority," Kohn believed, "in return for security and respectability," and they taught their children accordingly. The unspoken assumption (by the "experts" though) was that middle class child rearing was superior.

However, as reflected upon by Helen, a working class maid in regards to her employer's method of parenting: Her employer's believed that children who were taught to respect authority were enslaved to the status quo, but to Helen, children raised in a permissive household never learned the virtue of mutual respect. "In that house," she told Robert and Jane Coles, "the kids speak back to their parents, act as fresh and snotty as can be. I want to scream sometimes when I hear those brats talking as if they know everything." And middle class advocates of liberation in the 60s rebuked working class Americans for their "primitive" devotion to discipline, their acceptance of authority, and their uptight refusal to follow their impulses.[32]

Another important feature of working class culture in Chicago was the existence of the nation's largest parochial school system and of which many Chicago policemen were products. Founded, whether Catholic or Lutheran, along ethnic lines and religious traditions brought over from Ireland, Italy, Poland or Germany, they essentially reinforced and advocated the emphasis on discipline, obedience and respect for authority in the school, the home and society at large.

As in the working class home, corporal punishment was often times wielded in order to promote and maintain a controlled learning environment. Showing disrespect or displaying unruly or impulsive behavior within the school was routinely rewarded with slaps, kicks, the "board of education" or severe tongue lashings. Working class parents had no qualms with these methods it was the way they had been brought up, and if they did they had no recourse except to take their children out of the school. As noted by Mike Royko above, many Chicago policemen had served in the military, and whether in wartime or not, usually in services like the Marines or the Army (which like the police department attracts a certain type) where the standards of physical discipline are the most stringent.

No One Was Killed!…

These sociological profiles do not account for all of the actions of either the protesters or policemen who confronted each other or explain all of the violence that occurred at the DNC. However, they can be considered representative of both, and they allow one to more easily interpret, clarify and understand the surcharged, violent energy that surfaced that week. That no one was killed can be attributed to the fact that in coming to Chicago in order to provoke confrontation with the police, no guns, knives, clubs or pipes were wielded or a real blood-bath would have resulted, for the police would have been legally justified in using their firearms at the riots on the West side in the wake of the King assassination the previous April.

As ugly as it appeared to many unfamiliar with the nature of policing, the police reacted as they have always done with unruly subjects—active and passive resisters in violation of the law—after verbal direction had been of no avail, they physically enforced cooperation—pain compliance in police department parlance. Force implies physical control. The DNC was just an example of this in a mass situation. That highly charged, volatile circumstances may provoke in a police officer actions or reactions that overcome his training and get the better of him, is part and parcel of the self-preservation instinct inherent in all human beings. That this occurred all too often at the DNC there can also be no doubt.

However, given the sociological antagonism that existed between the police and the protesters that week, which put things on an "us against them" level, and all of the other undercurrents present that week, circumstances beyond the individual police officer's control, what occurred should not be considered surprising. That much of the police violence was "indiscriminate," in that innocent bystanders got "whacked" too, was unfortunate. But the police were the only ones in uniform and when confronted by the "hit and run" tactics employed by many of the protesters, especially those throwing projectiles from a distance, in their eyes everyone was suspect. And if they weren't, what were they doing down there in the first place.

Dissecting the Outrage, the Street Coppers' Line...

That these were middle and upper class protesters from "good homes" also factored in the outrage. Growing up in the city as most Chicago policemen did, they knew from their own experiences as youths just what questioning a policeman's authority, let alone provoking him via taunts or derogatory epithets, would bring, and for the most part there would be no sympathy extended on their behalf at home or at school. This then is not only a facet of their working class upbringing that distinguished them from the middle and upper class protesters, but one that can also be attributed to the way each side interpreted the controversy.

As far as many Chicago policemen were concerned, the "cake eaters" kids carrying the black banner of anarchy, the Viet Cong flag, the red flag of revolution, all the while burning the American flag and literally throwing bags of their own shit at them, finally 'got something they had needed for a long time—the rod-what was the big deal! At one point during

Convention Week, Dunn (C/O of the National Guard) said he regarded the kids in the streets no differently from the way he regarded his own children, maybe they just needed to have been spanked when they were growing up. Dunn saw it as mere adolescent rebellion.[33]

The Press Reports...

That the great majority of the media pilloried Daley and his police department was no surprise, for they were not only liberal, socially and politically, they were also representative of the middle and upper classes whose children, the protesters, were getting whacked around by Daley's police right before their very eyes.

During the convention itself and immediately afterward, neither the press nor television stopped short at reporting what happened. They took sides editorially, and the great majority took sides against the mayor. "The truth was," wrote Tom Wicker of the *New York Times,* "these were our children in the streets, and the Chicago police beat them up." And with Olympian solemnity, the *Times* editorialized on August 30 that "one Richard J. Daley" was guilty of "rigidity," "insensitivity," and "repression." As late as September 7, the *Washington Post* went a good deal further. It printed on that date a column by Leroy Aarons which compared Daley's real Chicago to the mythical gangland Chicago of Berthold Brecht's play, *The Resistible Rise of Arturo Ui.* The column ended with the play's last line, in which the actor who plays the gangster-dictator takes off his Hitler mustache and warns the audience that, though Hitler is dead, "the bitch that bore him is in heat again."[34]

But Not All...

On September 3, 1968, Joe Kraft wrote a column in which he asked, rhetorically and repentently, whether the press did not suffer from certain prejudices. "The answer, I think, is that Mayor Daley and his supporters have a point. Most of us in what is called the communications field are not rooted in the great mass of ordinary Americans—in Middle America. And the result shows up not merely in occasional episodes such as the Chicago violence but more importantly in the systematic bias toward young people, minority groups, and the kind of presidential candidates who appeal to them. "Kraft thought that this was because the press was dominated by an "upper class outlook" which could afford to be indulgent to rebellious Negroes and kids. The press was out of touch with the public. Then Chicago blew up in their faces. Beaten by cops and jeered by delegates, reporters found themselves openly detested as a biased, leftist elite. The violence radicalized a few journalists, but most of the newsmen were simply shocked and hurt to find out that a majority of Americans thought that the press sucked.[35]

America's Verdict...

Indeed, as the reactions flowed in from the reader's mailbag in newspapers across the country, it was only too apparent that the great majority of the American public sided with Daley and his police department. Surveys taken immediately after the convention established that most people polled thought Daley and his police had been correct. "Daley came out of the convention even more popular than before because "bust their heads" was the mood of the land."[36] According to Jack Mabley of the *Chicago American,* "80 to 85 percent of the callers and letter writers were cheering for Daley and the Cops."[37] "In the days that followed the convention, the Mayor's office received more than 100,000 letters, of which the ratio in favor of his policies, regarding permits for demonstrators and the police actions, was 20 to one."[38]

"Messages would start coming in from various professional organizations—from the American Psychological Association, for example—canceling their conventions in Chicago during the next year because of the disorders. Critical mail came from the professors and do-gooders who had vexed him all his life. But the great bulk of messages came from average Americans who were sick of demonstrations as Daley was, and who saw in him one of the staunchest defenders of everything in which they believed."[39] Thus the media was forced to reconsider their interpretation:

With honorable exceptions, most notably *Newsweek and Time,* many of whose reporters had been personally roughed-up and were not inclined to forget it, the press came to accept Daley's version of events more or less uncritically. Cars in Chicago blossomed with bumper stickers saying "We support Mayor Daley and his Chicago Police," and this reaction was by no means limited to Chicago. Partly this was a spontaneous reaction. Millions of Americans had become sick and tired of marches and protests and demonstrations. The belief in law and order was proving stronger than more permissive beliefs for them. Others were genuinely troubled by the question where the line should be drawn. In part, no doubt, Daley—like George Wallace and Richard Nixon—was the passive beneficiary of a real public mood.[40]

Together Nixon and Wallace managed 57% of the vote, and when considering Humphrey had been Johnson's man and to who Daley had delivered 400,000 votes, much to the chagrin of the New Left, the election—subsequent to what happened in Chicago at the DNC—as David Steigerwald noted, was strong evidence of "the public's fear that political radicalism and a breakdown in law and order were related."[41]

Of course, there was the obligatory study, the Walker Report (Rights in Conflict). However, even according to a *Life* magazine analysis, it "did not fully establish why police discipline collapsed." Although voluminous in eyewitness detail, its conclusions, that the police were provoked by word and act, but all too often their response was unrestrained and indiscriminate and were responsible for "violent acts far in excess of the requisite force for crowd dispersal or arrest,"[42] would change few perceptions for, as noted above, the overwhelming majority of the nation held otherwise.

Nevertheless, the nature of the police response can be seen not only as the primary source of a controversy that remains to this day, but one which also revealed a cultural and class fault line in America's perception of it. In retrospect then, Daley, and his police reacted exactly the way Tom Hayden, Rennie Davis, Abbie Hoffman and Jerry Rubin had intended. And, just as expected, the liberals, the media and their parents overindulged themselves and their kids in sympathy and outrage, the same way they had always overindulged them since birth. What unexpectedly backfired though was the rest of America's reaction. Much to their displeasure and embarrassment was the fact that "they didn't get it"—*America's sympathy and support for Daley and his police.*

Postscript...

It's interesting to note that upon the GI withdrawal from Southeast Asia in 1975, the ensuing genocidal and political mass murder (numbering 3-4 million) perpetrated by the North Vietnamese Communists in Vietnam and Pol Pot's Khymer Rouge in Cambodia caused scarcely a ripple of protest from Messrs. Hayden, Rubin, Hoffman and Davis at the time. Indeed, it might be asked, where did all the flower children go?

Author's Note

My sincere gratitude is extended to those police officers who related to me their individual experiences at the 68 DNC during the research phase of this paper. Having not been there myself, their collective experiences allowed me to grasp more fully the street coppers' perceptions at that time. Thanks then to Tom Fleming, Carl Sonne, Al Rogers, George Mikell, George Volkl, Bill Getz, Norbert Holzinger and Horst Zickenheiner.

Edited and condensed from a *De Paul University, Graduate History,* research/seminar paper written by P.O. Mike Haas (M.A., De Paul '98) of 019.

Officer Haas, a 13 year veteran, is currently the assistant editor of the *Chicago Police Star Magazine,* Editor of the *German American Police Association* and Editor of the *CPD's Educational and Training Division Bulletins.*

NOTES

[21] *John Schultz, No one was Killed* (Chicago, Big Table Publishing Co., 1969, 86, 87.

[22] Ibid, 117.

[23] Ibid, 118.

[24] Frank Sullivan, Legend, The only inside story about Mayor Richard F. Daley, 42-43.

[25] David Steigerwald, *The Sixties and the End of Modern America* (New York, St. Martin's Press, 1995), 250.

[26] Ibid, 248.

[27] Ibid, 134.

[28] Ibid, 140.

[29] Mike Royko, Boss, 178.

[30] William I. Gertz, Patrolman (New York, Vantage Press, 1977), 54-56.

[31] David Steigerwald, *The Sixties and the End of Modern America*, 117, 118.

[32] Ibid, 256-259.

[33] John Schultz, *No one was killed*, 160.

[34] Chester, Hodgson, Page, *An American Melodrama*, 592-593.

[35] Timothy Crouse, *The Boys on the Bus, Riding with the Campaign Press Corps* (New York, Random House, 1972), 129-131.

[36] Mike Royko, *Boss*, 194.

[37] Chester, Hodgson, Page, *An American Melodrama*, 594.

[38] Frank Sullivan, *Legend*, 50.

[39] Eugene Kennedy, *Himself*, 237.

[40] Chester, Hodgson, Page, *An American Melodrama*, 594.

[41] David Steigerwald, The Sixties and the End of Modern America, 32.

[42] Life Magazine, December 6, 1968, 37.

BIBLIOGRAPHY

Crouse, Timothy. *The Boys on the Bus, Riding with the Campaign Press Corps*, New York: Random House, 1974.

Epstein, Jason. *The Great Conspiracy Trial*, New York: Random House, 1970.

Chester, Lewis, Godfrey Hodgson, and Bruce Page. *An American Melodrama, The Presidential Campaign of 1968*, New York: Viking Press, 1969.

Getz, William. *Patrolman*, New York: Vantage Press, 1977.

Kennedy, Eugene. *Himself, The Life and Times of Mayor Richard F. Daley*, New York: Viking Press, 1978.

Mailer, Norman. *Miami and the Siege of Chicago*, New York: The World Publishing Company, 1968.

Miller, James. *Democracy is in the Streets, From Port Huron to the Siege of Chicago*, New York: Simon and Schuster, 1987.

O'Connor, Len. Clout, Mayor Daley and His City, Chicago: Henry Regenery Co., 1975.

Rakove, Milton. *Don't Make No Waves, Don't Back No Losers, An Insider's Analysis of the Daley Machine*, Bloomington: Indiana University Press, 1975.

Royko, Mike. *Boss,* New York: E.P. Dutton, 1971.

Schultz, John. *No one was killed*, Chicago: Big Table Publishing, 1969.

Sullivan, Frank. *Legend, The only inside story about Mayor Richard F. Daley*, Chicago: Bonus Books, 1989.

Steigerwald, David. *The Sixties and the End of Modern America*, New York: St. Martin's Press, 1995.

PERIODICALS

"Walker Report Discloses The Police Rioted at the Democratic Convention," *Life Magazine*, December 6, 1968.

BEST FRIENDS

by John H. Pappas

Michael R. Elias, Star No. 13848 was and still is one of my best friends. Mike and I were best friends from childhood. We also were in Nam at the same time. Mike was Army and I was in the Marines.

We subsequently worked tactical units in three different districts: the 010th (Marquette), 007th (Englewood) and the 008th (Chicago Lawn). Mike quit the summer of 1976 and moved his family to Oregon where they still reside. I stayed on and retired from the C.P.D. June 16, 1999, with 31 years of service. During those years I was assigned to 14 different units.

I'm very proud of my time spent, but am more proud of the friends I made on the C.P.D. during those

Michael R. Elias (he's on the left with shotgun) and John H. Pappas. The photo was taken approximately October 1969 while we were assigned to the Tenth (010) Police District. It had been decided to take the photo as we were both awaiting assignment to the district's Tactical Unit in plain clothes. At the time we were both fresh from Vietnam, having returned during 1967.

years. It was truly a privilege and an honor to work along with and know so many dedicated and outstanding individuals.

I believe that a lot of people fail to realize that big cities could not survive without a dedicated police department. *By John H. Pappas.*

BOUQUETS

Bouquets to Dr. Francis Peitch, principal of Ebinger and Stock schools, and to Roz Rubin, who developed a program of parent volunteers to assist in individualized instruction with Learning Disabled children. Considered successful after a trial period, the plan will probably be adopted in other schools.

Bouquets also to James Davern, who is a starring decoy member of the Chicago Police Department's much celebrated Mass Transit Unit. Jim was described in the *Tribune* as a "tenacious lawman, who not only wants to get his man every time but also will risk his life to get him in a 100 percent air tight arrest that will result in a conviction." For the further qualities of dedication and courage that Jim has, CACLD salutes him, and his family.

BUNGLED HIJACK TRY AT O'HARE

Chicago Tribune

Aug. 14, 1981, A Miami man was arrested Thursday at O'Hare International Airport after he reportedly pulled out a book of matches as he entered a

Republic Airlines jet bound for Green Bay and told a flight attendant: "Take me to Cuba or I'll blow up this plane." The flight attendant notified a nearby security guard who escorted the man from the aircraft and turned him over to Chicago police. The police then transported him to the Jefferson Park district lockup, according to officer George Pocius of the police detail at O'Hare. Pocius said Keith A. Allen, 21, reportedly an enlisted man in the United States Navy, was charged with disorderly conduct on a complaint signed by security officials for Republic. Pocius said the Federal Bureau of Investigation was notified but agents declined to bring federal hijacking charges.

HENRY P. BURTON

Cecil Ward and Henry P. Burton were assigned to the Public Transportation unit. The period of this assignment was from 1976 to 1993. They had the arduous task of keeping the peace at the south end of the Dan Ryan rapid transit line. The station was a point or connection where students from different high schools converged. Each school contained a different gang faction. The job of keeping the peace in this station caused Burton to be shot at. Thank God the gangbanger was a poor shot. Henry P. Burton is retired living in Las Vegas, NV. Cecil Ward is also retired.

THE CANINE UNIT

The Canine Unit was activated by Superintendent O.W. Wilson in 1961. I was a police officer with the Chicago Police Department from July 16, 1957 through Sept. 15, 1995.

I joined the Canine Unit as a handler in 1962. I was instructor-trainer of new man-dog teams from 1968 through 1972.

Henry P. Burton (left) and Cecil Ward

In 1972 I became a dispatcher in Communications of Chicago Police Department. I instructed new personnel for call-taking and dispatching policy and procedures for the 9-1-1 System until I retired as police officer Sept. 15, 1995.

I remained as civilian dispatcher with a group of other retired police dispatchers to work in the newly opened new 9-1-1 Communications Center located in a new building 1411 W. Madison St. I worked as civilian dispatcher from Sep. 16, 1995 through Mar. 1, 1999, when I retired.

CAPTURE SUSPECT IN O'HARE THEFTS

Chicago Daily Tribune

May 25, 1961. After a two day wait with binoculars and walkie-talkie sets, four patrolmen Wednesday captured a man accused of a series of thefts from trunks of autos parked at O'Hare Airport.

Alvery B. Willis, 34, of 1109 W. 63rd Street, was captured as he started to steal a spare tire from a 1961 sedan parked at the airport, police said.

Task Force patrolmen George Pocius, Ralph Gibson, Thomas McGovern and Edward Cashier captured him. They found five other stolen tires in the trunk of his car and a lock puller and screwdriver in the glove compartment.

The patrolmen had dressed in coveralls and mingled with construction workers to prevent recognition during the lookout.

Capt. Patrick J. Deeley of Jefferson Park District had requested the special help because of a recent series of thefts from autos at O'Hare.

HUGH E. CARROLL

This photo was taken at the Hudson Avenue Police Station, the old 36th District. The officer under the St. Jude's sign is Harold Walchuk with his dog, Prince. The other officer is Hugh Carroll with his dog, Baron, part of the first K-9 graduation class.

The three men in the center of the photo were arrested for armed robbery in the subway station at North Avenue and Clybourn. This arrest was made, I believe, around Christmas 1961.

Walchuk and Carroll were patrolling with their dogs late at night, under the elevator tracks at North Avenue and Clybourn. While patrolling under the tracks, the officers observed the three men running from the subway station into the alley where the officers just hap-

Harold Walchuk and Prince (left) and Hugh Carroll and Baron (right) guard prisoners, late 1961. (Chicago Tribune Photo)

pened to be patrolling. The men were ordered to halt and after seeing the police dogs, surrendered. Two of the offenders dropped their knifes, but were taken back to the subway station where the victim readily identified all three. A further search of one youth revealed the victim's wallet. All three youth confessed and were sentenced. I remember speaking to the victim who was in Chicago from California on a convention. He was so delighted in the fast work of the police.

CHICAGO POLICE DEPARTMENT 1874-2000

by Jack Rohan and Kevin Keefe

It was shortly after midnight, when Police Officer Kevin Keefe was shot by a sniper in Chicago's Rockwell Garden's housing project. Officer Keefe's wife, newborn baby, mother, father, and extended family waited impatiently in the intensive care unit of Cook County Hospital for news from doctors. We waited and summoned foxhole prayers. We watched cops mill convict's, shackled by wrist and ankle, about the gray corridors.

It was Mother's Day. We drank stale coffee, and spoke an occasional word or two. It was unusually quiet in retrospect, because we were silently rethinking our family history in the Chicago Police Department - Kevin is only the second to get shot in the line of duty in over 125 years of family service. We thought our history, like folklore, made us invincible. We thought wrong, but we reminisced anyway. Here is the story.

Andrew Rohan joined the police force in 1874 after emigrating here from Ireland to escape the potato famine and British oppression. He rose through the ranks to lieutenant, then chief of detectives in the early 1900s, and worked under the Police Chief, Francis

Lt. Andrew Rohan

O'Neil. Through this process, he acquired the nickname "Thief Catcher" and worldwide recognition for his work. A young and rising star had plans to exploit his popularity.

An emerging young magician named Harry Houdini challenged Lieutenant Rohan in a publicity stunt that Houdini staged, so Houdini could perform his shackled escape from a jail cell. Houdini had just invented the trick, and wanted to gain national exposure. According to a book, *Escape: The Life of Harry Houdini*, by Florence Meiman White, Lt. Rohan was skeptical of Houdini's trick. Who was this young wiseacre to challenge the Chief of Detectives anyway? A date and time was set for the stunt. When the time arrived, Lieutenant Rohan locked Houdini's handcuffs, and secured him in

Sgt. Andrew J. Rohan Sr.

the jail cell. Rohan then dealt a hand of cards to kill time while they waited with anxious newspaper reporters who hoped to muckrake the story.

The first hand wasn't fully dealt yet when Houdini walked out from the cell block. The reporters first thought Rohan had pulled a prank. Rohan was equally as stunned, and thereby quickly convinced them otherwise. The reporters believed it.

"We're lucky this guy is not a criminal, or we'd have real trouble on our hands," said Lieutenant Rohan. He also played poker with Jesse James. (We're currently searching for a book to document the Jesse James episode.)

Andrew Rohan had three sons. They all joined the Chicago Police Department. Andrew J. Rohan Sr. joined and rose to sergeant in the Detective Bureau. He retired at the age 40 (only 20 years of service required then) and became a bodyguard for Presidents Theodore Roosevelt and William H. Taft, and Emperor Hirochito of Japan and the Czar of Russia as well.

The Czar of Russia appreciated Rohan's presence as he met with the Russian people who rapidly grew fond of him, and offered him vodka as a Russian tradition of friendship. Who could refuse an ethnic toast? That would be rude - even to an Irishman. Mr. Rohan and the Czar toasted, and became good friends.

The third son, Timothy Rohan was on duty at the Saint Valentine's Day massacre. He was a sergeant at the old Sheffield Street station. As a young boy, Kevin Keefe loved the stories. This grim chapter of the story had just repeated itself, however.

Andrew Rohan's other son, William, one of three sons who also joined the department, was the first to get shot in the 1920s. The story was told to us when we were kids at Thanksgiving and Christmas dinners. William Rohan got shot in the cheekbone chasing a robber down an alley. The bullet remained lodged there because doctors had fewer resources in those days. He lived for decades, however, and coughed the bullet up years later at the dinner table.

Andrew Rohan Sr.'s son, Andrew J. Rohan Jr., became a policeman in 1946. Future Superintendent of Police, James B. Conlisk was among the graduates. Training at the time consisted of only two weeks of school at the old Chicago Avenue station. His first assignment was at the Summerdale Station followed by assignment to the old Roger's Park station. He was meritoriously promoted to detective, and transferred to the old area six headquarters at Grace and Damen where he worked as a homicide detective. He became known for his savvy techniques with descriptive language in his recollection of homicide scenes on his police reports. After 13 years of homicide, he moved to vice and gambling and retired in 1972.

Many stories were passed down to Kevin in the oral tradition from his grandfather, Andrew J. Rohan Jr. This inspired Kevin Keefe to join the Chicago Police Department. Today Keefe proudly wears his grandfather's star number: 6041.

Det. Andrew J. Rohan Jr.

Kevin Keefe, is mending well, and is expected to make a full recovery. He looks forward to returning to work in the Chicago Police Department.

Left: Swearing in ceremony, Navy Pier October 1997. of Officer Kevin J. Keefe (left). He is the grandson of Detective Andrew J. Rohan Jr., great-grandson of Sergeant Andrew J. Rohan Sr. and great-great-grandson of Chief of Detectives, Lieutenant Andrew Rohan. Kevin is wearing his grandfather's, Andrew J. Rohan Jr.'s, star #6041.

ANDREW ROHAN'S RETIREMENT SPEECH

North Shore News - 1910

"Gentleman, I stand before you in the capacity of lieutenant for the last time. Some of you, like myself, have grown old in the service of the police department. Others among you are just breaking in, and it's to the youngest of men that I wish to address a few words of advice.

There are two kinds of coppers. The honest kind and the dishonest - The grafter. I've traveled the road for 37 years, and I think I ought to know which of the two policemen you should choose. Be honest. That's the only way to get along in this business. You might go along grafting for a year or two, but you're bound to tumble. A grafting copper is soon found out, and he loses the respect of all, honest men. He even loses his own self-respect.

All policemen are not grafters, as some of our critics are prone to believe. In this respect, the department is much better today than it was a few years ago. There are men within the reach of my voice whose integrity will compare favorably with any set of men. They have performed their duties faithfully, and as a reward they have the satisfaction of knowing that no one can point a finger of scorn at them.

You young men who are on the threshold of a police career can rise to the highest ranks of the department if you follow the rules I suggest:

Be honest. Be faithful to your trust. Don't drink to excess and take good care of your families. A man who doesn't love and cherish his wife will never make a good policeman.

Drinking is the great pitfall of men in this line of work. More policemen get into trouble through drink than all other cases put together. I'll take a drink myself, but I know when to quit. Few men can handle it, and, if you can't, I'd advise you to leave it alone. I knew men once in the department who were sent to the penitentiary for crimes committed while they were drunk.

Policemen above all should always have a cool, level head. He doesn't know the hour or minute when he'll be called upon to face death at the point of a pistol.

I've put the best years of my life in this business, and what today I tell you I've learned in the school of experience, or from the sad experience of others. And another thing I want to impress upon you, and that is - be on the square with your brother officer. If you should meet a thief or former convict on the street, and you call him aside to speak to him; don't tell your partner that the fella is an old schoolmate of yours. That's the meanest kind of double crossing. Be on the square.

Now boys, I bid you good-bye. I wish every one of you success. And, I thank you for all the uniform courtesy you've always shown me. If my remarks have wounded anyone's feelings, I'm sorry. Good-bye. And God Bless you all."

CHICAGO POLICE DEPARTMENT HONORABLE MENTION

Presented To...
Police Officer Eugene McGuire
Star #2501
For...Strong Arm Robbery Arrest

On 2 December 1991 while you were stopped in traffic you observed a male black running and a female chasing him. The victim stopped and informed you that the offender had just taken her purse. You gave chase as the offender ran into a gangway. As you attempted to go around the building the offender ran from the gangway and jumped into the rear seat of the squad car, now realizing what he had done he attempted to exit, you immediately arrested him.

Congratulations on your alertness and dedication to duty!

COOPERATION NETS TRIO FOR BANK ROBBERIES

by Det. Donald E. Long, CPD (Ret)

In the early part of June 1975, information was obtained as to the whereabouts of several persons in the Chicago area who were committing bank robberies throughout the midwest. Sergeant Jerry Adams and Investigator Donald Long, Chicago Police Department, Area Two Robbery, were assigned to assist a senior agent of the FBI Chicago Bank Squad in a follow-up investigation of a bank robbery of the Gateway National Bank in November 1974, located at 7853 S. Stony Island Avenue which was one of the banks allegedly held up by this group of individuals.

On June 24, 1975, Sergeant Adams and Investigator Long accompanied several FBI agents in an attempt to serve a search warrant at 7740 S. Seeley. At approximately 8:00 a.m. Sergeant Adams and Investigator Long arrived in an unmarked squad in front of the two story house in this quiet residential neighborhood, along with two FBI squads. There were two more squads from the FBI positioned in the rear of the building. A call was made to the FBI office and they made a call to the house informing the female that answered the phone that the house was surrounded by the Chicago Police and the FBI, who had a Federal Search Warrant in their possession, and to open the door. The female shouted a few expletives into the phone and hung up. A few moments later semi-automatic gun-fire erupted from the second floor window in the direction of the officers and agents in front of the house. The squad car windows in the agents' autos in front of the house were shattered by gunfire.

The FBI swat team then fired back at the windows in the building. A pipe bomb was thrown into the back yard from the second floor, and exploded leaving a massive hole in the rear yard. Several rounds of tear gas were then fired into the house and the three individuals, two men and a woman, surrendered.

There were no injuries in this tremendous gun-battle which lasted approximately 30 minutes with shots fired back and forth, and the bomb thrown at the arresting officers.

Recovered from the house were another pipe bomb, an automatic 9mm carbine, two automatic pistols, a revolver, a large quantity of ammunition for the firearms, and the proceeds of a major hotel robbery.

One of the men was wanted for escape from a federal prison in Michigan, and one was on parole for bank robbery. All three were charged with assaulting federal officers. The female was charged with several bank robberies, after being identified in several bank robbery surveillance photos. The two men were also charged with several bank robberies. They were also charged with robbing the Continental Plaza Hotel on May 19, 1975, where a large amount of cash and checks were taken.

COP PROVES HE'S HIS DOG'S BEST FRIEND

by Patricia Leeds
Chicago Tribune

April 20, 1969. It isn't often that a policeman will give up a promotion to remain with his partner, but then Patrolman Frank Varallo, 37, felt Yank wasn't an ordinary partner.

Yank is a German Shepherd, and he and Varallo have worked as a team in the Chicago Police Canine unit for seven years.

When Varallo took the detective examination in July 1965, he placed high on the list and was called to attend the Police Academy for detective training. According to department rules, he had to give up Yank.

Policeman Has Misgivings...

Varallo had misgivings about turning in Yank to the canine training kennels where he would be retrained with another patrolman who would become his handler.

So it was with great reluctance that he left Yank at the kennel. Yank looked puzzled, then hurt.

"I never felt so bad in my life as when I had to turn my back and walk away from him," Varallo said.

"We had been through a lot together," he said. "There was the time we answered a report of a burglar in a factory. We got there, and Yank went bounding in with his usual zest for work. What we didn't know was that this was a mattress spring factory, and they have sunken vats of paint in which they dip their products.

Runs Into Vat...

"It was dark in there, and Yank was running too fast to stop in time. He went right into a vat of blue paint. We got him out, but what a mess. The only part of him that wasn't painted was his head.

"We tried everything to get the paint off, but nothing worked. Somebody said he looked like he was in uniform—it was the same blue as our uniform shirts. But Yank didn't think it was funny. It had hardened, and there was some danger of his skin being affected.

Experience Not Forgotten...

"There was only one thing to do. We had to shave off his entire coat."

Varallo said Yank never forgot his paint experience. He said that when he and Yank were sent to Wrigley field on a tip that a man sought for killing a policeman was hiding there, the dog searched everywhere except one closet. The closet contained paint cans.

Varallo tried to put these things out of his mind because a promotion to detective meant $600 a year extra pay. He went to the school, but each night when he came home he found the children crying and his wife sad. "I felt like a heel," he said. "Finally I took it up with the family."

The family consists of his wife, Anna, and four children, Joseph, 14, John, 10, Vivian, 8, and Victoria, 6.

"We decided we'd rather have Yank than my promotion," he said. "The next day I told the boss about my decision, and I went to the kennel to get Yank."

A Dejected Dog...

"When I got there he was lying in his kennel looking dejected. They told me he'd been that way since I brought him in. But the minute he heard my voice and I got him out, he leaped up and barked in such a way it was almost like he was saying 'Thanks boss for coming back'."

When it came time to take the exam again in 1967 (they're held every two years), Varallo took it again. Again he placed high and was called to report to school.

"It didn't take much thought this time though," he said. "I asked the family if they changed their minds.

I knew I felt the same and so did they, so I just didn't report for school the next day."

He and Yank are still working together, but now they're trainers at the police canine school in Des Plaines. Varallo, with Yank's help, also lectures at the academy.

Frank Varallo puts Yank through his paces at police canine school.

Frank Varallo holds leash, Yank bites padded arm of Patrolman William Wagner, assistant instructor at police canine school.

There will be a detective exam again this summer. Varallo doesn't plan to take it.

Cops-and-Robbers for Real; Cohen Watches

Ald. Christopher Cohen (46th) got an insider's look Thursday on how police handle crime in his ward and found them to be "highly professional."

Cohen went along with eight mass-transit unit plain clothesmen in their hunt for strong-arm robbers who prey on riders entering and leaving L stations along the Howard line.

At the Sheridan Rd. station, a man walked up to Patrolman James Davern, a decoy who has taken part in more than 100 arrests of strong-arm robbers.

"The man intended to rob Davern, no doubt about it," Cohen said. "But at the last minute he recognized him because he had been arrested by Davern just a few weeks ago."

The police stakeout, with Cohen following, moved to the Wilson Ave. station then to the Lawrence L. station. There three men pounced on Davern, grabbed his watch and $30 in cash and began beating him.

"Hit!" shouted Davern. The other plain clothesmen moved in. They arrested two suspects on the spot and caught the third a few minutes later in the 4800 block of N. Winthrop, about 200 yards away.

Davern was treated for minor injuries at Weiss Memorial Hospital and released.

One of the three suspects was identified as a 15-year-old West Side youth. The other two identified themselves as Willie Brown, 32, of 1211 W. Ainslie, and Terry Lee Nixon, 19, of 4805 N. Winthrop, police said.

Cop's Drunken Ruse Nets Thief

The police department's favorite drunk, James Davern, was stumbling about a subway station as usual Friday night, and as usual, his bleary-eyed, disheveled appearance led to the arrest of another accused thief.

According to police, Davern, a Mass Transit Unit patrolman who is the unit's top decoy, was using his favorite ruse, that of an inebriated businessman in the subway station at Clark and Division Streets, when he was allegedly attacked by Paul Ferrara, 36, of 1515 W. Monroe St.

Ferrara reportedly began rifling through Davern's pockets and was about to leave with his money when Patrolwoman Joyce Smith, who was backing up Davern, moved in and arrested Ferrara.

The 41-year-old Davern has been with the police department 15 years and has been playing the role of a drunk in subway stations for about five years. During that time, he has participated in over 150 arrests, police said. (*Copied*)

Cop's Hunch Was Better Than Decoy

The decoy act used successfully many times by Patrolman James Davern of the Mass Transit Unit failed to attract two robbery suspects Thursday on the Howard Street line.

But Davern and his partners, Patrolmen Wade Parrott and Ermilo Garza, got results — they made an arrest. They seized Arthur Stringer, 17, and Marvin Young, 18, both of 801 E. 62d St., a short time after the pair allegedly robbed George Pavlopoulos, 47, a waiter, of $116 and his watch at gun point.

Davern said the two youths are suspects in about six other robberies on train platforms in recent weeks. He said Pavlopoulos of 4826 N. Magnolia Ave. was robbed after he and the suspects left the northbound train at the Thorndale Avenue station.

Earlier the suspects had ignored Davern as he played a decoy role on the train, slouching in his seat and feigning sleep. Sensing that Pavlopoulos might be robbed, the policemen got off at Morse Avenue, the next station, and quickly returned to Thorndale Avenue aboard a southbound train. They arrested Stringer and Young, who were preparing to board the southbound train. Pavlopoulos was found unharmed on a roof overhanging the street near the station where he said the pair had forced him to go after robbing him, Davern said. (*Copied*)

* * * *

Mass Transit Unit police this morning arrested a Mutt and Jeff robbery team that allegedly has been plaguing riders on the CTA's Howard Street line for the past several weeks. Three patrolmen arrested 18-year-old Marvin Young, who is five-foot-seven, and 17-year-old Arthur Stringer, who is six-foot-two, after they allegedly robbed a 47-year-old waiter on his way home. The Mass Transit Unit has been seeking the two youths for quite a while and believe they may be responsible for at least seven armed robberies in the last few weeks.

COPS' SAFETY PLAN FOR "L" HIT BY ACLU

by Larry Green

A police crackdown on subway and L loiterers was criticized Wednesday by civil rights groups and legal observers who questioned its constitutionality and the possibility that minorities may be victimized.

Undercover police working with uniformed officers began working in the program Tuesday night concentrating on individuals whose "surreptitious actions present potential fear or threats to citizens."

Bob Howard, director of the Illinois American Civil Liberties Union (ACLU) police project, said the vagrancy statute under which Chicago police would presumably operate "appears clearly to be unconstitutional under recent Supreme Court decisions."

"Obviously, minorities and poor people for whom public transportation facilities are a normal place of gathering or hanging around are going to feel the special impact of this program," Howard added.

"It seems likely a high proportion of the people the police will stop will be innocent people," he said.

In announcing the new program, Police Supt. James M. Rochford said any suspicious person seen on an L or subway platform who lets two trains go by could be arrested. He defined loiterers as persons "who cannot reasonably explain their presence and who cause fear."

"There is a serious question whether even letting two trains go by could be grounds for a stop and frisk," Howard said, "because I doubt that that conduct would support a reasonable inference based on specific facts — required by law — that someone was about to commit a crime."

Andrew C. Barrett, executive director of the National Assn. for the Advancement of Colored People (NAACP) said the program, as described in newspaper accounts, "raises some very serious constitutional questions."

"If the police are going to use missing one or two trains as a basis for stopping, questioning or detaining persons we would be against that," Barrett said. (*Reprinted from Daily News*)

COOKIE LADY

by Christine C. Goduto, wife of Leonard P. Goduto

My husband and his partner are the first to arrive to a robbery call. The victim is an elderly woman whose purse was stolen. After getting a description and a brief synopsis of the event, the officers were in hot pursuit of the perpetrator. They quickly found a person matching the description and after searching him found the woman's money on the accused. The incriminating evidence was the fact that the victim recently withdrew money from the cash station and the officers were able to see the monies were in numerical/sequential order. He was brought in and picked out of a line up. Guilty as charged. The victim wanted to show her appreciation to the two officers who solved the case so; she baked cookies for them and sent them to the station with a letter of thanks and praise. Unfortunately, because they were working nights, by the time they reported for duty the cookies were gone and they had yet another case to solve. Who ate their reward?

CREDITABLE MENTION

Sgt. Thompson G. Phelps, (Ret.)

On Feb. 2, 1945, I was sworn in as a patrolman in the Chicago Police Department.

I have been commended several times by my commanding officers for good police work. To mention a few, Captain J. Hartnett for the arrest of Joe Gabryszak for the murder of T. Spinowski; by Captain J. Graney

Thompson G. Phelps, Sr. and Thompson G. Phelps, Jr. during police golf outing.

for the arrest of Levi Wilson for the rape of a nurse at the South Chicago Hospital; also Captain J. Graney for the apprehension and arrest of the two men that stole a squad car and for recovery of the sawed off shotgun that these men had stolen from the squad car.

I was awarded a creditable mention for the arrest of Dan McCarthey for the assault of three juvenile girls, with a knife and his fist in an attempted rape. He was apprehended after a 19 hour search.

Also a creditable mention and a share of a reward from the Illinois Bell Telephone Company for breaking the case, leading to the arrest of four juveniles who kidnapped and raped two telephone operators.

A creditable mention and a Mayor Daley Youth Award of $50.00 for tracking down and the arrest of a robbery and burglary of six juveniles. The youths beat two elderly women so viciously that both sustained broken legs. I traced the members of the gang through a watch I found in the possession of another woman. One juvenile turned state's evidence and the others were sentenced to two to five years in the penitentiary.

Another creditable mention and Mayor Daley Youth Award was for the apprehension and arrest of 19 adults and five juveniles, during which I worked 36 hours straight to break up a prostitution ring that was using juvenile girls.

My years were busy but I was proud to serve and protect.

CREDITABLE MENTIONS

George Pocius received about 60 creditable mentions and several honorable mentions. Following is a congratulations letter he received from Thillens, Inc. in April 1957.

On the strength of his recent outstanding performance in achieving six creditable mentions in less than two months while detailed with the Task Force, George Pocius of the Central District is compiling a record likely to dwarf that of the most illustrious policemen in the history of the Chicago force. Commissioner O'Connor first commended Pocius in General Order No. 556, dated Dec. 26, 1956. The sixth in the series of George's commendations came on Feb. 18 in General Order No. 581.

CTA ARREST

CTA Mass Transit Unit Police arrested and charged two South Side men with strong armed robbery this morning when the pair allegedly snatched a woman's purse near the 63rd St. and Harvard Avenue elevated station.

Sgt. Clarence Kerr, of the Mass Transit Unit, said as the men attempted to flee on foot, the decoy police who heard the woman's screams on the street, gave chase and captured the pair after a block's pursuit.

Kerr said the Patrolman James Davern, who made the arrests had to use his imagination in the chase because he was not armed and actually stopped the assailants by pointing his finger at them!

Kerr said that Davern, who had been acting as a decoy, dressed in civilian clothes and holding Christmas packages on the platform, heard Mrs. Ruby Blanchard, 49, of 6535 Normal Ave., scream and went down to investigate.

Kerr said Mrs. Blanchard pointed at the fleeing pair and Davern, followed by his four partners, took off in hot pursuit. Davern identified himself as a policeman and threatened to shoot the pair if they did not halt.

Kerr said on the dimly lit street, the pair could only see Davern pointing and assumed he had a gun. They abruptly halted and were arrested.

Police identified the duo as Robert Williams Sr., 20, of 6517 Yale Ave., and Gary Brim, 20, of 6423 Stewart Ave., both were scheduled to appear in South Youth Court today. Kerr said in addition, Williams was wanted on a burglary warrant by Mobile, Alabama authorities.

Kerr said Mrs. Blanchard had $1.50 in cash, and $.30 cents worth of food stamps in her purse. (*Reprinted from City News 35*)

CTA DECOY ARREST

CTA decoy patrolmen James Davern, 38, posing as a drunk this morning, made two more subway arrests, as he nabbed two men who roughed him up and robbed him beneath the Belmont Avenue L Platform.

Sgt. Clarence Kerr, head of the CTA Special Task Force, said Davern stumbled off the train and went downstairs close to the station entrance, where two robbers grabbed him from behind and snatched $9 dollars from his pocket.

"Get him, get his money," one of the men said to the other as they attacked the policeman, according to Sgt. Kerr.

As one man dragged Davern outside, the other riffled his pockets, snatching his cash, Kerr said.

The five man back-up team, also wearing plain clothes, stepped in and subdued the resisting offenders and Town Hall District police staked out at the scene had some trouble telling police officers from offenders, according to Kerr.

Police arrested Billie Ray Brothers, 42, and Ralph Long, 36, residents of the Wilmont Hotel, 933 Belmont Avenue, and charged them with strong armed robbery.

Brothers told police he was a fugitive from Arkansas and had served five years there for burglary. Long said he had done one year at the Vandalia Prison, also on a burglary conviction, according to Kerr.

Both men were scheduled to appear later today in North Felony Court and were being detained in the Town District Lockup, Kerr said. Damen Ave. area robbery unit investigators were continuing to question the two.

Kerr further explained that the backup squad members, as well as Davern, affect casual dress, with two of the policemen sporting long hair and two others affecting beards.

He added that occasionally one of the backup men rather than Davern the decoy is accosted but said that all members on patrol, except Davern, tote walkie talkies for communication and each man is always in sight of at least one of the others.

He said that the cover men go largely unnoticed. He also said that Davern's arrests this morning were his third and fourth since Friday and his 15th and 16th since joining the special unit on September 18, Kerr said. *Copied from City News.*

CTA DECOY IN BUSY WEEK

Chicago policeman James Davern, 38, has had a busy first week as a new member of the department's undercover transit unit.

He's already made four arrests. And there was more of the same this morning when he snared two men who tried to rob him. A third would-be robber escaped.

Some time after midnight, Davern posing as a tired businessman got off a southbound rapid transit train at the 43d Street station of the north-south route.

Police said two men—later identified as Jesse Scott, 27, of 5322 S. State St., and James Stewart, 24—spotted Davern.

The men then ran to a nearby pool room and got Stewart's cousin, Larry Dunklin, 19, of 4226 S. Indiana Ave., and ran back to accost Davern who was walking down the exit stairway.

They demanded Davern's watch and wallet. If he resisted they threatened to kill him, police said.

Davern announced he was a police officer and other policemen concealed nearby rushed in to make the arrest.

One of the three men reached into his pocket, but Patrolman Samuel Summer drew his revolver and fired two warning shots. Dunklin was arrested but Stewart fled. No weapons were found on the pair.

Scott and Dunklin will appear tomorrow in South Boys Court on a strong arm-robbery charge.

CTA DECOY MAKES FINAL ARREST

Patrolman James Davern made his 22nd and final arrest as a decoy with the Special CTA Task Force Unit this morning in the CTA Rapid Transit elevated station at Wilson Ave. and Broadway.

Davern, posing as a drunk and wearing his famous "silver wrist watch" was approached by a man identified as Lawrence White, 35 of 1630 Wilson Ave., on the stairs leading from the platform.

White asked Davern for a match and before Davern could speak White knocked the policeman to the ground, jumped on top of him and took his wrist watch, "all in one swift move," according to Sgt. Clarence Kerr of the Task Force Unit.

Kerr said White attempted to riffle through Davern's pockets but was surrounded by six backup patrolmen who had been waiting undercover only a few feet away.

White was charged with strong armed robbery and scheduled to appear in Holiday Court later today.

Kerr said Davern, who joined the unit Sept. 18, will remain on the elevated platforms, but as a backup instead of a decoy.

Kerr said decoy patrolman with assistance of backup policemen have been responsible for 109 arrests since the inception in June. (*Reprinted from City News 13*)

A DANGEROUS FELON

by P.O. Tamara Matthews and P.O. Donyal Williams

I would like to submit an experience by my partner and I, while assigned to the 004th District Gang-Tactical Unit. On Thursday, August 3, 2000, at 2131 hours, my partner and I responded to a call of a criminal sexual assault in progress at Rosenblum Park, located on the southeast side at 7500 South Baldwin Ave. Upon arrival we were met by a witness and the victim who gave us a description of the offender who had just sexually assaulted the victim. Working only with a description, we performed a grid search of the area and within minutes, apprehended the offender. The victim, a 16-year-old girl, whose face and head had been severely beaten and eyes that had been swollen shut, stated that she was swinging on the swings in the park when the offender walked up to her, grabbed her off the swings, threw her to the ground then began beating her repeatedly in her face and head then sexually assaulted her. The offender turned out to be Sandy Williams, 37, who, according to court records, was sentenced in 1985 and served 12 years of a 25-year sentence for aggravated criminal sexual assault, armed robbery and aggravated kidnapping for abducting a woman at gunpoint in 1984 after repeatedly raping her. Williams was paroled in February 1997. After this current incident, Williams was held on a $10 million bond and faces lifetime imprisonment. The present victim suffered severe facial trauma and numerous contusions to her head and was hospitalized for several days.

As a result of our quick response and investigative acumen, a dangerous felon was taken off the streets. The above incident was reported in the *Chicago Sun-Times* newspaper and my partner and I were featured on *Crime Watch* show #149.

Arresting officers: P.O. Tamara A. Matthews (#4640) and P.O. Donyal Williams (#10788).

Supervisors: Lt. Peter Piazza (#711) and Sgt. James O'Donnell (#2114).

004th District Commander Lamont Thompson (#524).

Davern Decoy Arrest

CTA Task Force Policeman James Davern, acting as a decoy in the Jackson Park subway station at State St., made his second arrest of the day this morning (Sun.) after a second man attempted to rob him of his gold watch. The man later told police he committed 25 other robberies in the subways to support his heroin addiction.

It was Davern's first day on the Task Force.

Davern, and his five partners, arrested David Comer, 35, 7959 S. Aberdeen St., after he allegedly attacked Davern and stole the watch.

Davern said he was sitting on a bench in the station when a man approached him and after waiting for a train to leave the station, jumped on top of him.

The man said "Give me your watch or I'll break your neck," and pulled the watch off Davern's arm. Supporting policemen then moved in and arrested the man Davern said.

Comer was charged with strong armed robbery and schedule to appear in Holiday Court today.

Police said Comer admitted to several other robberies, mostly on the Howard, Englewood and Congress subway lines.

Police say Comer has been arrested over 30 times and has spent over half his life in various jails.

The two decoy arrest today have pushed the decoy total arrest to over 80 since the beginning of the program in June.

Earlier this morning Davern and his partners arrested Nathaniel Wynn, 24, 4003 S. Indiana Ave. after he allegedly robbed Davern of the same watch. He was also scheduled to appear in Holiday Court today charged with strong armed robbery.

Decoy Police Nab 2 at CTA Elevated Station

An undercover policeman on the special Chicago Transit Authority Unit posed as a tired businessman and arrested two men after they tried to rob him in a stairway on the elevated station at 43rd Street and Calumet Avenue early today.

Sgt. Clarence Kerr of the special unit said Patrolman James Davern, 38, was acting as a decoy when three men approached him and demanded his watch and wallet. Davern told the men he was a policeman and all three fled. Two of the three were captured, Kerr said.

Charged with strong armed robbery were Jess Scott, 27, of 5322 South State Street, and Larry Dunklin, 19, of 4226 S. Indiana Avenue. (*Copied*)

Decoys Nab 3 in Thefts in Subway

CTA task force patrolmen spent a busy Friday night on the Englewood-Howard elevated line, arresting three men each of whom allegedly attempted to rob CTA decoy patrolmen in separate incidents.

The first arrest occurred at 10:00 p.m. at the Chicago Avenue station, where Patrolman Fred Stone, 33, posed as a drunk on the subway stairway. He was approached by James Caldwell, 45, of 4659 S. Calumet Ave., who allegedly pushed Stone down the stairs and riffled his pockets, taking a dollar before fleeing up the stairs.

Stone's four partners arrested Caldwell at the top of the stairway. It was Stone's 12th arrest as a decoy patrolman.

Shortly afterward in the same station, decoy James Davern, feigning sleep on a subway bench, was grabbed by a man who pushed him against a wall and snatched his wristwatch. Lester Ross, 34, of 673 N. Milwaukee Ave., attempted to flee up the stairs, when Davern's partners nabbed him.

The arrest, Davern's 27th, marked one of several times in which his silver watch has been pulled from his wrist.

Patrolman Phillip Hayman nabbed the last man at midnight on the platform at 58th Street and Calumet Avenue. Posing as a drunk, Hayman, 30, left a south-bound train at the station. He was approached by a man who spun him around, took $5 from his jacket pocket, and tried to run downstairs.

Hayman's four partners arrested Jimmie Hopkins, 37, of 6126 S. Woodlawn Ave. It was Hayman's fourth decoy arrest.

All three suspects were charged with strong arm robbery. They appeared before Holiday Court Judge Emanuel Rissman, who ordered them to appear to-morrow in Felony Court.

DECOY SEIZES TWO IN THEFT ON CTA TRAIN

A 17-year-old youth and his 16-year-old companion were arrested early yesterday after they allegedly stole a wristwatch and a wallet from a police decoy who was shabbily dressed and feigning sleep on a northbound Jackson Park CTA train.

Reginald Thomas, 17, of 3500 S. Lake Park Ave., was charged with theft from a person, and the 16-year-old was named in a delinquency petition on the same charge.

They were arrested by Patrolman Paul Siegfried, who was the decoy, and his partner, Patrolman James Davern.

DEMOCRATIC CONVENTIONS 1969 & 1996

by Sgt. Mike Siciliano, Area Four Detective Division

What a difference 27 years make. In 1969 I was just graduating from Schurz High School in Chicago ending a decade that witnessed such political and ra-cial unrest this country has rarely experienced; the Vietnam conflict (war), both Kennedys and Martin Luther King assassinations, Kent State, Black Pan-thers, all culminating at the infamous Chicago Demo-cratic Convention of 1969.

During the start of the convention the news media gathered from around the world preparing for what was promised to be a massive demonstration. The

Sgt. Mike Siciliano watches demonstrators from Area Four-Police Headquarters during Democratic convention, August 26, 1996

These 1996 demonstrators were too young, or had not been born when the infamous 1969 Democratic Convention took place.

promises came true. Grant Park turned into a Hippie and Flower Child love fest. Unfortunately, this love didn't transfer over to the citizens and property of the City of Chicago. The Chicago police, along with many other law enforcement agencies and National Guard, had their hands full with the massive crowds.

I and a few friends were very curious of the hap-penings at Grant Park. We were all just teenagers look-ing for something to do. We kept hearing about the "free love" the hippies were performing on the grass of Grant Park, so we had to go down and investigate. Four couples riding our baby motorcycles (back then, a Honda 305 was considered a big bike) to see the action. When we got to the Grant Park area, we never got to see any love making in the park, we were caught in the middle of tear gas drifting in the wind. We were all choking and decided that watching hippies fool around wasn't worth it.

After a few years out of high school I married my childhood girlfriend (who went with me to Grant Park that day) and decided to become a Chicago police of-ficer. After 27 years the City and the police depart-ment still carried the stigma around the world as being brutal. The news media always showed those isolated incidents, where demonstrators were being harassed and abused, they never showed what was happening prior.

In 1996 the City of Chicago hosted another Democratic convention. This time dissenting groups again vowed to cause havoc and disrupt the convention as they did in 1969. The City and all involved geared up for a possible major catastrophe occurring once again. What a surprise, guess what, demonstrations did happen but they turned out to be mere babies, in their early 20s. There were some older leaders that might have been around in 1969, but for the most part these young wannabe hippies had no clue why they were protesting. There was no war going on at the time. Many of the radical leaders are now the establishment and grandparents. The Black Panthers are now business men. So the whole Democratic convention gala went without any major incidents. Something that I was very proud to be a part of.

P.S. We did have demonstrators that camped out in front of the 011th Dist. Police Station for a few days (peace signs and the tie dye shirts) but somehow I had the feeling it was just a cool thing to do.

DETECTIVE EDWARD DOJUTREK STAR # 3477

The following is a brief biography of my police service on the Chicago Police Department. I was sworn in as a police officer on February 16, 1954, and was assigned Badge #3477. After completing 12 weeks of police training, I was assigned to the old 33rd District (Jefferson Park Station). I remained at this station for nine and one-half years mainly working on the wagon and three-wheel motorcycle, but also completed other district duties.

I then was assigned to the Internal Affairs Division. While on this assignment, I achieved the rank of detective and was then transferred into the Intelligence Division for a two-year period.

In February 1969, I was assigned to the State's Attorney Police, under the then State's Attorney Edward Hanrahan, as one of his bodyguards and also conducted various investigations handled by this office.

Det. Edward Dojutrek

After Hanrahan was defeated for re-election in November 1972, I remained in this office until March 1973 when I was assigned to the Area 5 Robbery Unit. Knowing nothing of Robbery investigating, I was somewhat leery of the assignment. However, I quickly adapted to the new position and found it to my liking as each day was a new and exciting experience. Of my 31 years of service, the nine years I spent in this unit were my most enjoyable and memorable ones. In 1981, due to a restructuring in the Detective Division, the Robbery Unit became a part of the Violent Crime unit.

Another warm feeling I have, is the time from 1969 to 1984 when I served as an elected trustee on the Board of Directors of the Chicago Fraternal Order of Police Lodge #7. This was a climactic period where the Lodge vied for, and subsequently won, the rights to be the sole representative and bargaining agent for the rank and file of the Chicago Police Department. Many improvements of benefits and general work conditions were the results of the combined efforts of the Board of Directors during this period.

Then in 1985, with the change in police structure and command, the job lacked the enjoyment and challenge of the previous years so on March 19, 1985, at age 54, I retired.

Following retirement, with my family, I moved to Buffalo Grove, IL, where we owned and operated a stained glass and antique store in a 100 yr. old barn for nine years. In April 1995, I moved with my wife, Jane, children and grandchildren to Austin, TX, where we are now enjoying our retirement to the fullest in God's Country.

DISTINGUISHED SHOOTER

by Robert J. Powell, Chicago Police (Ret)

Colonel Paul E. Cullinane, director of Civilian Marksmanship, U.S. Army awarded retired Chicago Police Officer Robert J. Powell the badge designating him a "Distinguished Pistol Shot" in 1990. Officer Powell, a member of Chicago FOP Lodge No. 7 who sponsored him at the National Matches, at Camp Perry, Ohio where he acquired his final points for the award.

The award was created in 1891 and Officer Powell was the 885th civilian to receive the award in 100 years of availability. In order to receive the "Distinguished Pistol Shot Badge" a shooter must earn a total of 30 points in various authorized pistol matches. Points are awarded to the top 10% of the shooters in each match.

The only authorized firearm is the 1911, 45 cal. pistol firing 45 cal. hard ball govt. ammo. Officer Powell earned points at matches at Tampa, Florida; Bradenton, Florida; Bristol, Indiana; and at the National Championships at Camp Perry, Ohio.

Only three other Chicago police officers have earned the Distinguished Pistol Shot designation. They are Sgt. Brian Lendzion, in 1979 at Camp Perry, Ohio; Lt. Al Henry in 1984 at the Wisconsin State Championships; and Officer John Leehey, in 1986 at Camp

Winners of "American Indian Trophy" 1985-86-87. Pictured with trophy from left: Robert Powell, Jacky Thomas, John Leehey, Al Henry and John Geldhoff.

Mrs. Josephine Dwyer

Perry, Ohio.

Officer Powell lives on the South Side of Chicago and still does some shooting as a 73-year-old retired firearms instructor. FOP Lodge No. 7 sponsored the Chicago Police Team since 1981.

MRS. DWYER'S REWARDING CAREER AS A POLICEWOMAN

by Michael Malone

Behind that Irish brogue and twinkling eye is a cool demeanor befitting one of Chicago's finest ... the policewoman.

I had the pleasure recently of meeting Mrs. Josephine Dwyer of Roseland who has spent 20 years serving the City of Chicago as a policewoman. Her husband, Michael, is a retired policeman and served in the traffic division.

The couple have two married daughters, Mrs. Patricia Malone and Mrs. Catharine Bentwell who have managed to give their parents eight beautiful grandchildren.

Josephine works out of the Youth Division from Area Two. She also has served out of the Fifth District. In the early days in her police career, she worked nights and her husband worked days. At that time the girls were required to wear long sleeved shirts with ties. Today, for comfort's sake, policewomen wear short sleeved shirts and no tie. Working conditions have also improved.

Eleven policewomen are assigned out of Area Two and deal with such things as missing persons, abandoned children or abortion cases. They work under Lt. Leonard Cody.

According to Josephine, "Each day brings something different." "Throughout the years as I worked with all the different cases dealing with children, I came to realize that there is good in all children. The ones who became delinquent became so when their parents do so in the home. The majority of cases came from broken homes."

Josephine recalled once when she had only been on the force a short time, she received a call to go to 11th and State to "follow a girl in red." It seems that the girl was a go-between with a wanted burglar. Josephine began following her on foot and on the subway. Later that day, the girl met her boyfriend and the police arrested the wanted man and a conviction was received.

She also worked on the now-famous call girl ring which made headlines a few years ago. Her job mainly was to work with the detectives with the search warrants. "You would really be surprised at the type of girls who were involved in this situation."

Requirements for becoming a policewoman call for a high school diploma. The training period runs 16 weeks and includes intensive training on the rifle range, ju-so and criminal law. There are approximately 87 policewomen working in Chicago. A few are in plain clothes in the Narcotic Bureau. A woman applying for the job must be between the ages of 25-30.

Mrs. Dwyer concentrates on her family and running a smooth household when she is not performing her duties as a policewoman. *(Reprinted)*

She wore star #4738 during her years on the job, and her grandson, Michael Malone, was assigned that number until his promotion to sergeant in 1998.

EXTRA POLICE ON ALERT FOR GANG FORAYS

Fifty policemen patrolled the Racine Avenue District in the vicinity of Noble Street and Chicago Avenue Sunday night to prevent disturbances which have broken out in the area for the last several nights, resulting in the breaking of several windows. Puerto Rican residents complained that roving gangs had been terrorizing the neighborhood, demanding the Puerto Ricans move out. They also said police protection had been inadequate. Twenty-six persons were arrested during sporadic violence Saturday night and police confiscated knives, clubs, chains and a revolver.

FOP SPONSORED PISTOL TEAMS

by Robert Powell, Chicago Police (Ret)

I think the FOP Lodge No. 7 History Book would be incomplete without some mention of the outstanding Chicago Police Pistol Teams sponsored by the FOP.

I have been a member of the Lodge since shortly after they received their charter, and a member of the Chicago Police Pistol Teams since they were formed.

In 1974 The Chicago Police Rangemaster, Sgt. Ray King, proposed the formation of two five-member teams to represent the Chicago Police Department in local, regional and national pistol matches. His proposal was forwarded to Deputy Director of Training, Lt. Mike Logan, who approved it and sent it to the Director of Training, John Jemilo, who approved it and sent it to the Superintendent of Police, James Rochford, who gave it his ok.

Try-outs were held and the two teams were selected. Some of the early team members were: Ptlmn. Robert Powell, Training Division; Sgt. Al Henry, 003rd Dist.; Det. Brian Lendzion; Det. Bill Struke, Bomb & Arson; Ptlmn. Dan Healy, Canine Unit; Capt. Bill Marschall, 007 Dist.; Lt. Andy Hilton, 005th Dist.; Ptlmn. Dick Alberts, Traffic Div.; Sgt. Roy Swanson, Training Div.; Sgt. Joe Celovsky, Crime Lab; Sgt. Davie Peters, 008th Dist.; John Geldhoff, Pat Quaid, Training Div.; Ignatius Grimaldi, 011 Dist.; Mike Griegel, Evidence Tech.; John Leehey, 022 Dist.; Ted Hadjuk, 011 Dist.; Dominic Vimarco, 005 Dist.; Jacki Thomas, Training Div. Shooting jackets and caps were provided to the teams by the department. Financial help was pro-

East Sider Bob Powell takes aim during the National Pistol matches he attended as a member of the Chicago Police Department's gold team.

From left, standing: Sgt. Roy Swanson and Sgt. Joe Celousky, from left kneeling: Ptlmn. Robert Powell, Lt. Albert Henry and Det. Brian Lendzion.

vided for entry fees to matches and ammo was provided to the members for practice.

In 1981 the Chicago Police Dept. said they would no longer be able to support the Pistol Team financially due to budgetary consideration.

At this time the Team asked the FOP Lodge No. 7 for their help. The Lodge, under then President John Dineen, was happy to come to the rescue of the Pistol Team.

From that time to the present the FOP Pistol Team has represented the Chicago Police at the National Pistol Matches at Camp Perry, Ohio, each summer in July. The matches started here in 1907. Many honors have been bestowed on the teams including the winning of the "American Indian Trophy" three times as the High Scoring Police Pistol Team in the National Trophy Team Matches in 1985-86-87. Without the help of FOP Lodge No. 7 Presidents John Dineen and Bill Nolan there would not have been a Chicago Police Team at the National Championship Matches.

All of the past and present members of the "Teams" wish to thank the Lodge and hope the year 2000 is good to the FOP and its members.

A Gift from God

by Franchesca Rathel-Williams. 015th Police District

Commander Otis M. Rathel served with the Chicago Police Department for 30 years, from 1955 until he retired in 1985. Otis Rathel was the first black police artist in the Chicago Police Department and went on to become the commander of the graphic arts section.

He drew thousands of sketches which resulted in an overwhelming number of arrests because of the uncanny resemblance of his sketches of offenders. His most famous sketch was that of Richard Speck who killed eight nurses July 14, 1966.

Otis was presented numerous awards, one of his most impressive was the Superior Public Service Award and the award presented on his 10,000th sketch. He received awards not only from the Chicago Police Department but from other police departments throughout the United States and other countries. He has appeared on TV shows, radio programs and constant newspaper articles including the Chicago Police Museum where his works are currently displayed. All of his original sketches are in my possession.

Otis never had any formal instruction or schooling regarding his art work, he had what is known as a gift from God. A graduate from DuSable High School, a WWII veteran, husband, father, grandfather and great-grandfather and a teacher of art.

Police artist Rathel draws sketch of suspect.

Commander Otis M. Rathel receives congratulations.

Otis died March 30, 1989, from Parkinson's Disease. His death was a great loss to me and those who respected and admired his work and him as a person. Otis M. Rathel was my father. I was blessed to have had him in my life, to have known him and blessed that he allowed me to share his work and be a part of his life and oh yes love him because he was my father.

Graduation Class, May 1955

The following named Probationary Patrolmen of the Police Training Division are hereby transferred to the districts set opposite their names:

Henry S. Zweir, Trf.
Thomas A. Beland, Trf.
H.E. DeBruce, Trf.
Malcolm B. Hill, Trf.
L.J. Freeman, Trf.
John C. Boeger, Trf.
Harry Kenerson, Trf.

Willie Johnson, Trf.
Edwin R. Broukal, Trf.
Thomas D. Porter, Trf.
K.B. Ephraim, Trf.
Richard G. Flint, Trf.
Willie A. Meeks, Trf.
Elmer L. Fox, Trf.
F.W. Kilcoyne, Trf.
John W. York, Trf.
Fred E. Reid, Trf.
Chester A. Zintak, Trf.
Edward J. Zolna, Trf.
Samuel C. Zroski, Trf.
Elmer L. Banks, Trf.
Leonard H. Klein, Trf.
David M. Murphy, Trf.
Phillip P. Casello, Trf.
R.C. Brown, Trf.
Alex L. Dybas, Trf.
K.A. Krueger, Trf.
Kenneth R. Kula, Trf.
A.A. Peterson, Trf.
Anthony Chiavola, Trf.
Lavoren Blakely, 1st
Henry Maxwell, 1st
George Brown, 2nd
H.L. Johnson, 2nd
Oliver J. Lake, 2nd
Richard Lewis, 2nd
L.H. Moaney, 2nd
William F. Fristoe, 5th
William J. Hightower, 5th
Homer Simpson, 5th
Wendell J. Smith, 6th
Joe L. Johnson, 6th
J.E. Fitzpatrick, 6th
Edward V. Willett, 7th
James P. Brooks, 7th
Bengt. A. Flood, 7th
James W. Craig, 8th
S.M. Kasprzyk, 8th
R.F. O'Connor, 8th
Robert E. Purcell, 8th
P.R. Fleming, 9th
Peter W. Doyle, 9th
George D. Tanner, 9th
Anthony J. Vuletic, 9th
Chas. H. Jackson, 10th
S.F. Peterson, 10th
James V. Price, 10th
James L. Martin, 10th
John J. Dwyer, 10th
Robert F. Reid, 11th

Maces L. Jones, 11th
K.T. Glover, 12th
Bennie E. Butler, 12th
Santo Bonaguro, 12th
Nick Buick, 12th
R.S. Posiadlik, 12th
T. Hortsman, 13th
Geo. Washington, 13th
M.C. Woods, 13th
John R. Placek, 13th
Jack G. Wallenda, 13th
Henry Jelderks, 13th
Thomas Eberhart, 14th
Joseph W. Kane, 14th
K.K. Knuckles, 14th
Irvin F. Simulis, 14th
Walter Saunders, 15th
Charles Williams, 15th
Orange Hudson, 15th
Richard F. Ryan, 15th
Joseph Botica, 15th
A. Mascolino, 15th
Henry J. Buba, 15th
Walter J. Clifford, 16th
Edward B. Earl, 16th
Ray W. Sperling, 16th
M. Grzeskiewicz, 16th
Warren Friedl, 16th
J.T. O'Malley, 16th
Frank Gallo, 17th
Phillip S. Pignato, 17th
Donald J. Carroll, 17th
Jack J. Meyer, 17th
Albert Robinson, 18th
James Coleman, 18th
L. Jackson, 18th
E.C. Jablonowski, 18th
James J. Gillen, 18th
S.E. Wisniewski, 18th
John Morgan, 19th
G. Washington, 19th
Felix Maliska, 19th
William J. Britton, 19th
Edward Carbone, 19th
John A. Jackson, 19th
Ralph C. Dunn, 19th
Harry Vafiadis, 20th
Clarence F. Smith, 20th
James V. Harlan, 20th
Daniel N. Scalia, 20th
H.W. Slawinski, 20th
S.H. Zyskowski, 20th
Donald Burns, 22nd

R.A. Perkins, 22nd
M.J. DeYoung, 22nd
Angelo L. Seno, 22nd
Fred Washington, 22nd
Howard A. Fertig, 22nd
Howard L. Bell, 23rd
Clifford Z. Butler, 23rd
Ulysses Honesty, 23rd
Robert F. Peppler, 23rd
Alvin W. Sholl, 23rd
Alvin B. McCune, 24th
John W. Watkins, 24th
Frank R. Lutchin, 24th
John J. Bogacki, 24th
William E. Calabrese, 24th
William Fox, 25th
L. Czechanski, 25th
J.A. Donovan, 25th
Ed. H. Conway, 25th
J.R. Finnegan, 26th
T.R. Finnin, 26th
William J. Sullivan, 26th
Bobby Bridges, 27th
William Simpson, 27th
Neil J. Francis, 27th
Edward R. Hunt, 28th
R.A. Hulsman, 28th
R.J. McCluskey, 28th
James W. Palmer, 29th
K.T. Anderson, 28th
Donald H. Herion, 28th
E.D. Cychosz, 29th
Robert B. Eis, 29th
R.A. Passeri, 29th
S.M. Weinstein, 28th
D.R. Lanners, 29th
Joseph Adamek, 30th
R.C. Charnow, 30th
L. Cichowski, 30th
L.A. Morgan, 30th
Victor P. Kamka, 30th
John D. Smith, 31st
T.J. Donovan, 31st
J.J. Lewkowicz, 31st
T.P. Matassa, 31st
August J. Dicaro, 32nd
M.J. Guerin, 32nd
Ronald A. Pabich, 32nd
R.J. Sullivan, 32nd
James A. Noto, 32nd
J.F. Seibert, 33rd
James A. Jack, 33rd
F.F. Peterson, 33rd

Owen J. Evans, 34th
Leroy J. Belt, 34th
W.L. Rivera, 34th
C.R. Isachson, 34th
Lester E. Izban, 34th
Wm. E. Havansek, 35th
Jerry Richards, 35th
Hyman M. Davis, 36th
A.S. Immordino, 36th
G.S. Kouvelis, 36th
Kurt W. Metzler, 36th

M.E. Paschky, 36th
Kenneth Johnson, 36th
Anthony Amici, 37th
Donald R. Kunz, 37th
Norman F. Rice, 37th
C.E. Ekenborg, 38th
Stanley L. August, 38th
Earl R. Johnson, 38th
John Kolb, 38th
Sam J. Florito, 38th
D.E. Crawford, 39th

George H. Penge, 39th
James H. Stewart, 39th
Geo. N. Volke, 39th
John W. Peterson, 40th
Donald J. Benson, 40th
John Blalocki, 40th
K.W. Tworeck, 40th
R.H. Thorniley, 40th
F.R. Podolsky, 41st
R.A. Roben, 41st
Mary King, Pol'woman

1955 Graduating Class. Also pictured seated: 1) Henry Hartman, 2) John McInerney, 3) Larry Marstan, 4) Lt. John Nelligan, 5) Lt. Mitchell Mall, 6) Clarence Jaeger, 7) John Lennon, 8) John Groark.

A Grateful Citizen

by Officer Chris Haralampopoulos

One winter, my partner and I were driving around patrolling our beat in the 24th district on the midnight shift. Suddenly, we were frantically flagged down by a 71-year-old cab driver who stated that a teenage customer of his had just bailed out of his cab without paying the $12 fare. We immediately drove around the block looking for the suspect without any luck and returned and informed the victim of the outcome at which time a look of sadness and grief came upon his face.

Without giving up hope, my partner and I came up with a plan and asked the cab driver the exact location as to where the passenger had fled out the vehicle. Pointing to a gangway, we picked up a trail of the only and unique pair of shoe prints. Leading us up and down the alley, we lost the trail several times before discovering it again when I noticed a fence door ajar with the same shoe prints leading into the backyard. We then traced the prints to the backside of the garage as if the offender were hiding there when we drove around looking for him 20 minutes prior. The shoe prints then led us to a rear patio deck when we noticed shoes sitting in a puddle of water just inside the glass patio doors. Cornered, we rang the bell to the house and startled the homeowners who themselves were victims of a rude awakening.

Explaining our situation, the parents summoned their son who arrived home minutes prior and was, needless to say, positively identified by the cab driver. Embarrassed, the teenager sheepishly gave the cab driver $20 and apologized profusely hoping charges would be dropped. The mother then downplayed the incident by telling us that it was probably something her son picked up while away at college as an innocent prank. I then looked to my partner and said, "I went to college and never did anything like *this*! How 'bout you? With my partner shaking his head the mother looked down understanding the point that we made. Happy to have received his cab fare, the victim reconsidered pressing charges and warned the boy on his foolish actions by humorously mentioning that the only thing worse than a criminal was a dumb criminal.

On the way back to our vehicles, the cab driver insisted that he treat us to a cup of coffee at which time my partner explained to him that it wasn't necessary because we were just doing our job. An incident like this can remind all of us of the great profession we are in helping others and some of the grateful citizens that appreciate our thankless efforts.

CINDY I. GUERRA

Cindy was born Aug. 19, 1969. Date of appointment: May 2, 1994. Districts/Units of assignment have included 011 District, November 1994; Bicycle Patrol Unit, summer 1996; 023 District, April 1997; Area 3 Gang Team, February 1998; and February 1999, Mounted Unit.

Her awards include the Fitness Award, 1995; Public Service Award, 1997; National Conv. Service Medal, 1997; 12 Honorable Mentions, 1994-99; and Appearance Award, 1999.

Receiving the Public Service Award from the 11th District Alderman, for rescuing a 5-year-old boy that was kidnapped, and returning him safely to his mother, was a major highlight. Graduating from Mounted Police training was another, after 940 hours on horseback and suffering a near fatal injury, the first week of school, when a horse kicked her in the chest. She was out of commission for four weeks but returned, despite the fact that she was terrified. For the first time in her career she can say she was terrified and it wasn't by a bullet, it was by a hoof, covered with a steel shoe that struck her chest and threw her some 10 feet back and six feet into the air, separating cartilage and causing internal bruising. Confidence is half the victory and she had to get it back. She was one of six to

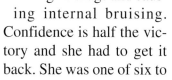
Cindy I. Guerra

graduate out of 19 officers, and the only female. The day she graduated was an incredible highlight, it was a pain/pleasure she'll never forget. To this day she is still on the Mounted Unit riding her horse "Skip." (Who, by the way, wasn't the horse that kicked her.) Although the fear has subsided, in the back of her mind the thought of what these animals are capable of lingers, it's a mutual respect they have for each other, he weighs in at 1100 lbs., her at 110 lbs.

HARD-STRIKING COMMANDO COPS TO MARK 1ST BIRTHDAY

by Walford J. Lewis
Chicago Daily News

March 9, 1957, Chicago's finest have dealt crime a hard blow in year. The police department's fast-moving "commando unit" - the special task force - will be a year old March 22.

And already some of its members have chalked up impressive records for the task force, and for themselves. Some of its members have moved to the front ranks of the department's most cited men. Others have switched from the force to choice assignments in other branches of the department with the aid of outstanding task force records.

The force was formed March 22, 1956, to serve as the police department's "Sunday punch" in areas where the crime incident rate is the highest.

Its 150 men work in two shifts and saturate selected police districts without advance warning.

In the first 11 months of operation the force's members have made 1,110 arrests, with 357 of these gun-toters.

Under a policy established by Commissioner O'Connor, members of the force automatically receive a creditable mention for each gun-toter they arrest. As a result some of the force's members have set new records for getting citations.

This has led to some grumbling in other branches where a policeman has to be recommended for a creditable mention by his superior officer in the case of an arrest of a man armed with a gun.

Top citation-getter of the task force is patrolman George Pocius, 26, a husky former Marine sergeant. He received eight creditable mentions in the five-week period from Dec. 10, 1956 to Feb. 20.

Runnerup is patrolman Donald H. Anderson, 31, who received seven between October and February.

Anderson might have had more but he has been confined to the Veterans Administration Research Hos-

He pointed out the task force's February record as an example of its work; 59 criminal arrests and 2,350 traffic summons issued, although many task force members were used on special details in connection with the Grimes murder investigation.

Its overall record includes 53,150 summons for traffic violations and 68 other arrests for carrying illegal weapons, including 17 blackjacks, seven bayonets and eight sets of brass knuckles.

O'Connor has indicated that he hopes to build the force up to 200 men sometime this spring.

HEROES

by Ofc. Edward J. Sullins

Most people will never understand the job we do. In today's society it's fashionable to hate the police. People's sense of value are warped. Sports figures are worshipped as heroes and we are demonized as monsters.

They pay these guys millions of dollars a year to play a child's game, while most of us have to work two or three extra part-time jobs just to put a decent roof over our families' heads and send our children to good schools. Yet we trudge on.

Well, let me ask you this. How many lives has Michael Jordan saved? How many murderers has Latrell Sprewell or Albert Belle caught?

I have more respect and admiration for a police officer than any of those people, for we are all that stand between life as we know it and utter chaos. We strap on our guns and pin on our badges every day and step into Hell's playground knowing that each time we do, it might be the last, and that we might not ever see our loved ones again.

We deal with the monsters lurking in your neighborhoods. The dope dealers, rapists, murderers, child molesters and gang bangers. All, so you can sleep safely in your beds at night. We see and deal with things that no human being should ever have to experience. Yet we trudge on.

We go down dark alleyways where others would fear to tread, chasing after people with guns, every day. We get shot at, attacked, spit on, vilified in the media, yet we trudge on.

We pick up dead babies out of dumpsters, stand in harm's way to protect the weak and injured. We see the very worst of society every day, of what evil men are capable of and then try to go home to our families and try to lead a normal life. Yet we trudge on, with nary a thank you.

Officer Edward J. Sullins #11093 outside old Maxwell St. Station during Democratic National Convention, Aug. 27, 1996.

pital, 333 E. Huron, since Feb. 8. He is a victim of spinal meningitis.

Creditable mentions count toward a policeman's efficiency rating when he is being considered for promotion.

The seven citations detective Edward H. Anderson, 31, received in the six months he was a patrolman on the force helped him when he was being considered for promotion.

Anderson now is assigned to the Marquette District as a detective.

To the policemen who grumble about the automatic citation ruling, Commissioner O'Connor has this answer: "The task force is the commando unit of the police department. It gets the most dangerous jobs, so we make life a little easy for them when we can."

O'Connor feels task force men probably have prevented many crimes by stopping suspicious persons and shaking them down for guns.

"It's dangerous business. They are working with the City's toughest criminals," O'Connor said. "I consider the task force the elite group of the department."

Yet, we don't complain. It's what we do. It's what we have dedicated our lives to. We trudge on.

God bless all police officers, for they are the true heroes. *Submitted by Ofc. Edward J. Sullins, #11093, 025 District.*

Hot Buttered Nostalgia

by Marcia Lee Masters
Chicago Tribune Magazine

"You've got to do something in life that isn't humdrum," says John S. Domanski, a tall, 35-year-old detective with the powerful grace of a bullfighter and the visionary face of the 19th century poet. He builds and handcrafts popcorn wagons when he's not on duty with the Chicago police force, perhaps chasing a dope-peddler up 16 flights of stairs. The sales record of his company, Antique Popcorn Wagons, at 12201 S. Indiana Ave., proves that many other Americans prize these symbols of our heritage too.

"I refuse to allow the nostalgic era of our country to die. Corn should still pop on city corners," he says.

Mr. Domanski's business, which started as a hobby eight years ago, now bustles with five assistants. The colorful hand-lettered wagons, completely hand-built, can be air-conditioned, offer either electric plates or old fashioned gas burners, and flaunt candy-striped awnings. There are two horse-drawn sizes, one for $7,200 and a larger one for $10,000. A pushcart sells for $2,100.

From the mills Domanski buys steel, forms it, and paints it. The assembled wagons can be delivered by trailer. In March, this builder of dreams sold 17. Where does he sell them? Ohio, California, Oklahoma, Texas, Japan, Europe, Hawaii. Anywhere.

Domanski also assembles motor-drawn vehicles, which he converts from old fire trucks. These sell for $17,000 and up and are called Model-T Popcorn Trucks. The fire trucks serve his purpose well because they don't have much mileage and he doesn't need to build fenders, radiators or headlights for them.

But not just anybody is allowed to buy an Antique Popcorn Wagon. Would-be popcorn men are screened. The applicant, of course, has to have character and credit references. Mostly, he has to be a "nostalgic person."

"The popcorn man must be very special," Domanski says. "A fascinating person, interested in preserving tradition. He has to be both sincere and

dreamy. Creating the illusion of a bygone era can't be accomplished by somebody who merely wants to make a lot of money.

"I have to know his family background and meet his wife before I conduct any business. If his wife doesn't want him to be a popcorn man, then he shouldn't be. However, selling corn can give people a new lease on life, especially retired people."

When I inquire further, he announces firmly: "No profanity. Popcorn men must have control and compassion because some days, especially those when corn is given away at exhibits, get really rough. People have to want to be somebody. A popcorn man should want to build air-castles."

Dominski and wagon.

Another Dominski wagon. Photos by Charles Osgood of the Tribune.

In our violent world, where more guns are popping on more corners than corn, that man in the glass wagon has a big responsibility. And Domanski is as sensitive to picking the responsible person as he is to spotting the other kind in high crime neighborhoods.

In the meantime, his popcorn wagons light the dusty trail of practicality. Many a college student, buying an Antique Popcorn Wagon on the installment plan, works his way through school selling popcorn. An ex-banker in Peoria now manages four popcorn wagons. A man in Ohio calls himself "the popcorn king." Others rent the wagons at $125 a day, including the cost of the operator and 500 bags of corn.

As far as Domanski knows, he has no competitor. Right now, he and his manager, Mrs. Arlene Leonard, are also taking orders for coaches, carriages, and black-powder cannons for the 1976 bi-centennial celebration.

As Domanski says, "You have to do something in life that isn't humdrum." Busy days and busy nights for him.

He has learned to sleep standing up.

IT'S A FAMILY TRADITION

Police work in Chicago is fast becoming a matter of family tradition. Eleven sons of police personnel were in the group of 75 veterans sworn in as temporary patrolmen yesterday. They began a two-week school at the Chicago Avenue Station today.

And now two other veterans, sons of a Chicago detective who was slain in a gun battle with a bandit, have filed applications to join the force.

The pair, Jerry, 23, and James O'Connell, 22, both of whom served overseas in the Army, are awaiting their physical examinations.

Their father, Jerry Sr., was shot to death July 30, 1928 when he came upon a bandit robbing a Negro minister on the South Side.

How does the mother and widow feel about her sons joining the police department? "I think they're both old enough and responsible enough to know what they want." Mrs. Irene O'Connell said.

THE JOB

Written by Leonard A. Muscolino II, February 2000

We come on this job usually young and green, filled
    with nervous anticipation of incidents to be seen.
Individual colors make up the Department's hue,

But when we're mixed together the shade you see is
    blue.
A mix of veterans and rookies working together to
    fight crime,
Continuously replacing the other, as a clock's hands
    move with time.
Never knowing in advance the call we're about to re-
    ceive,
But unlike the anonymous citizen, we cannot up and
    leave.
Handling each situation with professionalism and
    grace,
Hiding our true feelings behind an expressionless face.
The job is very real; filled with excitement and some
    fear,
It's hard for us on the street and those at home who
    care.
Our office never closes, that is the police way,
But our main objective is to come home safely at the
    end of each day.
Building lifelong bonds with our partners of friend-
    ship and trust;
Working always together as we handle each bust.
So next time you see us, the men and women in blue,
Stop and think for a moment of what it is that we do.
Under oath we swore to serve and protect,
And all we ask for in return is a little respect.

KARATE PAIR GETS 'COP-CHOP' ON THE CTA

It took eight policemen to subdue two karate experts Sunday on the CTA L platform at Lake and Cicero.

Patrolman James Davern, newest member of the CTA task force was credited with his 12th and 13th decoy arrests after the karate fighters, who are brothers, finally were subdued.

Davern pretended to be drunk as a westbound L train stopped. Two of the passengers, Donald Taylor, 20, of 9719 S. Prairie, and Rubin Taylor, 21, of 3133 W. Lexington, walked over, and one of them began punching Davern in the face, police said.

Davern yelled for help, and his five task force partners came out of hiding, Police said. They were met with a flurry of karate blows.

Davern and Patrolman Samuel Sommer, 25, suffered bruises and cuts. They were treated at St. Anne's Hospital and released.

Sgt. Clarence Kerr, head of the task force unit, said two Austin District policemen on routine patrol duty joined in the fighting, which lasted several minutes before the brothers were subdued and handcuffed.

Both were charged with battery and resisting arrest. Police found no weapons on either man. They are to appear Monday in North Youth Court. Holiday Court Judge John Ouska set bond at $1,000 for each. *(Reprinted from Sun-Times)*

KEN-TU

by Bernie Irgang

My partner and friend, Frank Balzano, was killed while making an arrrest at the Harlem Irving Shopping Mall.

This canine photo was taken in 1973 at the Sears Store at Damen-Lawrence after the search of the building. Bernard Irgang and K-9 dog, Ken-Tu, are on the left and Frank Balzano and K-9 dog, Bullet, are on the right.

Officer McGuire was an Evidence Technician when this photo was taken. He retired in 1995 after 30 years on the CPD. October 1972. (Chicago Sun-Times Photo by Jack Dykinga)

Ken-Tu, my dog, was also my partner and friend. During his career, from February 1970 through April 1979, Ken-Tu found and assisted in the apprehension of 112 criminals. He too was a hero!

A LANDLORD YIELDS TO SIX POLICE SQUADS

Six police squads arrested an irate landlord who had forced two policemen from his building with a shotgun. Taken into custody was Jack Neffert, 31, of 1006 N. Ashland. Neffert admitted to police he routed Motorcycle Policemen Robert Kendzora and John Ryan when they went into the building on the complaint of a tenant.

The policemen said they were talking to Mrs. Helen Walczak, 37, in the hall outside her apartment. She said Neffert and another tenant, Eugene Swiatkowski, had been annoying her and her daughter, Diane, 13, all morning. Then Neffert appeared with the shotgun. After he was disarmed, Neffert said he had been trying to evict Mrs. Walczak for nonpayment of rent and had a court eviction order.

LANE TECH BOMBING FOLLOWS ED COX TALK

Oct. 27, 1972
Chicago Sun-Times

A homemade bomb exploded at an exit of Lane Technical High School Thursday an hour after Edward Cox, President Nixon's son-in-law, finished talking to student leaders.

The bomb, which was thrown between two exit doors of the school's west corridor, broke the plastic shield over an overhead light and put powder burns on nearby walls. No one was injured.

School officials received two bomb threats after the explosion. They ordered students to leave the building on a fire drill at about 12:30 p.m., and they dismissed the students about an hour later.

Donald J. Racky, the principal at Lane, 2501 W. Addison, said there was no evidence that the bomb was connected with Cox's visit.

"But who knows?" he said. "Maybe somebody was disgruntled with the school for even allowing him here."

Cox held a question-and-answer session with 75 students from 9 to 10 a.m. Shortly before 11 an anonymous telephone caller warned, "A bomb will go off and another will go off later. People will be hurt."

School officials immediately began searching the school, Racky said, but the bomb exploded before anyone found it.

Ten minutes after the first call the same anonymous caller warned that a second bomb was placed in a locker. Then a second person phoned in still another bomb threat.

At that point, Lane was evacuated. Police searched the school but found no more bombs.

LAST HIT I QUIT!

Monday, June 9, 1975
Chicago Tribune

A top decoy of the Chicago Police Department's Mass Transit Unit was knocked unconscious Saturday night when a robbery suspect smashed a beer bottle in his face.

The patrolman, James Davern, 42, who has been beaten and pushed around often in the years he has posed as a drunk to decoy robbers, was treated at Henrotin Hospital for a cut under his left eye.

Posing as an intoxicated businessman Saturday night, Davern was leaving the subway station at Chicago Avenue and State Street when a man offered to call a cab for him, police said. The man pulled Davern to an empty lot behind 2 E. Chicago Ave. and smashed a beer bottle against Davern's face when he refused to hand over his money, police said.

The suspect was arrested by a backup team as he was taking $4 from the unconscious policeman's pockets, police said.

The suspect, Bobby Jefferson, 27, of 6238 S. Martin Luther King Dr., was charged with armed robbery.

LATIN DRAGONS GANG

by PO Tamara A. Matthews

On March 27, 2000, at 1700 hrs., after an extensive CAPS Problem #0423-00-001 gang/narcotics investigation, we learned through numerous interviews and surveillances, that drugs were being sold by the Latin Dragons Criminal Street Gang on the 8700 block of South Escanaba. We further learned that the drugs were being sold from the 8749 South Escanaba from the first floor apartment and the narcotics were being stored at the second floor apartment located at 8747

James Davern (center) with unidentified officers.

004th District Gang Unit narcotics arrest. Top from left: P.O. J. Knezevich, P.O. T. Matthews, P.O. C. Medina (top center), P.O. V. Law and P.O. J. Bravo. Bottom from left: P.O. R. Palomino, P.O. D. Williams, P.O. C. Kirby and Sgt. D. Jarmosz, March 27, 2000.

South Escanaba. The 469 Gang Team set up a narcotic surveillance on the two addresses then made a narcotic and UUW arrest from 8749 South Escanaba and during said arrest, we confirmed that the narcotics were being stored at 8747 South Escanaba. Armed with the affirmed information, we relocated to 8747 South Escanaba and obtained a CPD Consent to Search form. Upon initial entry we were met by the strong odor of cannabis. We then recovered from the front bedroom of the apartment nine bundles of tightly wrapped cannabis and 50 large zip-lock freezer bags of cannabis totaling 250 pounds and secured two arrestees.

As a result of our dedication to duty, teamwork and continued service to the community a dangerous weapon, a large quantity of narcotics and two members of the Latin Dragons gang were taken off the streets.

Arresting Officers: 004th District 469 Gang-Tactical Members P.O. Jaime Bravo, #4123; P.O. Ralph

Palomino, #18743; P.O. Victor Law, #15539; P.O. Charles Kirby, #12335; P.O. John Knezevich, #13165; P.O. Tamara Matthews, #4640; P.O. Donyal Williams, #10788; and P.O. Carlos Medina, #14593.

Supervisor: Lt. Arthur Parra, #439 and Sgt. David Jarmusz, #1718; 004th District Commander Noreen Walker, #225.

A LOT OF BULL

by 008 District CPD

My partner and I received a radio call of a big bull running loose in the vicinity of 63rd and Artesian at approximately 2:30 p.m. (Artesian is one block west of Western Ave., a major street in the City of Chicago.)

We arrived on the scene and a 1500 lb. bull was in the alley. We called for assistance and blocked off the alley with the squad. The sergeant came in the other end of the alley. All he had to do was place his squad car sideways in the alley and the bull was trapped. But no, he parked it long ways in the alley. Naturally the bull just jogged right by the squad car and out on Artesian and was slowly running down the sidewalk.

Other squads came and the sergeant ordered us to shoot the bull because children would be getting out of school at 3:00 p.m. and they could get hurt. All the shooters were running alongside the bull pumping bullets in him. Then the bull turned around with all the shooters still shooting. My partner and I did not shoot. We ran in the gangway. They must have fired 50 bullets. Finally the bull dropped and all the shooters left. Probably to reload, and my partner and I had the paperwork.

A man came out of the house and told us to slit the bull's neck and let the blood run into the sewer drain. That would save the meat. We told him what he could do with the meat.

In the meantime three people came up to us and said they had bullet holes in their cars. We called the shooters on the radio and told them to leave (shots fired reports) and for someone to handle the three damage to property reports while we called the stockyards for a truck to remove the 1500 lb. dead bull. The bull got loose from a truck delivering him to the stockyards.

The sergeant made captain later, naturally. It sounds like a lot of bull but it's true.

MCAFEE ARREST

An alleged wristwatch thief saved police the trouble of transporting him anywhere this morning when he was captured in the State Street-Roosevelt Road subway station—a half block from police headquarters.

The suspect, Lewis Joe McAfee, 21, of 117 S. Rockwell St. allegedly grabbed Mass Transit Unit Patrolman James Davern's watch and was bolting for the exit as the northbound CTA train pulled into the station, when he was stopped by undercover Patrolwoman Virginia Cronk.

Mass Transit Sgt. Clarence Kerr explained that Davern, the city's most frequently robbed and mugged decoy, was in his usual role as a sleepy, inebriated businessman, when McAfee entered the Englewood-Howard St. train at 35th St., and sat behind him in the rear of the car. Davern's partner, 28-year-old blonde Cronk, dressed as a hippie, was seated in the front of the car covering Davern.

When McAfee made his move, Cronk made hers, and drawing her .38 caliber snub nosed revolver, ordered the unarmed McAfee to stop which he quickly did.

McAfee was then taken to the Central District, A 11 E. 11th St., and charged with theft from a person. He was being held in Central Detention and was scheduled to appear later today in South Felony Court.

Kerr said McAfee told police he thought Patrolwoman Cronk was "too pretty to be a cop." Kerr added that she had recently joined the Mass Transit Unit, and that this was her second felony arrest in less than a week.

There are four women working under cover in the MA Mass Transit, along with a number of other uniformed women. (*Reprinted from City News 11*)

MANY GRIEVE LOSS OF THEIR POLICE BUDDY

Cop On School Corner 28 Years Dies. A lot of the kids will be on hand Monday to say their last good-by to Johnny the Cop. Johnny's funeral services will be at 1 p.m. that day in the chapel at 2114 Irving Park Rd., just half way down the block from the corner of Leavitt Street and Irving Park Road, where he was stationed 28 years.

Johnny was Policeman John J. Komerska, 62, late of the Damen Avenue district. He died of a heart attack in his home at 3630 Kimball Ave. Thursday.

"Johnny the Cop" and "his kids."

The kids—some of them in their 40s—are from Coonley Elementary School, 4046 N. Leavitt St., and St. Benedict's parochial school, 3938 N. Leavitt St. Their Johnny worked the corner and saw to it that they crossed safely for those 28 years, until he retired on July 1, 1959, because he loved them.

Kids Loved Johnny...

And they loved him, too—tens of thousands of them. Twice, when the police administration tried to transfer him away from his kids, they rose up to prove it.

In the spring of 1952 he was put on the night shift, and 1,400 children who signed a petition pleaded to the police commissioner, "Send our Johnny back." Back he went to his kids.

He was assigned to a newly formed sanitation detail at the end of the school year in 1956. This time, 1,800 names went on a petition. Again he went back.

Things Johnny Did...

There were little incidents which told graphically what Johnny meant to the kids. When ice was on the corner, he would bring salt and sand, to make sure no autos slid into the children crossing to school. On cold mornings the patrol boys would be sent to a nearby drug store to warm up and have hot chocolate on Johnny.

Perhaps the mother superior at St. Benedict's explained it best when she told of passing Johnny the Cop on a subzero morning in 1952.

"I asked Johnny why he didn't have his gloves on," she said. "He told me one of the patrol boys had left his gloves at home, and he just couldn't have the boy standing out there with cold hands."

Johnny had no children of his own. He is survived by his widow, Jane; a sister, Margaret; and three brothers: Joseph, Charles and Edward.

John Komerska, Star #5459, received his badge on May 26, 1924, and retired from the force on July 6, 1959 (35 years of service).

A Minimum Auto Runs into Maximum Trouble

The Richmobile Special, an open-air vehicle that might be described as the minimum possible auto, made a short and inglorious run this past Wednesday.

Its designer and builder, Raymond Richmond, 34, rode it from his home at 503 N. Wells three blocks north to Chicago Ave., where Patrolmen Richard Gorecki and Edwin Pokoj halted it.

The Richmobile consists mostly of two bicycles welded together side by side, allowing room between for the operator and a one-cylinder motor.

A Variety of Charges...

Ingenious as this is, the policemen claimed that the Richmobile repeatedly violates the ordinances of the City of Chicago. They charged Richmond with driving an unsafe vehicle because it has no windshield, no fenders, no tail lights, no turn signals—and "the steering gear is faulty."

Moreover, the Richmobile bore state license plates and a city vehicle sticker which had been issued for a motorcycle. The Richmobile, said Gorecki, cannot be a motorcycle because it has too many wheels—four.

Gorecki directed Richmond to push his vehicle home. He is to defend the Richmobile against the legal objections to it at a hearing May 17 in Traffic Court.

Gets Good Mileage, Anyway...

Richmond, father of three children, made his first cruise in the Richmobile last September 8, when he was arrested for failure to have state license plates, a city sticker or a driver's license.

Richmond is an employee of Western Motors, a used car lot at 3950 N. Western. He said the Richmobile has one advantage—he has traveled 40 miles to the pint of gasoline out of it.

Patrolman Gorecki was not impressed. "I don't know why Mr. Richmond just doesn't go ahead and buy a car from the fellow he works for. It would be a lot cheaper in the long run."

"The 'Richmobile' was assembled from scrap metal—two old bicycle frames and a lawn mover motor.

'Richmobile' Cycle Junk to Junk...

The "Big Three" of the auto world can rest easy. The "Richmobile Special" has been banned from Chicago's streets.

The "Richmobile" was built by Raymond Richmond, 34, of 503 N. Wells St., who modestly conceded that it just might "revolutionize" motor traffic in the Windy City.

But Traffic court Referee Melvin Kanter agreed with Policeman Richard Gorecki that the "Richmobile" was unsafe because it lacked the following:

Brake lights, turn signals, windshield, bumpers, and proper steering apparatus. (It balked at turning to the right.)

Kanter fined Richmond $25 and gave him until June 20 to pay. He warned: "Don't ever try to drive that thing again!"

"The 'Richmobile' was assembled from scrap metal—two old bicycle frames and a lawn mover motor.

It had a license, though—a motorcycle license. The fine was for improper use of that, too.

MTU ARREST

Patrolman James Davern, Chicago's most famous police decoy, made his 100th arrest this morning as a member of the Mass Transit Unit.

Davern, 33, who has been in the unit for two years, took on his best "easy pickens" posture and nabbed two robbers at the top of the subway stairs at Chicago Avenue and State Street.

As he climbed the stairs to street level, he was confronted by two men who asked how much money he had.

Davern told them he had none, and one man grabbed him while the other went through the patrolman's pockets, according to Sgt. Clarence Kerr.

After the bandits took $17 from the victim's pocket, they started to fight over the bills when they blew away. When Davern tried to collect the wind blown bills, one of the men kicked him in the groin, and both robbers struck him.

But quickly two other MTU patrolmen rushed over to arrest the pair, identified as Komingo Quijano, of Dallas, Tex., and Louis Brantley, 19, of 9133 Cottage Grove Ave.

Kerr said Brantley is presently under indictment for a January armed robbery, and this was his fourth robbery arrest. Quijano has a minor police record.

Davern was treated and released at Henrotin Hospital. Meanwhile Brantley and Quijano were charged with robbery and scheduled to appear in North Youth Court later today. (*Reprinted from City News 22*)

Designer and builder, Raymond Richmond, March 31, 1963.

Various guises are adopted by decoys. Goal is to make muggers wary about attacking anyone on transit system.

Chicago cop listens to two-way radio as he keeps watchful eye on fellow officer acting as decoy outside subway booth.

A NIGHT WITH CHICAGO'S DECOY SQUAD

, by Jack Star

Special police decoy James Davern finished his career with the CTA Decoy Unit by making his 22nd arrest in the last two months. Davern has been reassigned to undercover work, protecting other decoys in subway stations.

A MOST UNIQUE AND UNUSUAL EXPERIENCE

by Youth Officer (Ret) J. Marcellus Burke #14350

The most unique and unusual experience of my entire police career that spanned from May 16, 1956 until March 11, 1988 occurred during the 70s. I was assigned to the old Area 3 Youth Headquarters that was located at 3900 So. California Ave. The district in my charge for most of the time I spent in Area 3 was the 8th District. I was informed that I was the first black youth officer to be regularly assigned to the 8th District, I guess it was my good Irish name.

During the Marquette Park riots of the 70s I was assigned sometimes in uniform but most of the time in citizen's dress (suit and tie). The incident that I consider the most unusual over all my other unusual incidents occurred on one quiet, warm, beautiful and sunny day. I was driving solo in my unmarked squad car, in citizen's dress, westbound on 71st St. from Western Ave. As I approached Rockwell Ave., the location of the headquarters of the American Nazi Party, I observed a group of men dressed in their brown shirts, wearing their swastika arm bands standing in front of the headquarters, some at parade rest in front of the entrance, others conversing with each other. The sight was something to behold, I was in awe, for a moment I imagined myself in a time-warp, having been transported to pre-war Germany during a Nazi Party rally. I pulled to the curb across the street from the headquarters and parked there, I was stunned. Some of the uniformed men came over to me and formed a semi-circle around me sitting in the squad car. They all raised their clenched fists, jabbing in the air and chanted repeatedly: "Hoop!, Hoop!, Hoop!", and said nothing else. Another group of men wearing T-shirts, emblazoned with "White Power", came over to the scene to see what was happening. To their amazement they could not believe they were looking at a black police officer, alone, sitting in front of Nazi headquarters! They stared at me with such hatred in their eyes that was indescribable. I had never seen such hatred before and I have not seen such hatred since, and that occurred over 20 years ago. The men in T-shirts talked among themselves, loud enough for me to hear, using the vilest of epithets to describe me. One of the men stepped forward, he stared directly into my eyes, then stopped and began to flex his muscles. He then turned slowly around with his back toward me so I could read the message on the back of his T-shirt. The message read: "NIGGER BEWARE." In an instant I bolted from the squad car in a rage that overcame me and

overwhelmed me. We became interlocked and were engaged in the "Mother of All Battles," using only our bare hands and fancy footwork, giving no quarter and accepting no quarter. Suddenly police cars arrived on the scene and a horde of officers descended upon us and attempted to separate us. I yelled and screamed for them to not stop the fight, to let the fight continue, one by one the officers stepped back, releasing us, the uniformed Nazis made a circle around us, and I heard one of them command their people not to interfere, to let us fight to the finish. The fight continued until my adversary could not get up from the ground, incapable of any further resistance. I stood over him in an atmosphere of deathly silence, I then reached down and removed the T-shirt from his fallen body. Suddenly, with a release of emotion, I started yelling at the top of my voice and waved the T-shirt around and around over my head. I then heard my fellow officers cheering, but to my utter amazement the uniformed Nazis also began to cheer! The whole scene was unbelievable! As I visualize that scene today, it still seems unbelievable, as if it were a dream, a fantasy.

I return to reality however whenever I go to my safety deposit box and take out that same T-shirt, old blood stains and all, and hold it in my hands, caressing it, reliving the moment.

That T-shirt is my most prized possession, my trophy of trophies, fought for and paid for in blood and honor!

The epilogue of this entire incident is recorded as follows:

(1) One of the officers returned my service revolver to me, I do not remember losing it.

(2) I told the nearest sergeant to me not to arrest the man, that I would not press charges. I explained that I wanted his own men to deal with him, that their punishment would be more just and swift than that he would receive in any courtroom by any judge. He agreed and we all left the scene.

(3) When the commanding officer of the Marquette Park detail heard of the incident he ordered that I report to him immediately. When he looked at me standing before him, covered with dirt, bloody, my clothes ripped to shreds, my face misshapen with lumps and bruises, for a moment he was speechless. He then gained his composure and lashed out at me in a tirade, lecturing on the proper conduct of a police officer, the possibility of the incident growing to major proportions, he then interjected a prayer to the almighty that it would not, he then inquired as to the whereabouts of my prisoner! I told him the "prisoner" escaped into the crowd, as I held my fingers crossed

behind my back. A long moment of silence prevailed. Then the commanding officer told me he had heard about the outcome of the fight, he leaned over and he smiled with a broad grin and asked me if I wanted to take a good hot bath and get into some clean clothes, I assured him that I did. He then shook my hand and in a soft voice said: "Job well done." Then in a loud booming voice he shouted: "GET THE HELL OUT OF HERE AND DON'T COME BACK!" I quickly complied.

To all that are interested in seeing my trophy, I will gladly display it before them.

MUGGERS MEET ALDERMAN

Ald. Chris Cohen [46th] went on a stakeout with mass transit unit police last night that resulted in the arrest of two men and a juvenile charged with assaulting one of the policemen near the Lawrence Avenue CTA station.

Cohen said he accompanied the eight policemen because of concern over beatings and assaults on riders along the Howard Street line in his ward.

Cohen said he hid nearby with the other policemen while Patrolman James Davern, a veteran decoy of the special police unit loitered at the Lawrence Avenue station. Within minutes, three males approached and began beating Davern.

They grabbed his watch and took $30 from his pockets before the other policemen rushed in and seized two of the suspects. The third one was arrested a few minutes later in the 4800 block of N. Winthrop Ave.

Davern, who has been involved in more than 100 arrests as a decoy, was treated for minor injuries at Weiss Memorial Hospital.

The three arrested are Willie Brown, 32, of 1211 W. Ainslie St., and Terry Lee Nixon, 19, of 4805 N. Winthrop Ave., and a 15-year-old West Side youth.

The policemen began their tour last night at the Sheridan Road station, then moved on to the Wilson Avenue stop before staking out the Lawrence Avenue station.

Cohen said one man walked up to Davern at the Sheridan Road station, apparently intent on robbery, but backed off at the last minute when he recognized Davern, who had arrested him a few weeks ago.

Cohen frequently accompanies policemen in his ward and thruout the city as an observer. Last year, while acting as a decoy, he lost his watch to a robber who escaped. *(Copied)*

Veteran decoy feigns drunkenness.

Sprawled in a seat with a cigarette in his hand, this passenger doesn't look like one of Chicago's finest.

NAB SUSPECT IN AIRPORT TIRE THEFTS

May 25, 1961, Chicago Daily Tribune

Five policemen using walkie-talkie radios nabbed a suspected tire thief in the O'Hare International airport parking lot early yesterday.

A lieutenant and four patrolmen had been watching the lot for two nights at the request of Capt. Patrick Deeley of the Irving Park District. Deeley said that tires and wheels had been stolen from 20 late model cars in the last week.

Uses Binoculars...

Patrolman George Pocious was stationed with a pair of binoculars atop one of the buildings under construction at the airport. He thought he caught a glimpse of someone loitering between parked cars, and radioed the information to Lt. Robert Arnold, Thomas McGovern, Ralph Gibson and Ed Cashier, who were in the lot. They closed in on a man who said he was Alvery Willis, 31, of 1109 W. 63rd Street.

Willis was grabbed, the police said, just as he was loading a tire and wheel into a parked car. He admitted under questioning that he had driven two friends to the airport in the car, which is owned by Marguerite Felter, 6631 May Street.

The policemen said they found three other tires in the trunk, trunk locks from four cars, and a lock puller.

Denies Taking Tires...

A check of the area revealed that locks had been pulled off four cars and that the tires and wheels were missing, Lt. Arnold said.

Willis was taken to the state's attorney's office where he denied taking the tires. Police said they found another lock puller in his pocket. He was charged with petty larceny and possession of burglary tools.

NEWSMAKERS

by Daniel McCaughna

No easy pickings. Patrolman James Davern made his 99th and 100th arrests early yesterday as a member of the police undercover decoy unit working at Chicago Transit Authority stations. Two youths were nabbed when they tried to rob Davern at the street entrance to the subway station at Chicago Avenue and State Street. Davern, as usual, wore old clothes and looked the easy pickings. He wasn't. (*Copied*)

ONE BULLET - TWO HITS

There is the story about Eddie Delso who shot two fleeing felons with one bullet. However, I have spent

Officer Edward Delso's Chicago Police Graduating Class, October 16, 1935.

the last two months trying to track down which of his six children still had the newspaper article relating the incident, to no avail.

From my recollection, it was in the 40s and two men had just committed an armed robbery. Officer Delso happened upon the scene just as they were making their getaway on foot. Officer Delso immediately gave chase. When one offender turned to shoot at him, Officer Delso instinctively fired, striking offender #1 with the bullet going "through and through" and hitting offender #2, downing both of them. Officer Edward Delson was in Chicago Police Graduating Class of October 16, 1935.

ONE OF CHICAGO'S FINEST

by Patricia Leeds

Jaconetti lives up to his billing and then some. Bill Jaconetti, one of Chicago's most decorated policemen, has a genuine concern for people and believes the slogan "We serve and protect" applies to all.

"When Bill Jaconetti is on duty, we feel safe," one repeatedly hears on the beat he covers: the Milwaukee-North Damen Avenue shopping area and surrounding neighborhood.

Here the stores are not posh or quaint. They have bars on the windows, and the shopkeepers control their doors with buzzers.

Jaconetti and his partner, Al Kohl, are assigned to the Shakespeare or 14th District, on what is called a walk and ride patrol. They park the squad car and Jaconetti takes the north end and Kohl the south. Occasionally they patrol together. They have their walkie-talkie radios and get the police calls on their zone. When they need the car, the one closest to where it is parked picks up the other.

The other day, the two officers took along a reporter on their beat.

"Bill's friendly, but professional too," said Frieda Schwartz, co-owner of Morry's Jewelers on Milwaukee Avenue. "He never forgets he's a policeman. Al's wonderful, too."

"We were in the middle of a conversation when Al suddenly ran outside and onto a bus," said Morry Schwartz. "He saw a man snatch a purse and get on the bus, and he followed him and caught him. Later he came back, and we finished our conservation. See what I mean? They're professionals."

"Bill suggested we install a plastic shield in the window so it couldn't be broken by 'smash and grab' thieves," Frieda said. "And it was his idea we install the buzzer system so we wouldn't let in anybody who looked suspicious. He's always coming up with ideas to help people. There should be more like them."

The group stopped for coffee the other day in Sophie's Busy Bee restaurant, 1546 N. Damen Ave., a family cafe known for serving fine Polish food for 50 years. The Busy Bee is a gathering place for senior

Jaconetti on the job.

citizens who have lived in this one time predominantly Polish neighborhood most of their lives: young Hispanic couples, lawyers and judges.

Sophie Madej, the owner, wanted to know how she could get Jaconetti to work on Saturdays. "We need you then," she said. "Or why can't you at least work until 8 o'clock at night when we close?"

"Because my wife and children like to have me home at that time," he said, smiling. "We can't work all the time."

Walking into Norm Levin's Singer Sewing Machine store, Jaconetti said, "Norm's my eyes and ears when I'm not around. He's street-wise and can tell right away if anything or anybody looks suspicious. Across the street in that fast-food restaurant he saw a couple of guys try to hide a gun. He got hold of me, and we prevented a robbery.

"He came to my rescue a couple of times," Jaconetti recalled. "I caught a purse-snatcher—he was a big guy, and he kept flailing around and I couldn't get the cuffs on him. Norm helped me cuff him."

Norm, a husky, middle-aged man, has a profound respect and admiration for Jaconetti and Kohl. "Did you know that in 1979 Jaconetti was named "Policeman of the Year?" he asked. "They take pride in their work."

Jaconetti and Kohl like working a foot patrol. "You get to know the people and their habits. Like the time there was a silent alarm in a clothing store down the block," Jaconetti recalled, "The man on the squad who responded reported that a black man behind the counter said the alarm went off accidentally. Kohl told them to send the squad back. He knew there weren't any black employees in that store."

"The concept of policemen who work the car is entirely different from that of the patrolman who walks a beat and gets to know the people. It brings the people together." Kohl said.

In Phillips Jewelry, Jaconetti saved a policeman from being shot and freed 13 hostages. He himself was shot. For his heroism he won the highest honor awarded a policeman—the superintendent's Medal of Valor and the City's Carter Harrison Award.

"I was walking my post," Jaconetti recalled, "when I heard the call. I knew if that alarm went off it had to be the real thing. They just assigned a one-man car, thinking it must be a false alarm. I knew I had to get over there fast. Through a side window I saw a man holding a gun to a policeman's head.

"I kind of crouched until I was at the door and shouted. 'Don't do it!'" He had the door partly open with his foot, and he swung around and started firing; I fired and kept firing until I emptied my gun. He dropped to the ground—dead.

"I heard the policeman calling into his radio. 'Send help there're two more robbers here and people in the back.'

"I moved back and crouching down, I reloaded my gun, then sidled over to the window with my gun pointed at one of the other robbers. He saw me and shouted, 'Don't shoot!' and put up his hands and the other one did the same. They threw their guns down.

"Thirteen people, including six employees, had been lying on the floor in the small back room, so cramped they were lying on top of each other. One elderly employee said, 'I'm so scared.' I told him, 'So am I.'

"We also found a couple of bags with thousands of dollars' worth of jewelry that the robbers had ready to take with them.

"And then I recalled, I'd been shot. I remembered the impact when the .38 hit me. But all I had was a bruise. The bullet was stopped by my leather jacket and was imbedded there."

This happened Feb. 16, 1979. The jacket is now on display in the Chicago Police Museum. Also a room at the Police Training Academy was named for him—it has a bronze plaque with his name and picture.

Despite the fact that the robber who shot at Jaconetti was an ex-con and wanted for other serious crimes, Jaconetti still agonized for almost a year over killing him.

But after receiving letters from two of the robber's terrified victims, Jaconetti said, "I finally was able to realize that he would never again be able to hurt anyone and perhaps I had saved someone's life."

At a recent ceremony honoring policemen, Jaconetti was the only one to receive two awards. One was a department commendation for apprehending a man who was observed behaving suspiciously just before a message was broadcast that a man fitting his description was wanted for the attempted murder, rape and robbery of a nun. Officers John Wasco and Russell Ruggero shared the award.

The other was a lifesaving award, shared by Kohl, for taking a stabbing victim who had been given up for dead to a hospital and administering first aid on the way.

Jaconetti has numerous other awards and letters of commendation.

"My parents were immigrants from Italy, and they instilled in me a respect for all people," Jaconetti said. "As a result of this I hate bullies, and I hate to see anyone take advantage of the disadvantaged. I like old people, and it burns me up when they are ignored or patronized."

He has also helped young people who were in trouble. "You listen to their problems and try to help them. A few former gang members are now working,

Marshall Robinson of the OTS Unit pictured with the Anheuser-Busch Clydesdales.

respectable citizens because somebody listened and helped straighten them out."

Jaconetti has been a Chicago policeman 16 years. He and his wife, Donna, have three children.

Jaconetti has one regret. "I'm so sorry my parents didn't live to see me become a policeman. They would have been so proud. They never heard of the police department slogan, but long ago they believed a policeman's job is to serve and protect."

OTS UNIT

by Marshall Robinson

I came on the police department March 16, 1957. When I left Police School I went to traffic and went to a unit called OTS that pulled out of a warehouse at 14th and Indiana. We were all on three-wheel bikes.

The districts I worked: 17 the Old Cragin, Filmore, 20th Dist., Town Hall and I retired out of the 19th Dist. in July 1966 at 65 years of age.

MORE COPS, DOGS TO START SCHOOL

Six more policemen and their dogs to be trained for the K-9 Corps will start school Monday, according to Police Supt. O.W. Wilson and Sgt. Edward Rhoerick, director of the special canine unit.

The patrolmen, William Duffy, James Gillen, Russell Holt, Hugh Carroll, Harold Walchuk and

Arthur Hajek, will be under the direction of Sterling Jantz at the training farm, 7900 County Line Road, La Grange.

Jantz was in the initial group of six who completed their training two weeks ago.

Nine dogs will be available for training Monday, according to Rhoerick, who said:

"We're going to have three additional dogs available in case some are not amenable to training.

"So far, we have a field of 3,000 dogs, but we only have been able to select 17 for training."

When six complete their seventh week, another six will begin. This schedule will be maintained until 150 handlers and their dogs are ready for duty.

THE PIPES AND DRUMS

by James Healy, President and Band Manager

The Pipes and Drums of the Emerald Society Chicago Police Department was formed in May 1982, with the assistance of then Mayor of Chicago, Jane Byrne, and the Emerald Society of Illinois, our parent organization, for the primary purpose of honoring police officers and firefighters killed in the line of duty. Since the formation of the band, we have had the honor of participating at the funerals of 40 policemen killed in

Two of Chicago Police Department's canine members are escorted by their new handlers on a stroll in front of police headquarters, 1121 S. State. German shepherds Von Jackson and Stormy enjoy airing with (from left) Policemen Russell Holt, Hugh Carroll, Harold Walchuck, William Duffy and James Gillen. Men and dogs will train together at Bridewell farm. (Chicago Sun-Times Photo)

The Pipes and Drums of the Emerald Society Chicago Police Department, Nov. 11, 1999.

the line of duty, including the two Capitol Police Officers killed in Washington, DC in July 1998. We have also had the honor of participating at the funerals of 27 firefighters killed in the line of duty. Besides the 67 line of duty funerals, the band has participated in literally hundreds of benefits for injured or catastrophically ill policemen/firemen or members of their families.

This volunteer group of musicians are all law enforcement officers from police departments throughout the Chicago Metropolitan area. Although the majority comes from the Chicago Police Department, suburban, county, state and federal agencies have Emerald Society members representing their department also.

In addition to honoring slain police officers and firefighters killed in the line of duty, the Band has expanded its purpose—to promote Irish culture and music. The Band has performed at functions as far north as Ottawa, Ontario, to as far south as Florida, and New Orleans for Mardi Gras. The Band has been featured in movies using the Chicago skyline, including *Backdraft, The Package, The Fugitive,* and *The Negotiator.* The Band has appeared on *The Tonight Show* with Jay Leno, and in Milwaukee, Wisconsin, with Doc Severnson and the Milwaukee Symphony Orchestra.

The Band also plays on the steps of the Illinois Capitol in Springfield and Washington DC during the month of May for the Annual Police Officer Memorial Ceremonies.

POLICE OFFICER OF THE YEAR

by Pam Proctor, Oct. 15, 1989
Parade Magazine

Wounded in the leg by a deranged gunman who had just slain three persons, Chicago Police Officer Gregory Jaglowski staggered toward the school where the killer had fled.

He heard gunfire. His partner, Officer Irma Ruiz, was in there, along with nearly 200 children and teachers.

For his ensuing actions, in which he killed the gunman and thereby saved perhaps dozens of lives, Gregory Jaglowski, 39, has been named the Police Officer of the Year by the International Association of Chiefs of Police. The award, also sponsored by *Parade,* will be presented by the association on October 17 in Louisville, KY.

"Had it not been for Greg," says Bernard Karlin, principal of the Moses Montefiore School, where the incident took place, "it could have been a massacre. We owe him our lives."

Officer Greg Jaglowski, with students at school where fatal shootings took place.

Chicago Police Supt. LeRoy Martin concurs: "Anybody who crossed the assailant's path that day was going to get shot and killed. He had already killed innocent people, two in an auto parts store and one of the engineers at the school. He was hell-bent on destruction."

Greg Jaglowski's story is also the story of a partnership between two officers.

"Greg was a shining example of what a policeman should be," says Karlin, who worked closely with Jaglowski and Ruiz during their four years together as school-patrol officers." He treated all the kids much the way he treated his own daughters," says Sgt. Tom Fuller, a police supervisor.

Jaglowski's partner was like a mother figure. With four children of her own at home, Irma Ruiz "knew exactly what to say to kids," says Victor Zapatka, a guidance counselor at Montefiore.

Typical was the time Ruiz and Jaglowski came upon a woman scolding her 8-year-old son. "If you're not good," the woman warned the boy, "these policemen will put you in jail."

"Oh, I'd never put you in jail, replied Ruiz, looking warmly at the child. "I know you're too good a boy."

On September 22, 1988, Montefiore reported that a student had assaulted a teacher, but by the time Ruiz and Jaglowski got there, the boy had gone home.

Then came the report of shots. Jaglowski was first out the door. A bullet hit him in the leg, knocking him down. He dove for cover as the gunman raced into the school.

"I thought Irma had gone for cover," says Jaglowski. "I hoped she had."

As a shot rang out, Jaglowski headed back inside the school, dazed and bleeding from his wound.

There, in a pool of blood, lay his partner. Irma had been shot in the chest. She was dead at age 40. The gunman, later identified as Clemmie Henderson, had ducked into the school library to reload. As Jaglowski looked up, he came out shooting from only a few feet away.

"It looked like fire coming out of his gun," recalls Jaglowski. "It was like slow motion; I could almost feel the bullets going by me."

The cop fired back, trading bullets with the gunman, who shot him in his other leg, severing an artery. Jaglowski kept pumping rounds into the man.

Nothing seemed to stop the gunman. But with his last bullet, Jaglowski finally dropped Henderson, a jobless neighborhood figure with a history of erratic behavior. In his blood and urine, according to the medical examiner, were traces of the drug PCP, also known as angel dust.

For Jaglowski, a new battle was just beginning.

"Sometimes I still can't believe that Irma is dead," says the 16-year police veteran. "You get angry when you think about these things. Sometimes it bothers me why God would take someone like that."

"His wounds are healing," says Jaglowski's wife, Diana. "He's walking and he's functioning. But what's rough is the mental part of it—losing Irma and seeing her kids not having a mother and her husband not having a wife." Today, more than a year since the shooting, Diana adds, "it's still as fresh as it was then."

Jaglowski could have remained outside the school, tending his own wounds and calling for help, says Cmdr. Ettore DiVito, his chief in the Youth Division. "But the fact that he did go back into the school—that's what separates a hero from just a good, solid police officer."

Today, Gregory Jaglowski accepts such accolades with a self-effacing smile and then sets the record straight.

Officer Irma Ruiz

"Remember Irma," he tells the kids. "Never forget what she did."

Det. Jaglowski remembers her as "a great woman, best friend and the greatest partner you could ever have."

Honors and Awards of Gregory M. Jaglowski...

Police performance job situation featured on the TV series *Top Cops* and TV special "Badge of Courage: Police Officer of the Year."

Recipient of Police Officer of the Year Award (1989-90) from Parade Magazine/International Association of Chiefs of Police, American Federation of Police, and inducted into Police Hall of Fame.

Selected to break ground in Washington, DC for the National Law Enforcement Memorial and honored by President George Bush as a special guest of the White House.

Recipient of Carter Harrison Award (City of Chicago's highest award for bravery), Chicago Police Department's Medal of Honor, Superintendent's Medal of Valor, 100 Club Medal of Valor and Blue Star Award (for injuries sustained in the line of duty), Illinois Police Association's Award of Valor, Distinguished Services Awards from the Chicago Crime Commission, Chicago Association of Commerce and Industry and other organizations.

Recognized for public service and police career achievements by U.S. Congress (named entered into Congressional Record) and President Ronald Reagan.

A POSITIVE ID

In late fall of 1965, we had an offender who started robbing and sexually assaulting women as they walked on the street, late at night. A pattern started to develop in which the women were accosted shortly after they got off of a C.T.A. bus and when they began walking down a side street. These incidents occurred on the far N.W. side of Chicago. This pattern continued into the early winter and spring months of 1966.

The incidents began to get more violent with each attack. The offender was armed with a hunting knife and wore a stocking cap. He first started threatening them with the knife and then progressed to stabbing them in the arm or other parts of their body. The offender would also take the victim's purse and tell them he would find them and rape them again, if they called the police. The victims were unable to aid us with a description of the offender, other then he was a M/W.

In two of the incidents, the victims informed us that while they were on the bus, they saw an old dark colored automobile and it appeared to be following the bus.

On March 30, 1966, at 10:00 P.M. a 32-year-old woman got off the bus near the intersection of Milwaukee Ave. and Elston Ave. She proceeded to walk to her nearby residence and was attacked and dragged into a passageway. The victim started screaming and at this time the offender began slashing her across the back of her neck. An off duty officer, Sgt. Charles Adamson, heard the victim's screams and came out of his residence. This caused the offender to flee on foot. Sgt. Adamson, chased the offender but lost him in a nearby alley.

Sgt. DiMaggio and Det. Evans were notified of this incident and the fact that the victim had been transported to the Resurrection Hospital for treatment of her wounds. These wounds to her neck area required 50 stitches. After interviewing the victim and learning that the offender had fled on foot, we proceeded back to the area of the assault. We hoped that the offender had abandoned his automobile in the vicinity of the attack. Five vehicles were located in the vicinity which did not belong to local residents. We started investigating these vehicles and later learned that they had been left in the area for tune-ups to be performed by one of the local residents.

Approximately two hours later, we finished checking out the last of the five vehicles. As we approached the intersection of Milwaukee Ave. and Elston Ave., we observed an older black vehicle stopped at the light facing north bound. Since it fit the description of the auto described by two of the victims, we decided that a street stop should be made. As we turned around to get behind this auto, another vehicle came up behind us and started honking his horn. A quick glance back, showed that it was Det. Clepp, in his own personal auto. Det. Clepp, kept pointing at the old car in front of us. We learned later that Clepp, who was familiar with this crime pattern and the offender's M.O., had observed this older dark automobile following a C.T.A. Bus.

When the light turned green this vehicle, proceeded north and then turned onto a side street and into an alley. A stop of the vehicle was made, and the driver now known as Gregory Hall, got out. A quick glance into the interior of the auto showed both the stocking cap and a bloody hunting knife on the front seat. We then informed Hall, that his last victim was in the hospital in serious condition. Hall, stated that he had not meant to hurt her. Hall, was placed under arrest and at this time told us, that there were several purses belonging to other victims, under the front

Rear: Sgt. John Dimaggio, front from left: Det. Larry Evans and Det. Louis Clepp show evidence retrieved from suspect's vehicle.

seat of his auto. Eight more victims' purses were then recovered. As the investigation continued more purses and personal items taken from the victims, were recovered from Hall's residence at his direction.

The next afternoon, a showup was conducted at the Area 5 Robbery section. Hall, was positively identified by 14 victims. Upon being identified by the victims, Hall, made oral admissions and apologized to all of the victims. Hall, subsequently plead guilty to all charges and was sentenced to 12 years in the Illinois State Penitentiary.

A PROUD MOMENT

by Edward J. Sullins–#11093.

This commendation was for an off duty shoot-out, that myself, Officer Chris Anderson, and Officer Daniel McCarthy had with a gang banger who had pulled out a gun on a kid in a parking lot. He then tried to kill us after we announced that we were the police and tried to intervene. In what turned out to be a running gun battle, the scumbag fired eight rounds at Officer Chris Anderson and me at close range, luckily missing all eight times. Three of those rounds struck a car next to me. The scumbag gang banger was not so lucky, we shot him twice. Good guys—2, bad guys—0.

Attending the presentation ceremony were my stepfather, retired Det. Jim Capesius, Area 4, violent crimes, a highly respected and one of the best detectives there ever was and my commander, Thomas Walton, a stand-up, take charge, and fly into the heart of chaos type of boss-one of the best.

An odd note: I have my stepfather's old Patrolman's Star #11093 which we had put away years ago in case a family member ever came on the job. I was hired on Nov. 22, 1993 (11/93) - coincidence or fate? I have tried to up hold the example of fine tradition and excellence set forth by my stepfather. I hope I have made him proud.

QUEEN FOR A DAY

Queen Elizabeth II of England paid a brief visit to Chicago on July 6, 1959 and received a royal welcome from Mayor Daley, Illinois Governor William Stratton, and an estimated two million well-wishers who lined her parade route.

The queen and her consort, Prince Philip, arrived at 10 a.m. aboard the 400 foot long royal yacht *Britannia*. The queen had sailed down the newly-opened St. Lawrence Seaway to Chicago, the only U.S. city she visited on a seven week, 15,000 mile trip. Her stay in Chicago would last only 14 hours.

In sunny, 80-degree weather, the royal party motored from the lakefront to the Loop, then back to

Edward J. Sullins receives commendation. Group includes Sullins stepfather, Ret. Det. Jim Capesius and Sullins commander Thomas Walton.

July 6, 1959: England's Queen Elizabeth arrives in Chicago for a 14-hour visit.

Navy Pier where the International Trade Fair was in progress.

The queen found the fair "frightfully impressive." Philip chatted with the crowd; Elizabeth threw a quarter into the CARE-benefit wishing well. The prince, spotting a Rolls-Royce, called it "the best car in the show."

Later, the queen and her entourage arrived at the Drake Hotel where they freshened up, using 95 rooms on two floors. Then it was on to the Ambassador Hotel for a luncheon hosted by Gov. Stratton and attended by Chicago's elite, including Mrs. John T. Pirie Jr., who said of her meeting with the queen: "I had such a lump in my throat when I looked at that little girl." (Elizabeth was 33 and Philip 38.)

At 3 p.m. the royal couple visited the Museum of Science and Industry where the queen heard a recording of her voice played back as it sounded on the telephone. "Oh, look! A Spit!" Elizabeth exclaimed when she spotted the English World War II fighter plane, the Spitfire, suspended from the museum's ceiling. A bomb threat turned out to be a hoax and failed to interrupt the museum visit.

At 4:15 p.m. the queen arrived at the Art Institute where she admired the 13-foot-high painting by El Greco, "The Assumption of the Virgin." Meanwhile, several blocks away, police were stationed at bridges warning skid-row residents to stay west of the Chicago River during the queen's visit unless they were sober.

The evening brought a reception for Midwestern governors at the Drake Hotel, followed by a banquet hosted by Mayor Daley at the Conrad Hilton Hotel. Conrad Hilton himself inspected the kitchens before the event and personally greeted the queen.

In his remarks following the meal, Mayor Daley hailed the "great charm and serene dignity of Her Majesty, Queen Elizabeth." Daley drew applause when he suggested, "Your majesty and your royal highness, Prince Philip, come back and see us again and bring the children."

Queen Elizabeth and Prince Philip were back aboard the *Britannia* by midnight, and the yacht set sail at 12:10 a.m. bringing to an end their whirlwind Chicago visit.

RAGGED BANDIT ROBS STORE THEN RETURNS, WELL CLAD

A six foot colored bandit returned to the scene of a crime yesterday and committed another one. He took $30 from James Hoffheimer, manager of a grocery at 4505 Cottage Grove Avenue. Several weeks ago he robbed Hoffheimer of a smaller amount. At that time he was ragged and unkept. Yesterday he was well dressed.

A RESOLUTION

*Adopted by The City Council of the
City of Chicago, Illinois
Presented by Alderman Robert T. Kellam on
May 20, 1987*

WHEREAS, the citizens, friends and members of the 40 & 8 of the American Legion request that the day of June 20, 1987 be designated (in Chicago) to be known as Jim Ahern Day who was selected as the Nation Wide Law Officer of the Year in Portland, Oregon in the fall (September) of 1986; and

WHEREAS, Officer Jim Ahern of the Organized Crime, Division, Vice Control Section, has exemplified not only to those in law enforcement but also the citizens of Chicago, his state and nation those attributes which exhibit dedication, honesty, and service for the betterment of his fellow man; and

WHEREAS, Jim Ahern was selected from 23 finalists from across this nation for the honor bestowed upon him by the 70,000 members of the 40 & 8, a fun and honor society, of the American Legion as the outstanding officer of the year; and

WHEREAS, Jim Ahern has received a total of 29 honorable mentions and has won the following medals and awards:

Junior Chamber of Commerce Award - December, 1981

Officer of the Month Award - April, 1984

Police Medal - May, 1984 (Highest medal presented by the City of Chicago)

Superintendent's Award of Valor - May, 1984

Lambert Tree Award - Highest medal presented by the Chicago Police Department

James Hoffheimer, manager of A&P Grocery Store, pictured here the year before he got on the Police Department (April of 1940).

Fraternal Order of Police Medal of Valor - 1984 Illinois Police Assn. Valor Award - 1984 Four time winner of the Blue Star Award - which is similar to the Purple Heart Award by the Army Personnel; and WHEREAS, the above biography shows Jim Ahern to be one of Chicago's finest, we hereby

Jim Ahern

request that June 20, 1987 be declared as Jim Ahern Day (in Chicago) who has never wavered in his dedication, faith in human beings and service to his fellow man; now, therefore,

BE IT RESOLVED, that the Mayor and the City Council congratulate Jim Ahern on this accomplishment and wish to present him with a suitable copy of this resolution.

A RESOLUTION

Adopted by The City Council of the City of Chicago, Illinois Presented by Alderman Ray Suarez on February 9, 1994

WHEREAS, the Reverend Adolfo Lopez, an ordained Deacon whose professional experience as a Chicago Police Officer, has given him unique qualifications for outstanding service to his fellowman, was able to offer strength and succor to the victims in the kidnapping of 6-week-old Crystal Guerrero last December; and

WHEREAS, in a much-publicized kidnapping in which little Crystal Guerrero was taken from the Uptown Neighborhood Health Center by a woman whom Crystal's mother allowed to hold the baby, Adolfo Lopez eventually played a key role in comforting the mother and father, Maria Alvarez and Jose Guerrero, and no doubt in inspiring the perpetrator, as he has reached out to so many, to return Crystal to her parents; and

Adolpho Lopez

WHEREAS, born in Mayaquez, Puerto Rico, and raised in Chicago, Adolfo Lopez is a graduate of John Marshall High School and of St. Xavier University, and has also attended DePaul University and Malcolm X College. He joined the Chicago Police Department in August of 1972 and has been involved in Prison, Youth and Retreat Ministries over the years. He is an Assistant Chaplain of Cook County Jail, is a part-time Police Chaplain as well, and has received 13 Complimentary Letters, over 90 Honorable Mentions and 2 Department Commendations. The Reverend Adolfo Lopez is a friend to many, and his inestimable help in the Crystal Guerrero kidnapping case is the latest example of his intelligence, perception, and of the care and concern he has long shown the people of this City, now, therefore,

BE IT RESOLVED, that we, the Mayor and members of the City Council of the City of Chicago, gathered here this 9th Day of February, 1994, A.D., on behalf of all our citizens, do hereby express our gratitude and congratulations to the Reverend Adolfo Lopez of the Chicago Police Department for his dedication and service to the people of this City, and we extend to this outstanding citizen our fervent wishes for his continuing success and fulfillment.

BE IT FURTHER RESOLVED, that a suitable copy of this resolution be prepared and presented to the Reverend Adolfo Lopez.

ROBBED 176 TIMES, COP ASKS FOR MORE

by Larry Ingrassia Chicago Sun-Times

Oct. 8, 1974. James Davern has been robbed 176 times in the last three years, and he has no one to blame but himself.

He travels around the city on a Chicago Transit Authority train at night, often impeccably dressed in a sports coat and tie, wearing a handsome wrist watch.

Davern, 41, knows he is asking for trouble, but he won't stop — it's part of his job. He is a decoy, a Chicago patrolman on the Mass Transit Special Operations unit.

He stumbles around CTA platforms and trains appearing drunk or drowsy, an open invitation to robbers who prey on the weak and vulnerable. Hidden in the wings however, are at least two of Davern's plain clothes partners.

"Whenever I get robbed," Davern said, "we recover the property - our evidence — from the assail-

Luring a robber. Appearing to have had one too many, James Davern leans against a subway vending machine in his role as a decoy. Davern is a Chicago patrolman on the Mass Transit Special Operations Unit. (Sun-Times Photo by Bob Black)

ant no more than 10 or 15 feet away from me. If there was ever anything such as an air-tight case, this is it."

Davern does not always dress like a businessman. Sometimes he wears a gas station attendant's suit, a soldier's uniform, a supermarket employee's coat or a department store delivery uniform.

Although he often changes costumes, Davern is always cast as a typical victim of crime on CTA train lines. He has studied the part since the mid-1960s when he was a plain-clothes patrolman.

"When this special unit was created in 1971, I interviewed people who actually were robbed on the train. I found out what they were wearing, where they sat, who they were with. I have to be convincing or we'd never fool anyone," said Davern, a Chicago policeman for 14 years.

An expert victim, Davern added that he knows how not to get robbed, too. He advised CTA riders, "There's safety in numbers. They should always sit near somebody, even if it's someone they don't know."

"And be alert. These people (robbers) are bullies. They like to pick on defenseless people who are tired or have had too much to drink."

While on the job, Davern breaks his own guidelines. He always appears alone. "When a robber comes up to me, I have to let him take something before yelling 'Hit,' to call my partners," he added.

Davern has avoided serious injury, but he has been punched in the head more times then he can remember and once his eardrum was punctured. He does not carry a weapon, because an experienced robber might spot it, he said.

"If I get hurt it's because of something I forgot to cover, because I was overconfident. You have to be ready for anything," Davern added.

He and his partners often apprehend robbers by following potential victims on a train. But those arrests do not lead to so many convictions as arrests by a decoy, because the victims are not willing to take the time to testify against the robbers, Davern said.

"Apathy of the victims is the biggest problem we have," he said.

Still Davern's boss on the midnight-to-8 a.m. shift, Sgt. Clarence Kerr, said crime on CTA trains has been cut in half since the special unit was instituted. "As a special unit, we've been able to develop contacts who tell us what's going on. The robbers don't get away from our decoys," Kerr said.

Davern said the existence of the decoy unit is a deterrent in itself. He remembered seeing a well-dressed man walking past other men on a CTA platform recently.

"These guys looked the other one up and down," Davern related, "motioned to his friend, as if to say, 'Let's get him.' But his friend replied, 'Naw, he's probably one of them decoy cops.'"

Davern added, "It wasn't, but it could have been and that's what stopped them.

ROCHFORD LINKS CRIME RISE TO HIRING FREEZE

By Harry Golden Jr.

A year-old freeze on hiring has left Chicago police 764 men short and has unmistakably boosted crime, Police Supt. James M. Rochford said Tuesday.

Rochford said the freeze — voluntarily ordered by Rochford pending the outcome of a U.S. District Court battle over charges of racial discrimination in police jobs — clearly contributed to a current increase in the city's crime rate.

He commented in an interview during City Hall ceremonies saluting heroic actions by members of Chicago's uniformed services.

In separate interviews, Ald. Edward M. Burke (14th), chairman of the City Council Committee on Police, and 1st Deputy Police Supt. Michael A. Spiotto also said part of Chicago's crime increase has been brought about by the thinning of ranks.

All three said the department has made determined efforts to keep squad car and foot patrols at full strength despite the manpower strain.

They acknowledged that the detective divisions and units such as those concentrating on youth and organized crime have suffered.

The most recent statistics show total serious crime in Chicago has risen so far this year by 7.8 percent.

"Naturally, we presume we wouldn't be up as much as we were if we were at full strength," Spiotto said. "We are trying to take care of our basic needs first by maximizing use of the manpower we have."

Burke said "the citizens aren't getting maximum protection.

"Because patrolmen are so crucially required, patrolmen aren't being promoted to investigator. I understand that one police area is operating with detectives at half-strength," the alderman said.

Also focusing on police manpower, Ald. Tyrone T. Kenner (3d) called for a special city police patrol to stem rising crime and "want-on shooting" at Robert Taylor Homes on State between 39th and 54th.

Kenner told a reporter he will appeal to Rochford for the patrol Wednesday.

In separate incidents within a month, Kenner said, Deputy Sheriff Joseph Law and a young girl were killed and several other persons have been wounded.

Since last Jan. 1, a force of 13,978 sworn officers has been authorized. But no police have been hired since October, 1973.

City Corporation Counsel Richard L. Curry, also present at ceremonies in the City Council chamber, said U.S. District Court Judge Prentice H. Marshall is expected to rule Oct. 15 on the long-standing lawsuit.

Rochford said, "We are keeping patrol at full strength as our No. 1 crime-fighting unit. Until we get stronger evidence we disagree with a consultants' recent study in Kansas City in which it was found that patrol had little or no effect on crime rates. (*Copied*)

ROCHFORD ORDERS ALL-OUT DRIVE ON CTA CRIME

by James Murray

A new "aggressive approach" to the fight against crime on the Chicago Transit Authority and a stepped-up drive against arsonists were announced today by Police Supt. James M. Rochford.

At a press conference today, Rochford said Chicago police will "concentrate our efforts to insure the security of all citizens who ride the subway and elevated trains on the rapid transit lines."

He said undercover tactical unit policemen and uniformed men will increase surveillance at eight CTA stations with a record of high crime incidence.

These stations, he said, "will be manned around the clock."

Four undercover policewomen have been assigned to CTA patrol as part of the new effort, Rochford said.

Loiterers who let two or more trains pass without boarding at stations will be challenged, he said, commenting: "We're after the criminals—not kids out after curfew."

Although the crackdown will be directed at "L" and subway platforms plagued by criminals, the Police Mass Transit Unit will continue to protect bus riders. Beat patrolmen will be ordered to keep a close check for loiterers at major bus transfer points, he said.

"We want the public to feel it is safe to ride the CTA," he said.

Rochford said that in the first six months of this year, there were 445 major crimes reported on the CTA system, 353 of them robberies. Last year, in the same period, there were 343 major crimes, of which 279 were robberies. As of yesterday morning, the total number of robberies on CTA lines was 409.

The sharp increase touched off the new crime-control effort, he said.

The superintendent also revealed that Deputy Supt. Michael Spiotto has completed a survey of West Side arson cases and has "established a definite pattern" in such crimes.

After the survey, concentration on arson cases led directly to two arrests, Rochford said, and strict policing of affected areas will continue. (*Copied*)

The chief tracks down the answers. Loopbound on a Dan Ryan train Tuesday night, Police Supt. James Rochford sits next to a passenger, asking about train safety. CTA chairman Milton Pikarsky (left) has some questions, too. News crews accompanied the two officials only on the Ryan leg of the ride from Northwest Side to South. (Sun-Times Photo by Duane Hall)

ROCHFORD, PIKARSKY GET ON CTA, THIEVES GET OFF

by Jay Branegan

At the 63rd Street stop of the Dan Ryan Rapid Transit line late Tuesday, Police Supt. James Rochford, Chicago Transit Authority Chairman Milton Pikarsky, and 20 newsmen, photographers, and TV cameramen boarded the northbound train.

At the next stop, all the pickpockets and jackrollers got off.

That was the view, anyway, of one hardened train conductor, a nine-year CTA veteran, as he watched the last leg of a "CTA inspection trip" by Rochford and Pikarsky.

"Didn't you see those people crouching in the corner and hiding their faces when the cameramen came on?" the conductor asked quietly. "Sure, people who are asleep or drunk have their pockets picked all the time."

But there was none of that Tuesday, as Pikarsky and Rochford took to the rails and talked to the people who ride the CTA at night. They wanted to learn the public's feelings about safety on the CTA and get suggestions on how to improve it.

Rochford was dressed casually in slacks and a sweater instead of his police uniform, while Pikarsky wore a white shirt and brown business suit.

The dozen passengers on the first car appeared perplexed as Rochford and Pikarsky went around introducing themselves and tried to make conversation over the noise of the train and the shoving of the reporters.

Pikarsky and Rochford completed the major portion of their trip alone, without the benefit of the media. They said they interviewed 50 people on two elevated lines and one bus route and found only one woman who said she had ever been harassed.

Earlier Tuesday, a CTA bus driver and a supervisor teamed up to rescue a 19-year-old woman who was being attacked near a bus stop at Belmont and Cicero Avenues.

Herman Lang, 62, the driver, needed 26 stitches to his mouth after he fought with the assailant, said a CTA spokesman. (*Copied*)

ROCHFORD RIDES CTA FOR NIGHT, FINDS IT SAFE

by F.K. Plous Jr.

"Can I talk to you?" said the middle-aged man in the baby-blue sweater and tan topcoat.

"Uh—sure," said the bewildered passenger on the Dan Ryan CTA train.

The man eased into a seat beside the passenger, shook his hand and introduced himself. "I'm Supt. Rochford of the Chicago Police Department," he said. "I'm just trying to find out how you feel about the CTA. Do you feel secure?"

It was indeed Chicago's top cop, and he really was out riding the L and the subway and the bus Tuesday night along with CTA Board Chairman Milton Pikarsky. Starting at the Jefferson Park rapid transit terminal at 10 p.m., the two officials rode to the Dearborn and Washington subway station, walked through the pedestrian tunnel to the State St. subway, took a southbound A train to 63rd and Ashland, transferred to an eastbound bus, boarded a northbound Dan Ryan train at 63rd and State and finally disembarked at Clark and Lake.

Only on the Dan Ryan trip were they accompanied by newsmen.

"The commissioner and I rode the trains and the buses and walked the tunnels," Rochford said. "I want the public to know I'm vitally concerned about their safety when they use the system. Between us we talked to 40 or 50 people."

Rochford said he asked people how they feel about conditions on the CTA, especially passenger safety and "whether anyone had ever bothered them."

"Surprisingly, most of them say it's safe and well lighted and they can usually see the conductor or motorman or a uniformed policeman in an adjoining car," Pikarsky said.

"Of the 50 people we talked to, only six or seven said they felt apprehensive all the time. No one complained of having been robbed."

Rochford, clearly the more garrulous of the two men, initiated most of the conversations and frequently fell into his habit of putting an arm around the person he was talking to. The technique elicited plenty of response from the passengers.

"I told him I have to ride every night and I never have any problems," said Marjorie Brewer, 29, a nurse at Northwestern Memorial Hospital.

"It's quite an experience," said Leandrew Major, 34, of 4044 W. Lexington, after he finished talking with Rochford. "It feels kind of good. I told him how on one occasion I dozed off and when I woke up a pickpocket was just about to go to me."

Just south of the Loop, Rochford had to use all his charm on one passenger. Despite the white glare of television lights, "no smoking signs," and a dozen witnesses, the young man refused to extinguish his cigarette. Rochford identified himself, smiled and said,

"Don't you think it would be nice if you put it out?" The man complied, and Rochford shook his hand.

At journey's end, Pikarsky said the CTA and the police department have entered into a "direct liaison" to increase passenger safety, even though statistics show people are "3 to 13 times safer on the CTA than on the streets." Rochford said further efforts to protect passengers are about to be made.

"Chairman Pikarsky and I are going to discuss the things we saw tonight," he said, "and in the near future we're going to make an announcement to the public." (*Copied*)

LOENDRI RODRIGUEZ #19440

"You were part of the great coalition, the great coalition of forces determined not to let a petty dictator, no matter what size his army, no matter how many tanks he had, no matter how many men he had armed, despite the fact that you were badly outnumbered, you were determined to show a petty dictator and his forces they just can't get away with bullying their neighbors and taking what they want because they are so tough.

"... but don't forget to make sure that everyone understands that we did it as part of a team. We all did it together, we all paid the price."

It was March 8, 1991, I had lived through the Persian Gulf War ... 30,000 American casualties had been expected in the "first hour" of the good fight ... and General H. Norman Schwarzkopf's farewell remarks began to stir a deep sense of purpose inside of me. It was shortly after, that I decided to become a Chicago police officer. I knew that the "petty dictator" and the criminal were of a congruous mind.

I carry star #19440. It stands for D-Day, June 6, 1944, the Liberation of France, the most decisive date in the historical course of the world and it also marks the first strategic combat engagement of the 101st Airborne Division, the Screaming Eagles, my alma mater.

Policing is one of the few noble tasks still existing in our "society of relativity." It is a profession that challenges one's spiritual, moral and ethical fiber; for the work of evil one will witness. To those who wonder about the essence necessary in the "Profession of Arms," I paraphrase from British King Henry V's speech to his battle tired troops moments before personally leading and engaging a fresh French Army that frightfully numbered five times greater ...

"- that which hath no stomach to this fight, Let him depart ...

Leondri Rodriguez, checking his equipment prior to a night operation during the Persian Gulf War in South Iraq.

- We would not die in that man's company that fears his fellowship to die with us.
- This story shall the good man teach his son ...
- ... we in it shall be remembered -
We few, we happy few, we band of brothers.
For he today that sheds his blood with me shall be my brother ..."

To future generations of police officers, know that good men and women have gone before you ... that many a young soldier in military or civilian life, has fought to the bitter end with the faith that you would stand in rock solid and free moral and ethical ground, so to you may protect our sacred "right to life, liberty and the pursuit of happiness."

Godspeed and good luck!

SANTA COP

by Christine C. Goduto, wife of Leonard P. Goduto

My husband graciously accepted the offer to play Santa at our church's Christmas party. The only problem was since I had taught Sunday school for 12 years, my husband was pretty well known with the older children who attended classes. Upon seeing him dressed for the occasion, our fears were confirmed, the older children did indeed recognize him and began to question if Santa was real. With quick thinking we were able to ease their minds. We simply told them: Since you're now old enough to understand, we will let you know just how Santa operates. They were sworn to secrecy to allow the younger children to still believe that Santa himself was here. After they agreed we proceeded to let them know "the truth." At this, the busiest, time of the year there is no way Santa could leave the workshop at the North Pole. So he has asked the best guys around (policemen) to help him by posing as Santa while he and the elves prepare for Christmas. These men are on a special division of the police force, and their code name is Santa Cop. The children were amazed to know "the truth" and quickly restored their faith in jolly old Santa Claus. And if there were any doubters in the crowd my husband made sure to convince them by asking their parents what Santa has brought them. As doubting children sat on Santa's lap he whispered in their ear, "Since you were such a good boy/girl Santa sent you this _____ which you asked him for." When they opened up their gifts and saw it was exactly what they wanted and exactly what the Santa Cop told them they too believed that Santa is real.

SECOND HIGHEST COMMENDATION AWARDED

One police officer was presented the Award of Valor and two others, the Award of Merit, by Superintendent O.W. Wilson.

Both awards are of equal importance and are considered the second highest commendations to be given a sworn member of the Chicago Police Department. Awardees of both commendations are eligible for the Police Medal, the highest citation awarded by the Department.

The Award of Valor, "for outstanding heroism, personal courage and devotion to duty," was conferred upon Patrolman BERNARD IRGANG, #7186, Task Force, Area #6 Headquarters. Patrolman Irgang was cited for his "prompt actions and bravery" on two occasions when he responded to "robbery in progress" calls—one in which he engaged in a gun battle with an armed robber.

Ptlmn. Bernard Irgang, Award of Valor Task Force Area #6, Commander James Holzman, Chief of Patrol James Rochford and Deputy Supt. James B. Conlisk.

Present at the ceremony which was held during the Superintendent's Tuesday morning press conference were: Task Force Commander JAMES B. HOLZMAN; Lt. JAMES GRENDER, Commanding Officer, Task Force, Area #6, and Lt. CLIFFORD RIORDAN, Commanding Officer, Area #4.

In one case on September 25, 1965, Patrolman Irgang responded to a "robbery in progress" in a northwest side tavern. As he entered, followed by other policemen, he was confronted by one of three armed robbers who pointed a revolver at him and repeatedly pulled the trigger. Fortunately, the revolver failed to discharge. Faced with a situation of apparent death, he reacted swiftly, firing at the man and fatally wounding him. Other officers on the scene then apprehended the robber's two companions.

Patrolman Irgang was also cited for exceptional bravery in a second "robbery in progress" call on February 21, 1966. When he got to the scene, witnesses directed the police to a hotel on the 3200 block on North Sheffield Avenue where the robber had fled. Patrolman Irgang and the other officers fanned out in various directions to search the hotel.

Patrolman Irgang went to the third floor where he found the offender hiding at the end of the hallway. He ordered him to drop his gun and surrender. Instead, the offender ran down the stairs to the first floor where he took cover behind the room clerk's desk in the lobby and started firing at Patrolman Irgang.

The officer held his fire until several persons who were in the lobby were able to reach safety. He then returned the gunman's fire. When he heard the gunman's weapon click twice, Patrolman Irgang assumed it was empty and taking this opportunity, Irgang charged the gunman and knocked the weapon from his hand.

Later, it was discovered that the .38-caliber revolver used by the gunman still had one live bullet in the cylinder which also held five spent cartridges.

The gunman, however, wounded by three of Officer Irgang's shots, was taken to the Illinois Masonic Hospital.

Superintendent Wilson said: "Patrolman Irgang displayed bravery and aggressiveness above and beyond the call of duty. In withholding his return fire when the gunman repeatedly fired at him until innocent bystanders could reach safety, Officer Irgang displayed great presence of mind and great courage."

Patrolman Irgang, 31, appointed to the Chicago Police Department on March 12, 1962, has 17 honorable mentions on his record.

A SHINING EXAMPLE

by PO Lorna M. Leslie #19607

Howard Brian Patterson was a shining example of what a police officer should be. He joined the Chicago Police Department in 1985. His outgoing personality, excellent work ethic, and unique ability to communicate with people from all walks of life made him not just competent, but exceptional at this job that he loved so much. During his career, Howard worked as a patrol officer, tact officer, Gang Crimes South, and school patrol. His diligence earned him several accolades, including a Department Commendation, and a Department Life Saving Award.

Howard came from a police family. He followed the footsteps of his father, Howard Patterson, who retired from the C.P.D. in 1997, and is currently the Chief of Police in Dolton, IL. His cousin, Elliott Matthews, retired in 1992, and he worked in Englewood as a recruit with my brother-in-law, John Arnold, who retired in 1995. His cousin, Susan Madison, joined the department in 1982, and is a sergeant in District 005. After years of harassment by my family members, I joined the department in 1996 and am currently assigned to Public Housing South. It was Howard that finally convinced me to take the exam.

Howard was a police officer, but he was so many other wonderful things. He was a husband, a father, a brother, a model son, a role model, and the most loyal friend that anyone could ask for. Howard was six years older than I, and he was my hero and protector in so many ways. When I had my confirmation in the Catholic church, Howard was my sponsor. When I was in high school he came to rescue me from a strange man that had been following me around the mall.

When Howard started college, he would scold me for being at the same parties he attended because I was still in high school, and tell all of his friends how old I was so that no one would ask me out. I wasn't very pleased about that at the time, but I came to realize that he had my best interests at heart.

When I was really old enough to hang out with Howard, we would go to different parties together. One night we went to a bar in the sixth district, and as we approached the front door, a disorderly patron was being escorted out. The guy began backing out of the door, cursing, and pulled out a revolver. Howard told me to run, but before I could even move, he had the man disarmed, cuffed, and

Howard Brian Patterson

on the ground. When the sixth district officers arrived, they just started laughing, and said, "Patterson, I should have known it was you! Do you ever take a day off?"

A few years later, Howard had a New Year's Eve Party. He made his sister, Angela, and I spend the night, and she and I woke up in the top bunk of his daughter, Ivory's, bunk bed, wondering how we got there. He let me have my 30th birthday party at his house, which lasted about 16 hours, and he never once complained. He was so proud of me when I graduated from the police academy, and by the time I arrived to work for my first tour of duty, he had already instructed his friends in the fourth district to look out for his "little" cousin. This was a few years after my 30th birthday, mind you.

Howard Brian Patterson was born into eternity May 9, 1998, just one month shy of his 41st birthday. His untimely death left a tremendous void in the many lives he touched, but his spirit lives on. His memory lives on in his children, Ivory Michelle, and Howard Brandon Patterson, and his stepchildren, Shawanaki Wade, Tiffany and Joshua Gills.

As those of you that knew Howard read this, I hope that you also will reflect on your own memories of him and smile, because that is what he would want. I write this tribute to celebrate the life of Howard Brian Patterson ... NEVER FORGET!!!!!

SNIPER SLAYS TWO POLICEMEN, SHOOTS FOUR...GIVES SELF UP

by Brian Boyer and James Casey

Chicago Sun-Times on April 15, 1969. A berserk former marine combat veteran killed two policemen and wounded four others Monday in a six-hour gun battle on the southeast side of Chicago.

The sniper, who held off hundreds of policemen with gunfire, hand grenades and black powder bombs, surrendered to police shortly after 9:00 p.m.

He was identified as Frank Kulak, 40, of 9251 S. Exchange, a veteran of World War II and the Korean War.

Ducking sniper's fire, two armed policemen race to move in closer. (Sun-Times *Photos by Bill Mares and Bob Black*)

Michael J. Neary, Star #3942, 1930.

The two policemen who were killed were Jerome A. Stubig, 40, a bomb and arson squad detective, and Sgt. James R. Schaffer, 48, of the 4th District.

Wounded, Then Killed...

Chief of Detectives Michael A. Spiotto said that the dead policemen were among the first on the scene. They were injured by the blast of a bomb thrown by Kulak, he said.

"Kulak emptied his carbine into both men and killed them," as they lay injured on the pavement behind the building, Spiotto said.

Spiotto gave credit for Kulak's surrender to Deputy Supt. James A. Rochford, whom he said "went up to the second floor and talked for more than an hour with Kulak before he surrendered.

STAR #3942

by John Neary

Michael J. Neary joined the Chicago Police Dept. in 1923 and retired in 1960. He was born in Ireland, and when he arrived in Chicago in the 20s, he had an uncle, Michael Neary, on the job (he was a detective in the Homicide Division) who encouraged him to become a police officer.

He came on the "job" in 1923 and retired in 1960. He had Star #3942 during his years on force. When he retired in 1960, I acquired his star and carried it for 42 years until I retired in 1998, whereupon, my nephew (my sister's son), Scott McKenna, who is an officer with the Narcotics Division of Organized Crime, took over Star #3942. Thus far, a member of the Neary family has carried this star number for approximately 79 years.

My brother, Peter J. Neary, was on the Chicago Police Dept. for 32 years before retiring in 1997. Not counting my dad's Uncle Mike, the Nearys have contributed 111 years to the Chicago Police Dept.

SUBWAY ARRESTS

The Police Mass Transit Unit made two arrests early Thursday morning in separate incidents in the same subway station at State Street and Chicago Avenues.

Police said it was the 25th and 26th arrests for Patrolman James Davern, who acted as the police decoy in both incidents. Davern has been with the special unit, aimed at stopping muggers—since its inception in June.

Chicago Avenue District Patrolman George Davis said police arrested 33-year-old James Taylor, after he allegedly took Davern's wristwatch, while Davern pretended to be asleep on a station bench.

When Taylor, of 4925 West Adams Street attempted to flee with the watch, he was stopped by Davern and five "back-up" men from the unit who had been hiding in the station.

Two hours later, six foot four inch 34-year-old Willie Davis, allegedly tried to get away with the "sleeping" Davern's watch, Davis said, but he too was overtaken by Davern and the others.

Both Taylor and Davis, of 5003 South Morgan Street, were taken to the Chicago Avenue District Police Station where they were being held on strong armed robbery charges. Both men were scheduled to appear in North Felony Court later today. *Reprinted from City News.*

SUBWAY ROBBER PICKS ON A 'DRUNK'—DIES

by Harold J. Tucker

A veteran thief working the subways today chose the wrong man to rob and was killed. He was shot by an undercover policeman whom he had just stabbed.

The incident took place in the State Street subway tunnel at Jackson Boulevard.

The robber, Ervin Martin, 27, of 5440 S. Prairie Ave., died when he was struck by two bullets fired by Policeman Fred M. Keto, 33, who is in Henrotin Hospital with a slashed arm that required several stitches to close. Martin had used the alias John Black when he was shot in a robbery in 1962 and when he was indicted for another CTA robbery on April 8.

Keto was one of four patrolmen of the mass transit unit assigned to CTA subways and platforms under the command of Sgt. Clarence Kerr. All five men were in the subway at 1:30 today when the robbery attempt and killing took place.

Although regulations specify a policeman's dress and appearance on the job, Keto is a decoy who pretends drunkenness or sleepiness to flush out would-be muggers and robbers.

He has long red hair, a full red beard and a Fu Manchu mustache. He wears the clothing associated with hippies, and is adept at feigning drunkenness.

Keto was putting on his act in the tunnel between the State Street and Dearborn Street subways, in view of the other men of his unit, when Martin made his mistake.

Martin stepped up to Keto, held an open pocket knife to Keto's stomach and said, "Give me your money."

Keto reached with his left hand to a hip pocket where he carried a wallet full of marked money and handed it to Martin. As he did so he said:

"I am a police officer. You are surrounded. Drop your knife."

Instead, Martin slashed Keto's arm. Keto drew his revolver and fired twice. When Martin did not fall, Keto fired a third shot. Martin fell.

Kerr and Patrolmen Emilo Garza, John Wright and James Humphrey all drew their revolvers and had started running toward Keto when they saw the knife in Martin's hand.

Kerr said the unit has made 30 robbery arrests in the subways in the last 60 days. One of the robbers has been convicted.

SURPRISE!

'Pretty Woman' Proves She's Pretty Good Cop. A thief scanned an L car on the South Side early Wednesday, decided it was safe, and robbed a male police decoy in full view of a woman seated in the front of the car.

The woman, he told police later, "was too pretty to be a woman cop."

After the robbery, the "pretty woman," Patrolwoman Virginia Cronk, 28, jammed a .38-caliber revolver in the suspect's face and arrested him.

"He just couldn't believe it," said Mass Transit Unit Sgt. Clarence Kerr. "He had never seen an undercover policewoman who was that pretty."

Lewis McAfee, 21, of 117 S. Rockwell, was charged with felony theft from a person after he allegedly took a wristwatch off undercover Patrolman James Davern, who was dressed as a businessman.

While Davern feigned sleep, Officer Cronk, dressed casually, sat in the front of the northbound Englewood-Howard L train, Kerr said.

Just north of 35th St., McAfee grabbed the watch, struggled briefly with Davern, and then ran to the front of the car, where Officer Cronk arrested him, Kerr said. (*Copied*)

THEY PUT BITE ON NIGHT CRIME

by Patricia Leeds
Chicago Tribune

It's an unlikely looking group. No two of the 10 men and a woman look as though they belong together as they pause to consult with a man carrying an attaché case.

Likely looking potential victims of subway crime? These late-night riders are actually undercover Chicago police.

Ophair Williams #12852 (left) and Ralph McKay (Nov. 1941-Jan. 1990) in the 7th District,E Dec. 24, 1972. Inset: Officer Williams, Vice Control, 1998

The historic old Maxwell Building which housed the 7th district. Al Capone was once held prisoner here.

However, they are members of one of the Chicago Police Mass Transit Unit's tactical teams conferring with their sergeant as they leave headquarters at 54 W. Hubbard St.

Sgt. Clarence Kerr and his crew are one of four tactical teams who ride the subways and elevated trains, check platforms and stations, and have been instrumental in cutting crime on the CTA in half.

Each team works different hours. Day teams concentrate on thieves, such as pickpockets and purse-snatchers; late teams watch for the more violent offenders they refer to as the "night people"—robbers and rapists.

Their boss, Capt. James Delaney, and Lt. John Collins, coordinator of the tactical teams, let them develop their own methods of operation, and some of them could be method actors.

Ptlmn. Paul Siegfried dresses and looks like a hippie with his beard and long hair, and when he goes into his drunk act, he usually makes a "hit."

When a decoy is robbed or assaulted, he calls out, "hit." This signals other police officers nearby in their various disguises that a crime has been committed.

Sgt. Kerr and most of his team have been together a long time. They know exactly what to expect of each other and how to protect each other. The policewoman, Mrs. Virginia Cronk, is new.

Policewomen have recently been added to the program, and they rotate, staying with a unit three months, then transferring to their regular assignment. The teams hope to change this and keep four permanently.

THIRTY-TWO YEARS

by Ophair Williams aka OW, Big O and Over Rap

My 32 years with the department were some of happiness and some of sadness. The sad times were anytime one of my brothers in blue was killed and when two of my friends were killed in the line of duty. Henry Peeler was killed in 1968 and Fred Echols in 1984.

The happiest time was when I made a traffic stop at 69th and Ashland while on my lunch break. You see, I was dedicatedly working on my lunch break when I met my wife, Dorothy, who is my soul mate for life. Another happy time was when I met Ralph McKay who became my partner and best friend in 1968. Our friendship lasted until his death in November 1990 at the young age of 49. That also was a very sad time, but the happy times outweighed the sad times.

I had great times with the department for 32 years. I thank God for blessing me with a job that was very enjoyable and the department for giving me the opportunity to serve the people of Chicago.

My friends and family asked me if I would do it all over again. My answer was yes, over and over. Again, I thank God for blessing me with that opportunity.

'Those Robbers!'

Alderman witnesses capture. Celia Nemerow, operator of newsstand at the Lawrence Avenue station of the Howard 'L,' reported to Ald. Christopher Cohen and Police Sgt. Ivar Rittenberg how she was assaulted last week by strong-arm robbers. Three men who matched the description she gave were arrested at the same location last night as they robbed Patrolman James Davern, on his 118th mission as a decoy for the mass transit police unit. Cohen was with the unit when the arrest was made.

Too Few Men – A New Feint at CTA Crime

by James Elsener, a Tribune reporter.

Police Supt. James Rochford's announced crackdown on crime aboard Chicago Transit Authority vehicles and property is nothing new.

Periodically, during the last few years, police, city, and CTA officials have "vowed to put an end to crime on the CTA."

They have promised installation of new security devices such as closed circuit television cameras which still have not seen their first subway despite two years of discussion.

They have held public hearings from which printed transcripts were sent to the police telling them about the violent crimes the police already knew were being committed. And they ordered security studies costing as much as $148,000.

In the meantime, "Monkey Slim," "Johnny Red," and other well-known [to the police anyway, since most are repeat offenders] thieves and muggers continue to ply their trade despite harassment from a beleaguered staff of policemen assigned to the Mass Transit Unit [MTU].

Rochford announced there would be around-the-clock uniformed patrols at eight high-crime transit stations in addition to 24-hour patrols in Loop subway stations.

But later Rochford admitted that MTU would not receive additional men. These patrols would have to be made out of the existing staff, which is already far too short of manpower.

Chicago has just over 200 policemen in the MTU to cover the CTA's 193 miles of rapid transit track with 143 stations, and 2,000 miles of bus routes. In comparison, New York City employs 3,168 policemen for security alone on its mass transit system.

The manpower problem is probably not entirely Rochford's fault. He is already understaffed because of a ban on hiring until settlement of a federal court suit against the department.

"What can we do?" commented one MTU undercover policeman, showing his frustration. "We're just so many, and we do what we can. But it's not enough. The only answer is more men."

One of Rochford's answers is not more men, but more women. He said at least two women would be assigned to MTU undercover units to work as decoys. The men of MTU believe the women can play an important role, and unlike some units are looking forward to their arrival. But two women can hardly be expected to reverse the trend of rising crime.

Another move designed to increase police effectiveness seems at the same time to decrease police presence. Officers patrolling Loop subways will now work in pairs rather than alone. Instead of one policeman at each station, two policemen will patrol a number of stations and the trains stopping there.

Rochford's men praise the move, saying it makes them more aggressive and able to handle situations with increased boldness. A lone policeman can rarely control an incident involving more than one individual, they claim.

Rochford also announced a "new" aggressive attitude toward individuals loitering on CTA station platforms. Any person, he said, who allows two or more trains to pass while standing on a platform will be questioned if a policeman is present.

However, undercover policemen said that policy has always been in effect. If a suspect was not questioned, he was often kept under surveillance until he left CTA property.

The strategy behind Rochford's announcement, however, may be sound. Faced with limited manpower, courts forced to allow repeat offenders on the street time and again, and limited finances to install electronic security systems, he seems to be employing the only alternative left to him: public confidence.

If he can convince people that it is safe to ride the CTA he may find the most effective crime preventive is increased ridership during all hours. Most crimes

Pictures show 18th District Sgt. and myself with the ticket box that I made in (1959).

Elijah Gilbert is flanked by Officers Donald Houihan (left) and Richard Borzych (left) after he was captured near his home.

are committed during hours when victims are alone on a train or platform.

With more riders, fewer of those situations would occur.

TRAFFIC TICKET BOX USED 41 YEARS

By Officer Richard Gorecki (Ret.), Star Number 10658, Chicago Police Department

In 1959 the 35th District Police Station (now the 18th District) was temporarily located at 321 North Clark Street, until the new station was built.

At the end of each shift, we put the traffic tickets we wrote for the day in a cigar box for someone to process them. This box was not big enough to handle all the tickets and some of them got lost.

When the new station was finished (1959) I decided to make a traffic ticket box to handle each watch tickets. I also put a lock on the box, so no tickets would get lost.

As of this date March 2000, the box is still being used, and that is 41 years of service.

I put a plaque on the box with my name and star number on it when it was put into service.

A new 18th District Police Station is now being built at a new location, and I'm told by the District Commander that the box will follow it to the new station. It will continue its purpose for more years of service.

TRIBUTE TO A FALLEN OFFICER

by John H. Pappas

Patrick J. Crowley, Star No. 3614, 006th District Tactical Unit was killed in action September 13, 1976, at approximately 7:00 p.m. He and two partners were in the process of a narcotic raid at 6247 So. Aberdeen Ave. The culprit was arrested and charged with Pat's murder. He is still in the state penitentiary.

Pat left behind a new wife, Joanne, and his mother, Joanna. He, Pat, was also one of my best friends.

My only son was born shortly after Pat's death. I named my son after one of the finest officers this city has ever seen.

Pat was 31 years old when he was gunned down.

TRIES TO KILL WIFE WITH AUTO

The following article appeared in the December 22, 1964 issue of the *Chicago Daily Defender*.

A 40-year-old southside father of six was arrested and charged with attempting to murder his wife by running over her with his automobile.

"Low pressure" tires, and the husband's "bad aim," were credited with allowing the 35-year-old mother to escape with only minimum injuries.

Englewood police are holding Elijah Gilbert, of 6416 S. Laflin Avenue, pending formal charges.

Gilbert's wife, Dorothy, told police that her husband tricked her into believing that he was taking her to buy toys for their children in order to get her into the car.

The woman said he drove to 105th Street and Constance, and then ordered her out of the car. She said he told her:

"Get out, I'm going to run over you and kill you." The wife added that she jumped from the vehicle and the car ran over her legs; thus, possibly saving her life. His automobile then became stuck at the side of the road, she added.

Police said Gilbert left the scene on foot after he attempted to free his car and failed. His wife, reportedly, was left laying screaming in the middle of the road.

Neighbors, who heard the woman's screams, came to her aid and rushed her to South Chicago Hospital where it was determined that she was not seriously injured.

Englewood police arrested Gilbert after getting a description from his wife.

An officer at the station said Gilbert shouted, "I didn't do anything" when the policemen approached him.

The couple's children are ranging in age from 3 to 9 years of age.

Truce Reached in Fight Over Driveway Fees

Gasoline Firms To Pay Pending Ruling. The City and the Gasoline Retailers Association of Metropolitan Chicago declared a truce yesterday in their war over sharply increased commercial driveway inspection fees.

The driveway owners agreed to deposit unpaid 1960 and 1961 fees in escrow, while the city promised not to barricade the driveways of those who make such deposits pending a ruling by Circuit Court Judge William V. Brothers on a suit filed by the retailers challenging the higher fees.

The suite charges that the disputed fees, which became effective January 1, 1960, are exorbitant.

Two Young Cops Beating Muller Ticket Game

by Joseph Morang, Chicago Sunday Tribune

They've Become New Scourge of Rush Street. If Jack Muller had not been forced to abdicate as champion ticket writer of the Chicago Police Department when he was promoted to detective, he would have been deposed by a team of young Turks who have become the scourge of the Gold Coast.

Edwin Pokoj and Rich Gorecki were assigned as partners in August 1959 by Lt. Francis (Chick) Rowder, then of the Chicago Avenue Station and now a captain in the traffic division.

Issue 13,000 Tickets in 3 Years…

Since then Pokoj and Gorecki have issued 13,000 traffic tickets.

In the waning months of 1959, the team issued a modest 500 tickets.

But with the arrival of Supt. O.W. Wilson in 1960, Pokoj and Gorecki really went into a ticket writing orbit. They issued 3,000 summonses, both of the moving violation and hang-on varieties.

In 1961 their total soared to 4,500 tickets. This year it will top 5,000.

How They Keep Count…

How do they keep track? Simply enough. As of December 15, Pokoj had 115 empty ticket books in his locker in the station at 113 E. Chicago Ave. Grocer had an equal number in a closet of his home. Each of the books had contained 20 tickets.

Neither ever has difficulty with his testimony in court, for each makes detailed notes on the back of his own copy of each summons given—relating when, where, and why the circumstance of the ticket.

Busiest day the pair ever put in occurred in November of this year when they handed out 251 tickets—44 of them for moving or hazardous violations.

Targets of Threats…

"We've been threatened lots of times," Pokoj reports. "So far, though, nobody's had us transferred.

Policemen Richard Gorecki (left) and Edwin Pokoj checking books they emptied while issuing 13,000 traffic tickets. Dec. 24, 1962

Naturally, we pay no attention to the people who call us over zealous."

The most tickets ever given one driver by the pair was seven, issued to a violator taken into custody at 35th Street and Lake Shore Drive after a high speed chase from Oak Street and the Drive. When grabbed, the motorist faced further grief in that a number of dynamite blasting caps found in his pocket occasioned a session with the bomb and arson squad as well as in traffic court.

Pokoj and Gorecki cover a beat from Chicago Avenue to the river and from Rush Street to the lake. *Submitted by Richard C. Gorecki.*

UNDERCOVER COP IS TOPS IN THE NATION

by J. Carole Buckner Staff Reporter

CHICAGO — For James Ahern, a Chicago Police Department undercover investigator assigned to the organized crime division, life on the job is a cat-and-mouse game.

"They know your job is to catch them, and you know they will do what they can not to get caught," said the highly decorated officer.

After a nationwide search, Ahern, 49, has been named National Law Officer of the Year by the 70,000-member Forty and Eight, an honor society of the American Legion.

Even though the Southwest Side resident said bird-dogging organized crime figures can get "a little boring," it remains the "epitome of police work" for the 19-year veteran, who is one of only two Chicago police assigned to the special detail.

"Sometimes it's boring, but when the surveillance pays off, it makes it worth the time and hard work," he said, his gentle eyes gleaming with satisfaction.

Undercover Investigator James Ahern (center).

Despite physical danger and erratic hours often filled with tedious surveillance vigils, Ahern said he has "never not wanted to go to work."

"I don't really know what it is I like about it — maybe it's the idea that it's thought of as a romantic position. I don't know.

"To me, it is the epitome of police work and I know I want to keep doing it until I retire," he said.

Romantic, maybe. Glamorous, doubtful. During a routine vigil to observe a suspected illegal gambling operation, the burly Ahern transformed himself into a nondescript average Joe in short order, something he says he does to avoid being spotted.

He has learned to go from crawling around in alleys to hobnobbing with the powerful in a matter of minutes, making any quick change necessary to follow a suspect.

As an undercover investigator, Ahern tracks the likes of organized criminals involved in narcotics, gambling and prostitution.

Danger is a secret shadow always nearby, although Ahern says it's not something he thinks of much. "I don't think about that. I suppose if I did start thinking I'm going to get up one day and get shot or killed, I wouldn't be able to do the job."

Having faced weapon-wielding criminals several times both on and off duty, Ahern said it is more caution than fear, a "street-wise, alley-smart" way of thinking that has kept him from being killed — that, and a good aim.

Despite his caution, however, Ahern admitted, "I've got nine holes in my body from working this job."

Besides suffering gunshot wounds, Ahern has been stabbed several times, and said the mob once offered a contract on his life.

In February 1984, Ahern was shot while stopping a trio of armed robbers at a tavern at 79th Street and Talman Avenue. The robbers, criminals with extensive records, were mortally wounded. He was off duty at the time.

Ahern's performance in the incident earned him several department commendations, including the Lambert Tree Award in 1984, the highest medal presented by the Police Department; and the Police Medal, the highest medal presented by the city.

Other commendations include the Superintendent's Award for Valor, 1984; The Fraternal Order of Police Medal of Valor, 1984; The Illinois Police Association Valor Award in 1984; and four Blue Star Awards for officers wounded in the line of duty.

His record of arrests covers more than 1,000 violations and the seizure of millions of dollars worth of narcotics.

Ahern speaks proudly of the football accomplishment of his three sons — Jim, 22, just out of the Marines; Tim, 22, a student at Daley College; and Mickey, 17, a student at Brother Rice High School. Ahern and wife Sharon lost their only daughter, Kim, to cancer at age 17 in 1979, the only time he asked to work a beat, so he could spend time with her.

Ahern will receive the National Law Officer Award at the four-day Forty and Eight convention, which opens Wednesday in Oregon. *Copied from Southtown Economist Newspapers.*

VICTIM A REAL SLEEPER

by Larry Weintraub

Pickpocketing Class On L Arrested. Pickpocketing school on an L train was dismissed in a hurry early Monday when the sleeping man the students were practicing on turned out to be a real sleeper — a police decoy.

The two teenaged students and a 31-year-old man whom police described as their professor were arrested at the Chicago Transit Authority rapid transit system's 35th St. Station.

The man who seemed to be snoozing on the train was Patrolman James Davern, whose drunk-and-drowsy act has lured a number of transit bandits to jail.

He and the team of other policemen, which is never very far away on such assignments, made the arrests.

They reported to the mass transit detail that Thomas Wilson, 31, of 6318 S. Peoria, was instructing the youths in techniques of the "dip," the way Fagin did in Charles Dickens' book *Oliver Twist.*

The boys were doing fine in their studies, according to the police, but their teacher flunked out with his choice of a victim.

Police said Davern pretended to sleep for about 15 minutes in the speeding classroom while Wilson instructed the youths — aged 15 and 16 — in such arts as the "two-fingered reach" and the "wallet twistaway."

"His instructions were very explicit," according to Sgt. Clarence Kerr, "and he admonished them when they made a mistake in procedure."

He said they went through Davern's pockets after taking his wallet and removed such items as a ballpoint pen, a book of matches and a slip of paper "just for practice."

The two boys were named in delinquency petitions charging them with theft and pickpocketing.

Their mentor was held at the Prairie Ave. District station on a charge of conspiracy to commit a theft.

A WORLD RECORD PACE

by Nial D. Funchion

He swam a world record pace for four hours straight, became violently seasick, vomiting every stroke for the next nine hours. Pressing on without giving in to even a consideration of quitting. Landed in France delerious and hypothermic 13 hours and 17 minutes from the time he started. Earning in that same moment the "Robert Lysu" trophy for the fastest American time of the year. That was August 1992. Sixteen months later Nial D. Funchion entered the Chicago Police Academy (Dec. 13, 1993).

Officer Funchion trained in the 9th Dist. After his probationary period successfully bidded to first watch to continue coaching swimming at St. Ignatius High School as he puts it "to nurture his spirit." It was there he continued to privately and delicately nurture the possibility of owning the world record for swimming the English Channel.

Two years later Nial swam from 57th St. Beach to Michigan, a distance covered of about 26 miles. Although he never admitted it, at the time, Nial was gearing up for another channel attempt. This Lake Michigan swim was an extraordinary challenge, not only was it a long marathon swim (same distance and approximate route that Jim Moran in the 60s offered $50,000 to anyone who successfully completed the task—and at the time there were no takers). But Nial insisted it be swam at night in total darkness. Nial wanted to (and did) face and battle fears—what he calls owning and conquering the "phobia of the dark water." When he reached Michigan the sun was just starting to peak up. It became a moment of deep personal discovery and victory.

Finally in 1998 Nial made his intentions known, to press on and reach once more for that world record channel crossing. He took huge chances having to live on a loan, disconnect himself via a leave of absense to intensify his training. There were no guarantees and that included being allowed return to the police department.

August 1998 Nial's channel crossing attempt was started and halted three frustrating times in a period of 10 days by English officials. On the last day, the last remaining opportunity, Nial took a chance and was turned back, a decision Nial made based on 12 miles to swim in conditions that were unforgiving. Nial did not make that last swim, did not land in France but insists it is his biggest and brightest victory in his personal journey.

Nial was reinstated as a patrolman and was allowed to continue testing for the Marine Unit (a process he started three years prior).

Nial Funchion attempting to swim the English Channel in 1998. The White Cliffs of Dover can be seen on upper right.

A "Victory" for Nial was a stolen car recovery from the river during a "Black Water Dive" on February 13, 2000.

Currently Nial is positioned on the Police Marine Unit in the capacity of search and recovery (sometimes even rescue) diver! It is a position that he feels he earned, a position and moment he looks forward to - personal victories that he treasures. You see 80% of the diving is done in water that is called "black water."

WORTHY ARRESTED, CHARGED WITH 3 COUNTS OF ROBBERY

Chicago police have shot and slightly wounded an 18-year-old South Side youth this morning after he allegedly robbed the same ticket agent for the third time in the last week on the Dan Ryan elevated station at 47th Street.

Police say John Worthy, of 4525 South Federal Street, was wounded when he pointed a cigarette lighter shaped like an automatic pistol at them during a short chase across the Dan Ryan Expressway.

Worthy is being treated at Provident Hospital for a wound to the left thigh, a hospital spokesman says.

Due to a recent rash of stick-ups, police had staked out the 47th Street platform this morning when Worthy approached the ticket agent, 34-year-old Mrs. Lovey Watts after loitering on the platform for more than an hour.

Apparently recognizing Worthy police say, Mrs. Watts exclaimed, "You again!" Allegedly pointing the fake pistol at her, Worthy said, "Yup, hand me the money," and fled with five dollars.

Mass Transit Unit officers Virginia Cronk, Mario Loiacono and James Davern then moved in on Worthy as he ran north along the Expressway to 46th Street.

When Worthy allegedly pointed the fake pistol at them, police fired a total of six shots, hitting Worthy once.

Mrs. Watts identified Worthy as the man who robbed her of a total of $24 in two separate robberies on May 18th and 19th.

Police say Worthy may be implicated in as many as 10 other ticket agent robberies over the past month when a show-up is held later today at the Wentworth Area Robbery Unit.

Worthy is charged with three counts of robbery and is scheduled to appear tomorrow in Central Youth Court.

He is being held at the Wentworth Avenue District Lockup. (*Reprinted from City News 29*)

STATION 20

BRIGHTON P...

Captain John J. M...
Commanding

ALL MEMBERS of the 2... wish a speedy recover... James Kozumplik and P... Scalia, who were struck t... while on duty on three w... cles. Both accidents ha... same week.

Glad to welcome back... admirable sergeants fr... he 15th District, Ser...

Happy vacation... Hope you discove...

Park District Division News

WEST PARK DIVISION

Captain Owen Duffy Commanding

THE vacationers come and go but this year we have not heard of many interesting accounts of vacations spent in unusual places.

Patrolman Ed Bourke feels that very soon now he will "cash in" on the Little Fooler. A lot of us wish this would happen as we have been waiting patiently for that "treat" these many months.

Ptlmn. Timothy O'Con... man with a big family as... The latest edition to T... Patricia. The O'Connors... boy and four girls.

Our sympathy to Ptlmn... roll and his wife upon th...

We were saddened t... deaths of two of our re... Sergt. Charles Holbroo... Edward Bonfield, both... assigned to the West D... eral years.

We hope by this tim... Alex Levenson and Edw... were transferred from t... North districts respectivel... the new Patrolman assign... trict on July 1st, have l... the great West Side.

Congratulations to... Merit Award Winners:... Hinchy, Brendan Haga... Carroll, Eli Blumenthal, D... William Gunther, and Ken...

Little Susan Ruth Sexto... months old and no one coul... of her than her dad.

Profound sympathy to M... Patrick Hamill in their recen... ment.

...ee Deputy, Lawrence Markey shows Carl Peterson, 8, of 14159 Linder ... Township, how to hold a sparkler for celebrating 4th of July in safety. ...p guns, and caps were the only kinds of fireworks that could legally be ...ar. Sheriff's Police were ordered to confiscate all other types of fire... ...rrest those selling or using them. Looking on is Dep...

Dr. Higgins Named President of International Association of Women Police

THE roster of the newly re-organized International Association of Women Police, which came into existence in San Diego, Calif., May 22, 1956, shows a membership of over 225 women, representing 25 states and Hawaii, and 77 cities. Interest and inquiries have been received from several foreign countries.

The purposes of the association are to advance the police science among the women of this country and possibly to the entire world; to serve departments and communities more efficiently by exchanging ideas to promote a general study so all members may become more proficient.

There was an International Association of Policewomen which was founded in 1915 by Alice Stebbins Wells, the world's first "regularly rated civil service policewoman" (Los Angeles, 1910). Headquarters were in the Evening Star Building, Washington, D. C. The association was a dynamic force in giving impetus to the entire policewoman's movement, both here and abroad, during the period 1915-1932, when its largest financial sponsor who was also its president, passed away. The membership numbered some 600 women, from all parts of the world. Meetings were held regularly and conventions were held each year in various cities in the United States.

May 1985, March down Michigan Avenue honoring police officers killed in the line of duty. Lead by District Comm. Walsh and PO Ted Sparrow carrying 13th District Flag.

37th District-Sheffield, May 1957.

1927 Police School Graduating Class B. Officer Peter Garramone (standing) second from right. Photo courtesy of Barbara Grahm.

Peter Garramone 1900-1975. He served 35 years as a Chicago Police Officer. Photo courtesy of Barbara Grahm.

JAMES H. ALESIA, *United States District Judge, he is the only Chicago Police Officer in the history of the department to become a federal judge. He served as a police officer from 1957-1961 in the Traffic Division and at the old Fillmore District (old 25th District). He is a graduate of Loyola University (BS, 1956) where he was class president and received a degree in three years and of IIT/Chicago Kent College of Law (JD, 1960). He is married to the former Kathryn P. Gibbons and is the father of Brian, an attorney, and Daniel, an assistant publicist.*

GEORGE T. BRYJA, *Star #12557, was last assigned to the 22nd District. On July 27, 1986 George observed a burglary in progress and began to pursue one of the offenders on foot for several blocks. Upon catching up to the offender, he became involved in a physical confrontation with the offender and sustained a fatal heart attack. He is survived by his wife, Sharon, daughter Peggy and son John, who is a police officer wearing his star number, and a grandson, Daniel. Submitted by John T. Bryja.*

The "new" 1972 Dodge squad car, photo taken at the 2nd District/Area 1 Detective Headquarters, 5101 S. Wentworth Ave. sometime in March 1972.

Chicago Police Hockey Team, photo taken Feb. 18, 1995 at the University of Illinois Pavilion prior to the 2nd annual Chicago Police Dept. vs the Chicago Fire Department Charity Hockey Game. All donations received at this charity game will be split between the Maryville Academy and the Cook County Burn Unit. The members of both hockey teams would like to thank Dr. Richard Ward, Mr. Rick Harrigan and the University of Illinois at Chicago. Without their generosity, this charity game would not be possible. Also, we would like to thank the Chicago Police Emerald Society for volunteering their time to provide entertainment during the game. The Bulletts: PO Tom Graszer (Captain) #5, Forward/Defense; PO Bill Dougherty (Alternate Captain) #27, Forward; Sgt. Matt Tobias (Alternate Captain) #24, Defense; PO Rich Aguilar #14, Defense; PPO Jim Bailey #10, Forward; PPO Mike Black #16, Forward; PO Jim Buhrke #20, Forward; PO Joe Butney #44, Forward; PO Tom Conley #2, Defense; PO Darin Hoeger #33, Forward; PO Dave Joritz #21, Defense; PO Gary Lorden #3, Defense; PO John Milio #23, Forward; Sgt. Nick Roti #26, Forward; PO John Sullivan #32, Forward; PO Steve Suvada #31, Goalie. Chicago Fire (not pictured) FF Doug Vasilevich (Captain), Center; PIC Tom White (Alternate Captain), Defense; FF Kevin Clark, Forward; FF Tom Connelly, Forward; FF Tim Corcoran, Defense; FF Ed Cortes, Forward; FF Bill DeLuca, Center; FF Dan Fortuna, Goalie; FF George Howell, Defense; PIC Rich Jurek, Goalie; FF Tom Kurgan, Defense; FF Chip Lorenz, Forward; FF Carl Ostrowski, Forward; FF Kevin Peters, Forward; FF Charlie Petruzzi, Defense; Engr. Dan Polli, Defense; FF Mike Uczen, Center.

Feb. 2, 1996 at 11th and State. (L) Matthew Fencl receiving Star #6781 from his father, Dennis Fencl. Dennis Fencl retired on this date after over 35 years of service on the Chicago Police Department.

October 16, 1991 in the rear of the 10th District Station. (L-R) Dennis Fencl (father) and Matthew Fencl (son).

John Kowatti Star 4621, directs traffic at Michigan and Chicago Ave. in 1988. Appointed to the force in 1961, he retired in 1990.

1942 Police School Class 1, January 17, 1942.

August 1995 – Nial Funchion moments before 26 mile Lake Michigan swim in the dark. Start time of 7:15 PM.

Solo Escort Detail Traffic Radar Unit 1960-65. From left: Rich Swallow, Clarence Heerdt, Leo Ciscilski and Sgt. John Hadel.

Opening of Area 3, 3900 S. California, March 16, 1961. Pictured left to right: Detective Dan Rolewicz, Captain Cantonesse, Superintendent of Police, Orlando Wilson, Detective John McGuire, Detective Leary, and Detective James Winke.

JAMES P. BAILEY, *a detective with the Chicago Police Department and has been with them for 32 years. Carrying on a family tradition of father and son on the Chicago Police Dept. Officer James P. Bailey Jr. #13137, appointed May 2, 1994 and assigned to the 9th District with his father, Detective James P. Bailey #20390, appointed Jan. 22, 1968 and assigned to Area 1 Property Crimes.*

In August 1959, Queen Elizabeth and Prince Philip arrived in Chicago on the maiden voyage of HRM Royal Yacht. They docked in Burnham Harbor by the Buckingham Fountain. Present were Mayor Richard M. Daley and Governor Stratton.

Officer Ray Egan in first row in sun glasses; to his right, Officer Frank Mayfield. Both assigned to Unit TA5 detail.

Meadowdale Training Course, Meadowdale, IL July 13-17, 1970. Officer Ray Egan Unit TA5 standing with white hat third from right, successfully completed Police Pursuit Driver Training Course. This course was open to all Police Officers in the United States.

Officer Ray Egan and Officer S. Gorski on their Harley Police Motorcycles, Detail Unit TA5. Escorting President Lydon Johnson at the Hilton Hotel, October 1965.

Photo taken in front of Police Headquarters at 1121 S. State Street sometime in 1962. L-R: PO Nick Mastro now deceased; Retired Capt. Anthony Faklis (then patrolman); Superintendent of Police O.W. Wilson (deceased).

This picture was taken in the front alley alongside the house of Richard B. Flint. Naturally, his dog, "Tops," didn't have his ears up. The patrol car was a 1960 Ford 4-door, with the back seats taken out. My partner was Ralph Dunczyh. Courtesy of Richard B. Flint.

CHICAGO
DEMOCRATIC NATIONAL CONVENTION
AUGUST 26 - 29, 1996

```
Post #114 Location: Front of Podium
Fixed    Post    Responsibilities:
Monitor activity on the convention
floor and prevent access to the
podium   from   the   floor.  Provide
general law enforcement duties in
this area.  This post will include
a  Secret  Service  Agent  when  a
Protectee is in the building.

Administrative Office:    336-1635
Call #290 Across from      336-1636
Sec 109 Main Concourse
Communications Room:       336-1644
Command Post #50 Across 336-1645
from Sec 116 Main Concourse
Chief's Call # 50
Commander's Call # 5500
On-Session
Commander's Call # 5400
Off-Session
Captain's Call # 50A
Supervisor's Call # 170
```

Chicago Democratic National Convention. Det. Linda Flores guarding the front of the podium.

A description of assignments for Linda Flores' four days of duty at the Democratic National Convention.

August 29, 1996: Chicago Police Department personnel gathers around DNC front podium for a group picture. This was the last day of convention and after the United Center emptied out. Superintendent Hillard is located in the middle row to the left. Linda Flores is two spaces to his right.

"Checkered Hat Bands and Striped Pants." From left: David Crement, Dan Weyland and Ray Gardecki.

June 14, 1997: Blessing of the Fleet at Navy Pier, Chicago, IL, Marine Unit #1

Left to Right: PO Tom Jaguszewski and Sgt. Mike Burke landing at Meigs Field, Chicago, IL in a Bell 47 Helicopter, after a patrol over Chicago on Feb. 26, 1972.

May 22, 1984 representing the Chicago Police Marines, Chicago Patrolman Jerry Farrell (left) and Sgt. Jimmy Griffin assist Mary Carol Lemon in raising the POW/MIA Flag at the Vietnam Veterans Monument at Wacker and Wabash. Chicago became the only city in the world to display such a tribute to its sons 24 hours a day, 365 days a year. Mary Carol is the mother of Jeffery C. Lemon, USAF, shot down over Laos in 1971.

Canine "Rocky" working a Bear game during the Super Bowl season in 1985. He was handled and loved greatly by PO Larry Janiszewski, Star #7007.

Dan Weyland with Dunkin Donuts Coffee.

David Crement, "How do you work this phone?"

This picture from 1976 has just about the entire Prostitution Unit in it. From left to right: Sgt. Dan Scalia, INV Mike Fera, Prostitution Unit Commanding Officer Lt. George Bicek giving a "thumbs up," INV. Tom Strom, INV Bob Richards, INV Joe Macuba, Sgt. Jim McDonough, & INV Ken Burt. The bride is not an arrestee; she is Shirley Pecordo, the Prostitution Unit secretary, who had just married CPD INV Michael Pecordo.

Charles L. Knight, Star #5119, sworn in Oct. 1, 1957, retired August 1990. John C. Knight, Star #5119, sworn in Dec. 26, 1989, killed in the line of duty Jan. 9, 1999.

1970 photo shows Area 3 traffic officer, Joe Macuba (standing) and Area 4 traffic officer, Dennis Fencl (seated in car).

Joe Kortowski, "Old Wagon Man."

(Above) Marine Unit Commander Tom Rowan.

(Right) August 7, 1966: Officer Cornelius Morgan, Star #6067; Officer Francis Gutrich, Star #2389; Officer Charles Knight, Star #5119. Suspect arrested after he attempted to flee the area. Suspect was observed reaching into the weeds. A search revealed three quart bottles with paper wicks and a can of gasoline. Offender transported to the 006th District.

Officer Francis Gutrich, Star #2398; Officer Edward Toomey, Star #4665; Officer Charles Knight, Star #5119. After a systematic search of an area of a recent fire bombing, an arrest was made of a suspect. Suspect was in possession of the displayed evidence.

1957 Class #6. From left, bottom row: E. Williams, C. Stanley, J. Watts, A. Trocchio, J. Trunzo, J. Scalzitti, C. Seidita, E. Wooten, J. Ustasiewski. Second row: Sgt. B. Stein (instructor), C. Torrise, W. Ziegler, V. Alomia, L. Harris, J. Maentanis, R. Casale, R. Sloan. Back row: S. Boncimino, D. Melson, M. Valde, S. Thompson, R. Flatow, R. Spirko, W. Thigpen, M. Robinson, G. Raess, D. Clem Jr., J. Schaffer Jr., F. Visco.

From left: Rick Newman, John Duignan, Dick Binnder, Bob Campbell, unidentified, Leo Dineen, Bob Ruthruff, unidentified, Les Madsen, unidentified, unidentified, unidentified, John Hennesy, unidentified, and Art Manger. In water: Horst Zickenheimer being towed by Joe Picaro.

Days of Rage: Officer Otis Love (new Star #6758) and Sgt. Robert Suess of Area Task Force on post in 1971 during a racial demonstration by the Students for a Democratic Society (SDS) led by Bernadine Dorn. The Criminal Court Building at 2600 S. California in background. This photograph was taken by an oriental student demonstrator who in her humorous fascination, could not understand how in the world there could be a "Pig" (a name for police at that time) named Love.

Tug of War Team. John O'Connor in back row, 13th from the right. John was a Chicago Policeman from 1921 until retirement in 1957. His son, Joseph, became a policeman in 1953 and retired as a captain in 1988.

1924 Chicago Police North Division Champions Push Ball Team. John O'Connor is in the first row, second from left.

Chicago Police Department Clowns from left: P.O. Frank Jasch, Tim Sadler (became a Chicago Police Officer in 1991), P.O. Richard Speilman and P.O. Mike Acosta.

"A Good Day's Work." Taking the drugs off the street, and away from the gangs. Drug and money seizure from the southeast side of Chicago. Picture and seizure April 27, 1999. Pictured left to right PO Carlos Medina, PO Steven Maldonado, Lt. Arthur Parra, Sgt. David Jarmusz, PO Ralph Palomino, PO Jaime Bravo, and one ton of cannabis. Courtesy of Ralph Palomino, Chicago, IL.

Police Training School Graduation Class, Nov. 12, 1955 - Class #7 (1955). From left, top row: Sgt. E. Williamson, V. Faedtke, J. Bluras, S. Grybas, L. Shultz, R. Wrzesinski, R. Wiening, A. James, J. Leith, J. Patterson. Third Row: R. Billings, J. Tobler, J. Dukes, T. Riley, W. Tlapa, G. Pocius, W. Skonieczny, L.P. Smith, A. McKenzie, Sgt. L. Marston. Second Row: D. Brady, R. Rushing, E. Walsh, R. Sandore, D. Gunnell, J. Nielsen, D. Thomas. First Row: W. Tarnow, S. Sagalow, F. Zientara, E. Harrison, T. Ochol, O. Richard, G. McMahon.

Officer Eugene A. Simale was assigned to Traffic Radar Unit in 1969, detailed to solo motorcycle escort at Shriners Convention in Chicago.

Solo Motorcycle Unit Traffic Division. Otto Petriet in the photo taken in June 1955.

Chicago Police Motorcycle, a 1954 Harley-Davidson, motorcycle, 74 C1-Panhead Model. The 50th anniversary Harley motorcycle, the 50th anniversary medallion on the front fender. The list price for this motorcycle was $1,015 when the City of Chicago bought these motorcycles in 1954. Photo taken in June 1955 by Otto Petriet.

Police Commissioner O'Connor and Deputy to Commissioner Kyran Phelan watch over Illinois Delegation at 1956 Democratic National Convention at the International Amphitheater while Mayor Richard J. Daley and Col. Jacob M. Arvey are interviewed.

Former President Harry Truman with pals Sgt. John Peyton and Ed Egan (Truman's favorite Chicago bodyguards) reunite at the 1956 Democratic Convention.

1968 Democratic Convention rioters are arrested.

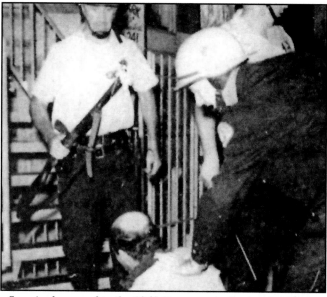

Seemingly no end to the 1968 Democratic Convention Riots.

Access Pass for Linda Flores. A new pass was issued every day.

Ptlm. George Pocius - last day on duty at O'Hare Field, Beat 1651. He served from Aug. 22, 1955 to Sept. 4, 1984.

Largest Cocaine Seizure of 1999 by Chicago Police Department. After a routine traffic stop, members of Team 1, Gang Investigation Section, Organized Crime Division, recovered numerous kilos of cocaine valued at approximately 19 million dollars! (Sep. 14, 1999. Standing from left: John Nee, Dennis Maderak, Robert Drozd, Benny Shields, Mike Bocardo, Bill Whitters, Sgt. Spratte, Steve Haras, Al Harris, John Capperelli, Eddie Yoshimura. Seated: Commander Hirum Grau and kneeling next to Commander is Mike Dyrasan.

Evidence Technician Class of 1965, James Gillen top row on right.

Officer Eugene A. Simale was assigned to Traffic Radar Unit in 1981.

First Lady Rosalynn Carter greets Officer Eugene Simale of Traffic Radar Unit in 1977. Simale was detailed to escort her while in Chicago.

Picture taken Aug. 28, 1996. Hillary and Chelsea Clinton going to their motorcade after a brief speech at UIC Baseball Field. During the DNC. We (Ed Sullins #11093, 025 Dist. and Ofc. Judy Castellanos) snuck into the inner perimeter to take these pictures and ended up talking to Mrs. Clinton. Believe it or nor, she actually thanked us for doing a good job at the DNC. Then we were yelled at by our Supt. Rodriguez right after that for being there.

Malcolm Woo in Washington Park, 1969.

Woo, a retired Chicago Police Officer, was born and raised in Chicago's Chinatown and joined the Chicago Police Department Sept. 8, 1969.

Malcolm Woo pictured here with Ron Howard on the set of Backdraft. He doesn't think he is the first person of Chinese ancestry to join the Chicago Police Department, however, he knows that in September 1969 he was the only Chinese Police Officer in the CPD. He thinks there was a gentleman named Frank Eng from the House of Eng Restaurant in Hyde Park who joined the Chicago Police Department before him. He doesn't have any more information on where Eng was assigned or when he quit the Chicago Police Department. He was the first Chinese police officer to be on Mayor Daley's bodyguard detail for 10 years. He was the first Chinese to retire from the Chicago Police Department. He retired from the bodyguard detail unit and the CPD in March 1999.

Ceremonies Open Calumet Skyway. Thursday April 17, 1958: First vehicle to traverse Calumet Skyway, a bus loaded with pupils from Jane A. Neil school for crippled children, as it moved thru one of the toll gates preceded by a police motorcycle escort. Mayor Daley dropped coin in receptacle to pay toll for the bus (Tribune photo). Submitted by Officer Eugene Simale.

Victory smiles are worn by members of the Shakespeare Ave. softball team after they defeated the Chicago Park District team in championship ball game. The score was 16-12. The players are (kneeling) Tony Delgenio, John Tyrrell, Pat Flannary, Dick Sullivan, Art Kelly and Stan Laskowski. Standing are Maurice Boissey, Joe Prindes, Dan Wise, Joe Ruskey, Walter Frontczek, Tom Walsh, Hank Gajda, Frank Kracker and Jerry Stubig. Copied from The Police Digest, September 1956.

Members of the 1922 Class of the Chicago Police Department. Seated from left: Deputy to the Commissioner Kyran Phelan, Capts. Joseph Healy, Thomas Harrison, John Golden, Michael Ahern, Philip Breitzke, William Ryan and Paul Johnson. Standing from left: Capts. John Walsh, retired; Bob Welling, retired; William Hennessy, John T. McAvoy, Redmond Gibbons and Chief John Olson of the State's Attorney's Police. September 1956.

Mike Maher (left) and Sal Sorci (right) check out a photo gallery of suspects as Sgt. Mead (center) looks on.

Join the CH

Chicago Pol

CITY OF

Department

announces an examination for:

POLICE OFFICER Grade P1

THE EXAMINATION will consist of written tests and an assessment center. Those candidates who successfully pass the written tests will be eligible for participation in the assessment center. Persons will be selected for the assessment center on the basis of written test scores in a manner that will adequately reflect the original candidate population. Candidates who successfully pass the assessment center must pass a pre-employment medical examination and background investigation.

Names of candidates passing all portions of this examination will be placed on an employment list on a continuing basis. Passing an examination does not guarantee an offer of employment. It is a statement of eligibility.

MINIMUM QUALIFICATIONS

Education: Applicants must be high school graduates at the time of appointment. A high school equivalency certification through G.E.D. is acceptable.

Age: As of the date of application, a candidate must have reached his/her 20th birthday and must not have reached their 35th birthday.

Physical Condition: Weight must be proportionate to height. Corrected vision must be 20/20 in each eye. Blood pressure must not be over 140/90. The medical standards for this position are available for review in the office of the Department of Personnel.

Driver's License: Applicants must possess a valid Illinois Driver's License at the time of appointment.

RESIDENCE REQUIREMENTS: As of the must be an actual resident of the C will be required at the time of app

STARTING SALARY: $17,604 per ye

CLOSING DATE
FOR APPLICATIONS: April 24, 1981

DATE OF EXAMINATION: Applicants wi time and date of examination.

DUTIES: Police Officers patrol an in order to observe conditions, to that require their attention, and b from occurring. They respond to a in progress, accidents, damage to p disturbances. Police Officers prot Investigators or superior officers evidence, and question suspects, vi gather information. They may have they may have to overcome forceful variety of emergencies and must pur of terrain and obstacles. They are persons and to carry people in vari transport bodies. They prepare case an incident, prepare arrest slips t testify in court. They perform a w directing pedestrian or vehicular t citations. Perform all other relate in order to serve citizens by enfor property.

AN EQUAL OPPORTUNITY—

CAGO POLICE

Department

HICAGO

Personnel

Recruiting flyer from 1981. Pictured are Joe Valez, Jan Readman, Alicea Iyaya, Malcolm Woo, Rose Olivery and Pat (?) Burke. Courtesy of Malcolm Woo.

plication a candidate
:ago. Proof of residency

ied by mail as to the

at by vehicle or on foot
n observed situations
ible to prevent crime
assignments such as crime
ls, domestic and other
scene until the
mine the scene for
itnesses in order to
h unruly persons, and
   They must respond to a
s on foot over a variety
o assist sick and injured
They must handle and
ecording all details of
   booking procedure and
   of other tasks such as
 issuing traffic
s required and directed
and protecting life and

TIVE ACTION EMPLOYER

NOTE:

Any person appointed as a result of this examination is subject to the provisions of Section 25-30 of the Municipal Code of Chicago which states: "All officers and employees in the career service of the city shall be actual residents of the city. Any officer or employee in the classified career service of the city who shall fail to comply with the provisions of this section shall be discharged from the service of the city in the manner provided by law."

APPLICATIONS:

Applications are available at the following locations:

Department of Personnel, Room 1100, 121 North LaSalle St.
Halsted Community Service Center, 1935 South Halsted St.
Trina Davila Community Service Center, 2550 West North Ave.
South Chicago UPC, 9231 South Houston Ave.
Uptown Urban Progress Center, 4554 North Broadway
Garfield Community Service Center, 10 South Kedzie Ave.
King Community Service Center, 4314 South Cottage Grove

For further information about this announcement, please write or call:

Recruitment Division, Department of Personnel
121 North LaSalle Street, Chicago, Illinois 60602
Phone: 744-4890

THE DEPARTMENT OF PERSONNEL RESERVES THE RIGHT IN ANY SECTION OF THE ABOVE EXAMINATION TO IMPOSE WRITTEN, ORAL, AND PERFORMANCE TESTS AND TESTS OF PHYSICAL QUALIFICATIONS AND HEALTH.

The 37th District pictured in 1954, located at 2742 N. Sheffield Avenue.

Today's Squad parked along the Illinois River.

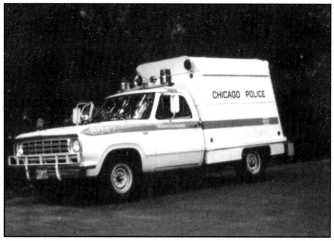

Clockwise upper left: Squadrols from the 1960s, 1970s and 1980s. Courtesy of Robert "Beats" Strzalka #5358 of the 18th District.

Nov. 1984, Oak Street Beach. While on routine patrol, unknown officer was swept into the Lake. Photo by Robert "Beats" Strzalka.

The first of the new Blue/White Squads after O.W. Wilson changed them from black, ca. 1962. Photo by Robert "Beats" Strzalka.

Democratic Convention, Aug. 29, 1968 19th District Tact Team. Courtesy of Det. Edward Valkanet (Ret.).

Kevin Keefe at swearing in ceremony, October 1997, Navy Pier: L-R: Jan Collins, wife of Detective Harry Collins; Joan Keefe, mother of Kevin, daughter of Andrew J. Rohan Jr., granddaughter of Andrew J. Rohan Sr.; Mary Rohan Nelson, great aunt of Kevin, granddaughter of Andrew Rohan, daughter of Andrew J. Rohan Sr., sister of Andrew J. Rohan Jr.; Jane Nelson Elrod, great-granddaughter of Andrew Rohan, granddaughter of Andrew J. Rohan Sr.; Melissa Daniels Keefe, Kevin's wife; George Keefe, father of Kevin; Suzanne Nelson Cronin, great-granddaughter of Andrew Rohan, granddaughter of Andrew J. Rohan Sr.

Ron Duske #9325, 25th District, with black and white squad, 1957.

Ron Duske #9325, 25th District, on 3 wheel patrol, 1959.

Max Steinmeier patroling the 2300 block of Monroe St., 1902. Grandfather of Arthur Steinmeier (Retired #681).

Officers Dan Shine and John Sullivan (007 Englewood) at the 1997 St. Jude Parade.

John Kowatt Star 4621, Traffic Control, 1988.

Lt. E. Wisniewski with Batman and Poster, 1976.

Officer John Franklin (now Sgt.) and Officer Tim R. Bridges partners on Beat 1822 (18th District),1996.

Joe LePore and Joe Rizzo (Foot Patrol 1281 and 1281A) at Jimmy's Hot Dog Stand, April 1997.

Arthur Steinmeier Star #681, and Gayle Steinmeier #2409. Arthur retired from Traffic in 1995 becoming an operations supervisor at Chicago's 911 Center. Gayle, injured on duty in 1995, is currently working in real estate.

Patrol Division Headquarters Staff, 1986.

Members of Capt. Phillip Iden's watch, 10th District – Marquette, Back row from left: Kaataczun, Delaney, Crock, Martin, Smejo and Morello. Front row from left: Gall, Pipello and Tororello. Oct. 1967.

Mayor Richard M. Daley (left) and Supt. Matt L. Rodriguez (right) with PO Tim Bridges #9755, recipient of the Recruit Class 94-5B Outstanding Recruit Award. Graduation at Navy Pier Ballroom, Jan. 20, 1995.

Unknown Police Officers directing traffic at scene of a fire at Reo's Restaurant in the early 1970s. Note Wagon/Old Squad. Courtesy of Chris Strzalka #5358, 16th District.

Officer Joe LePore foot Beat #1281B, merchant John Dollar, Officer Rich Mrozek Beat #1281 and Officer Joe Rizzo #1281A. Historical Maxwell Market ca. 1980s.

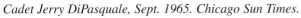

Cadet Jerry DiPasquale, Sept. 1965. Chicago Sun Times.   *Tom Sadler, 3rd Place in 3 Mi. Run, FOP Olympics, ca. 1983.*

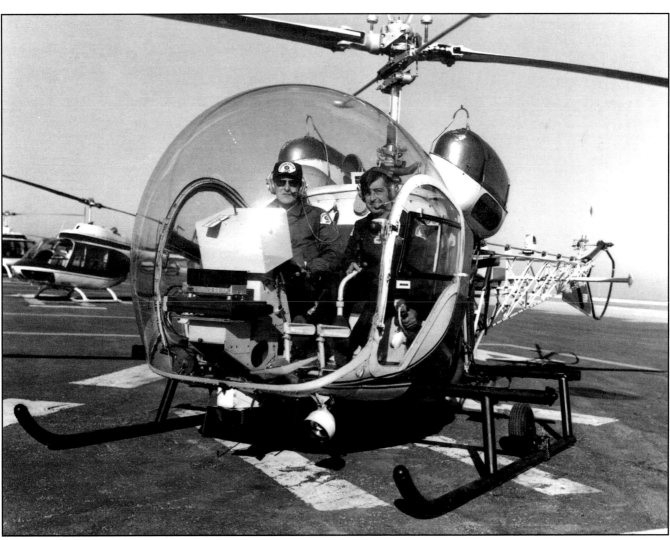

Left to Right: PO Tom Jaguszewski and Sgt. Gerald Weber ready for take off from Meigs Field, Chicago, IL in a Bell 47 Helicopter, Spring 1973.

James J. Gillen and police dog "Jack." All 1961 Canine Class photos from the collection of James Gillen. Courtesy of Maureen Schmidt.

Congratulations on Graduation Day for Jim Gillen and Jack.

Graduation Day for the first ever Canine Training Class.

Pictured on training course are Hugh Carrol and dog Max, Bill Duffy and Big Fella #1, Art Hajek and Big Fella #2, Russell Holt and Pinpoint-Major I, Harold Walchuk and Prince I (The Barracuda) and Jim Gillen and Jack.

Class members pictured with training course equipment in background.

1961 Canine Class. James Gillen and Jack pictured in bottom row, 3rd from right.

Jim Gillen and Jack by Squad.

Jim Gillen and Jack. A well trained team.

Norman Wiest and Clarence Heerdt, 1958.

Solo Motorcycle Unit Traffic Division, Otto Petriet, June 1955.

Nial Funchion coaching girls swimming class at St. Ignatius, 1994-95.

Nial Funchion back on land after 1998 rough weather attempt to swim the English Channel.

Chicago Police Marine Unit cruiser piloted by Sgt. Tom Rowan, Unit Commander, patrols the Lake Michigan waterfront.

Det. James Hoffheimer #2529 of A3/H & S (left) and Lt. McGuire of the 16th District (now 008th District). October 1951.

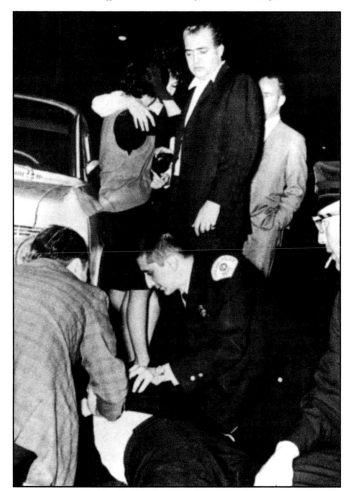

Patrolman Robert Strzalka #5358 assists accident victim, ca. 1960.

Policemen Harry Lopez and Edwin Ogonowski (right) holding Janie and David Garcia, whom they rescued from burning three-story building where they had been locked in an attic apartment, ca. 1969. Tribune Photo by William Kelly.

137

CITY OF CHICAGO / **DEPARTMENT OF POLICE**   1121 South State Street   Chicago 5, Illinois   WAbash 2-4747

RICHARD J. DALEY, *Mayor*
O. W. WILSON, *Superintendent*

Mr. John W. Reed
4850 Drexel Blvd.
Chicago , Illinois

Dear Sir:

You are hereby notified to report to the Police Training Academy, 720 W. O'Brien Street at 7:45 A.M., _____

__12 NOVEMBER 1962__ **for appointment as a Probationary Patrolman, Chicago Police Department, to begin recruit training at the Academy on that day.**

FOR THE SUPERINTENDENT

Jacque K. Boyer
Jacque K. Boyer
Director of Personnel

John W. Reed Appointment Letter, Nov. 12, 1962. Directions to the Police Academy accompanied the letter. (Inset)

Dailey Bulletin from Christmas Day 1962. Courtesy of George Pocius.

Mayor Daley, Police Commissioner O'Connor, Director of Police Personnel Nelligan and Lt. Marilyn Olson inspect Women Police in new uniforms during ceremonies at Grant Park, 1956.

The Lambert Tree – Carter Harrison 1989 Chicago's Medal of Honor recipient, Gregory Jaglowski, participates in the Ground Breaking Ceremony for the National Law Enforcement Memorial in Washington D.C. Pictured here with President George H. Bush, October 30, 1989.

Officer Greg Jaglowski and wife Diana, guests of President Bush at the White House.

THE LAMBERT TREE - CARTER HARRISON
CHICAGO'S MEDAL OF HONOR

Official List Starting In 1886

YEAR	CHICAGO FIRE DEPARTMENT	CHICAGO POLICE DEPARTMENT
1886	Edward W. Murphy	James Brennen
1887	William A. Cowman	Soloman C. Steele
1888	Charles E. Case	Open
1889	John Canty	Issac Odell
1897	Charles J. Rowe	Thomas J. Howard
1898	John J. Hennessey	Daniel Carey
1899	Robert Ambrose	James Keefe
1900	Patrick R. Sweeney	Frank J. McNamara
1901	G.H. Thompson	Open
1902	Jacob Heiselman	George Mengersen
1903	John Moran	William V. Blaul
1904	George W. Thompson	Joseph M. McGuirk
1905	Anton J. Leiber	Henry L. Bussian
1906	Frank W. Stoltz	Open
1907	George E. Dolan	Open
1908	Leonard E. Olson	Open
1909	Henry A. Joyce	Henry G. Decker
1910	Timothy Dillon	John Devaney
1911	John T. Moynihan	George Newheus
1912	Paul H.E. Riemer	Open
1913	Frank C. McAuliffe	Open
1914	Thomas W. Crockett	Open
1915	James Cowhey	Open
1916	Daniel P. Cullnan	Alumus W. Carlisle
1917	Michael Corrigan	Open
1918	John P. Stahl	Open
1919	Theodore R. Luedtke	John C. Griffith
1920	Allen V. Prunty	Horace C. Odell
1921	James D. Cotter	William F. McNaughton
1922	Otto C. Dahl	Hugh T. McCarthy
1923	Thomas H. Dwyer	John T. O'Malley
1924	William J. McMahon	John Kennedy
1925	Cornelius P. Baldwin	Demitry Cal
1926	John Enright	Benjamin McCarthy
1927	Michael J. Corrigan	William Drury
1928	Albert Zuris	Andrew Barry
1929	Charles H. Edmunson	Frank Renolds
1930	William C. Moir	Herman Meyer
1931	James Cowhey	Edward Hanus
1932	Martin Carney	John P. Conway
1933	Peter Hanrahan	Frank Renolds
1934	Robert J. Quinn	Russell L. Richards

YEAR	CHICAGO FIRE DEPARTMENT	CHICAGO POLICE DEPARTMENT
1935	George Flack	Samuel McDowell
1936	Lawrence Owens	John J. Freid
1937	Frank A. Kunz	William F. Ward
1938	Leo F. Kelly	John B. Asher
1939	Joseph Flahive	William Phillips
1940	Patrick J. Driscoll	Michael Curtin
1941	Otto W. Schlau	John A. Will
1942	Andrew A. Cafferata	Anthony T. Comiskey
1943	Bernard A. Morgan	Maurice J. Broderick
1944	John Ryan	Charles McGuire
1945	Timothy King	Raymond T. O'Hara
1946	Frank J. Kubek	Steven Barrett
1947	Harold E. Shortall	Anthony T. Comiskey
1948	Anthony Pils	Open
1949	Edward J. Wallace	Open
1950	Lee Walton	John J. Scott
1951	Russel J. Harper	Edward S. Klankowski
1952	John B. Windle	Michael L. Fitzgerald
1953	Willard N. Meeker	James Classon
1954	John C. Hough	Jack E. Hastings
1955	Karl E. Scheel	Clarence Kerr
1956	Thomas Linane	Henry O. Hartman
1957	Emmett J. Robinson	Robert Devitt
1958	James Kehoe	Ronald Nash
1959	John E. Ahern	Harry Lyons
1960	John J. Gallapo	Donald Hansen
1961	William Schreiner	John C. Grentzner
1962	Leroy Kelly	Open
1963	Richard Munson	Serges S. Joseph
1964	George E. Tannehill	Howard A. Spooner
1965	Walter Budde	Emmett F. Ebert
1966	John F. Kerechek	Gary R. Hettinger
1967	John Howson	Roland Charles
1968	John F. Kerechek	William Thompson
1969	Ronald Direnzo	Ronald Lillwitz
1970	Patrick Conley	Kenneth Fowler
1971	Frank Becka	Crossett Hamilton
1972	George Garant	Richard Drummond
1973	Ronald Clancy	William Lavin
1974	Raymond Graan	James Collins Jr.
1975	Joseph Baldwin	Patrick White
1976	William O'Boyle	Robert Osborne
1977	Michael Shanahan	Ramon Andersen
1978	Open	Robert Schaller
1979	Richard Keating	Miles Myers
1979	Donald Gavoni	William Jaconetti
1979	Open	Louis Trifilio
1980	Open	George Coleman
1981	Terrence J. Collins	Louis Washington
1982	Salvador Marquez	Robert Mantia
1983	John Sampey	Ronald L. Korzeniewski

YEAR	CHICAGO FIRE DEPARTMENT	CHICAGO POLICE DEPARTMENT
1984	Clarence Parker	James F. Ahern
1985	James O'Donnell	Robert Chernik
1986	Bruce Rheinwald	Austin W. Ware
1987	Patrick J. Joyce	David Kopala
1988	John O'Donnell	Edward Dolan
1988	Open	David Jackowiak
1989	Charles Hock	Gregory Jaglowski
1990	Terrence McShane	Jerry Eggers
1991	Raymond Caballero	James O. Love
1992	Robert Hoff	Paul W. Meyer
1993	James M. Purl	Joseph R. Sosnowski
1993	Open	Paul A. Lopez
1994	John V. Gariti	Francis A. Valadez
1995	Kevin Krasneck	Talmitch L. Jackson
1995	Open	Michael Robbins
1996	Edward Clafford	Ricardo Mancha
1997	Gary K. Coney	Hector Silva
1998	Robert Hoff	Edward T. Farley
1998	Open	John Kohles
1999	John J. Cunningham	Charles S. Jones
1999	Open	Brian D. Allen
2000	Open	Pactrick McDermott
2000	Open	Philip V. Rider
2001	Robert Martin	Jerry Farrell
2001	Open	Danny McGuire
2002	Raul Ochoa	Miguel Rios

Left: The Lambert Tree – Carter Harrison 1979 Chicago Medal of Honor recipient William Jaconetti.

Right: The Lambert Tree – Carter Harrison 1984 Chicago Medal of Honor recipient James F. Ahern.

THE POLICE MEMORIALS

Courtesy of the Chicago Police Star — 307th Issue — March 2001

Tributes to American Law Enforcement

THE NATIONAL LAW ENFORCEMENT OFFICERS MEMORIAL

Dedicated in 1991 by President George H. Bush, the National Law Enforcement Officers Memorial in Washington, D.C. pays tribute to all of America's federal, state and local law enforcement officers by honoring those of their comrades, past and present, who paid the supreme sacrifice in defense of the citizenry of this nation. Inscribed on the memorial's blue-gray marble walls are the names of more than 15,000 officers who have been killed in the line of duty, dating back to the first known fatality in 1792. The names on the memorial, however, appear randomly and are not listed alphabetically, by year or in any other systematic order. The rationale for this approach, according to Craig W. Floyd, Chairman of the National Law Enforcement Officers Memorial Fund (NLEOMF), is that it "reinforces view of the Memorial Fund that there is no difference between an officer killed 100 years ago or 100 years in the future. Their sacrifice is the same and they should be honored the same."

Rank and File Go Above and Beyond

All the funds necessary to design, construct, operate and maintain the memorial came from private donations which the NLEOMF was charged with collecting. No government dollars were used. The other law enforcement organizations comprising the NLEOMF included the Concerns of Police Survivors, Federal Law Enforcement Officers Association, Fraternal Order of Police, Fraternal Order of Police Auxiliary, International Association of Chiefs of Police, International Brotherhood of Police Officers, International Union of Police Associations/AFL-CIO, National Association of Police Organizations, National Black Police Association, National Organization of

National Law Enforcement Officers Memorial, Washinton, D.C.

Black Law Enforcement Executives, National Sheriffs Association; National Troopers Coalition, Police Executive Research Forum, Police Foundation and the United Federation of Police. Together, these organizations represented virtually every law enforcement officer, family member and police survivor in the United States at the time.

In Their Own Words

In the following pages, FOP representatives, CPD chaplains and Gold Star Family members discuss their involvement in and/or participation at the National Law Enforcement Officers Memorial, Illinois Police Memorial and Gold Star Family Memorial Park.

John Dineen
Former Chicago FOP President John Dineen recalls the early history of the memorial, including Lodge 7's participation. The first National Police Memorial was sponsored by the Fraternal Order of Police in Senate Park in Washington, D.C. in 1982. Some 250 FOP members from around the United States attended this service which was promoted by then FOP National President Leo Marchetti of Pittsburgh. Shortly after the first memorial service, the FOP along with other police organizations from across the nation

met with Congressman Mario Biaggi, a retired New York City police officer, to promote plans for the construction of a National Police Memorial. Congressman Biaggi and Senator Claiborne Pell of Rhode Island sponsored this legislation.

In October of 1984, President Ronald Reagan signed legislation establishing the National Law Enforcement Officers Memorial. The federal government donated the land for the site, but no federal funds were to be used to build it. The National Law Enforcement Officers Memorial Fund had been established to provide the monies for the construction of the Memorial, and police officers nationwide were solicited for contributions. Chicago FOP Lodge 7 promoted a voluntary one-time payroll deduction contribution from the membership to assist in the financing of the memorial. This effort resulted in Chicago police officers contributing tens of thousands of dollars to this noble cause.

In addition to the fund raising efforts of Chicago's rank and file, numerous other police organizations nationwide and several big name, individual and corporate, sponsors eventually raised the necessary capital to get the memorial built. In October of 1991, the National Law Enforcement Officers Memorial was dedicated in Judiciary Square in Washington. Every year on May 15, police officers from across the nation gather at the memorial to pay homage to our brother and sister law enforcement officers who made the supreme sacrifice. Chicago FOP Lodge 7 underwrites all the expenses for surviving family members of CPD honorees attending the memorial service for the first time. The National Fraternal Order of Police also sponsors the memorial service held on the lawn of the US Capital.

In recognition of the National Law Enforcement Officers Memorial Fund's efforts in honoring our nation's fallen police officers, the Chicago Police Department has recently authorized its sworn members to display the Memorial Fund's citation bar and lapel pin while on duty during the month of May.

ILLINOIS POLICE MEMORIAL

From conception to construction, the Illinois Police Memorial in Springfield developed at about the same time as the National Law Enforcement Officers Memorial in D.C. Though smaller in scale, the Springfield Memorial was built with the same inspiration, effort and wherewithal to get the job done.

Mark Donohue
Mark Donahue, the president of the Fraternal Order of Police of Illinois, tells how the Illinois Police Memorial in Springfield came to be built.

Officers at the Memorial Wall.

During the early 1980s, there was much interest in establishing a police memorial to honor members of Illinois law enforcement who made the supreme sacrifice on behalf of the citizens of this great state and to those who carry on in protecting our most cherished values and freedoms. This interest resulted in six police organizations coming together to form the Illinois Police Officers Memorial Committee. The organizations comprising the committee were the Fraternal Order of Police of Illinois, Illinois Association of Chiefs of Police, Illinois Sheriff's Association, Illinois Department of Corrections, Illinois Police Association and Police Benevolent and Protective Association.

The first goal of the Illinois Police Memorial Committee was achieved in 1986 when the first Police Officers Memorial Day was established. Ever since, the first Thursday in May has been annually designated as Illinois Police Officers Memorial Day. Several other groups joined the committee as they, too, recognized the need to honor our fallen brethren. These included the Illinois Blue Knights, Gold Star Families and Illiana Chapter of Concerns of Police Survivors.

This newly expanded committee then set out to make the memorial a reality. With the assistance of then Secretary of State Jim Edgar, the committee was offered an area at the southwest corner of the Capital Building as the site for the memorial.

Five Illinois art experts and two Police Survivors joined with the memorial committee to review the work of Illinois artists who specialized in statues. The idea was to design a monument that would not only capture the essence of the memorial but a piece of artwork that would conform to the general aesthetics of existing works throughout the state capital.

The committee decided to commission Keith Knoblock to sculpt the monument. Mr. Knoblock had been a sculpture instructor at Illinois State University in Normal since 1967 and liked working with bronze. The artist was paid $20,000 at the time of commission, $20,000 when the bronze was poured and $20,000 upon completion. An additional $60,000 was needed to prepare the base of the statue and the grounds around the memorial site. The costs of the memorial

Red carnations are placed within the star at the national memorial ceremony, each representing a fallen officer from that year.

The Illinois Police Memorial in Springfield.

were offset through the fund raising efforts of the organizations comprising the committee. To complete the construction of the memorial in an expeditious manner, however, the committee needed to procure a loan. The completed memorial was officially dedicated on October 29, 1990 with more than 1000 attendees. The six-foot tall statue atop the seven-foot tall, six-sided base depicts both a male and female law enforcement officer uniformed in common dress. Due to the fact that there were and are so many hat styles worn throughout the state, the decision was made to exclude the hat.

Attending the memorial also provides a great opportunity to convene with our fellow law enforcement members from across the state. If you have never made this trip, you should really find the time to do so. It's not only a part of our collective past, we must not forget it's part of a living history that will go on long after we ourselves are gone. Unfortunately, all six panels on the Memorial will one day be filled.

Chaplain Carlos Cortes

Carlos Cortes has attended and participated in numerous memorials as a police officer, an FOP trustee and a Department chaplain.

I'll never forget the first Illinois Police Memorial I attended in Springfield on 5 May 1993. I had been recently elected as an FOP Trustee and made the trip along with other members of the FOP Board. The procession from the church to the state capitol and then to the ceremony included hundreds of police and civilian vehicles which were lined up as far as the eyes could see. Blue ribbons fluttered on every vehicle and from the chests of every person in attendance.

The ceremony began with some words from the president of the Gold Star Families, the governor and other honored guests. The names of slain officers were read off. Wreaths were set into place and flowers were attached to the monument when the bag pipers started into 'Amazing Grace.'

I remember tears welling up in my eyes when Johnny Lyons' name was read off. Johnny Lyons was not only my friend, he was a living hero to me, as well as the kind of police officer everyone wanted to work with and be like.

I was making an etching of Johnny Lyons' name on the memorial for the 014th district and myself when I overheard a woman crying directly behind me. Somehow I knew this woman had to be Johnny's wife. I had never met his wife, but I had a strong feeling it was. When I asked her if she was, she nodded in assent. I then gave her a big hug and held her for a mo-

ment. I knew that Johnny was there and for that moment we were able to share our sorrow.

GOLD STAR FAMILIES

Father Tom Nangle

Father Tom Nangle of the Police Chaplains Ministry is also one of the founders of the Gold Star Families.

The Gold Star Families was started in the early 1980s by myself and Sgt. Robert Faust (now retired) of the Special Activities Unit. Since both of our duties included responding to every line of duty death, an intense bond was often formed with the families of slain officers during the hours spent together in their homes, the hospital and at wakes and funerals. After the white gloves and bagpipes were put away, though, and the CPD mourning flag was folded and stored, life went on – except for those families who had lost a loved one.

On one of these occasions when Faust and I were together, Bob mentioned that it would be nice if there was some way we could let these grieving families know that they weren't forgotten by the men and women of the Department. This fleeting thought became the founding principle of the Gold Star Families.

The Gold Star Families is not intended to be a 'mourning society' or a 'grief group,' but simply a gathering of the survivors of our city's police officers whose lives were lost in the line of duty. To show this remembrance and respect, the Police Chaplains Ministry hosts the Gold Star Families three or four times throughout the year. It might be a cruise or dinner on the lake, a trip to Great America or an evening of theater and dinner at Drury Lane. At an annual holiday dinner at the Drake Hotel, each guest is greeted by a member of the Mounted Unit and escorted into the hotel by an honor guard of police officers in dress uniform. One of the bright spots on

any of these evenings is to see some semblance of healing for family members who have endured the agony of losing a loved one and have moved on with their lives. We go first class for them, and we pay our own way thanks to the men and women of the CPD.

I also attended the first police memorial in Washington D.C. I attended because the names of so many Chicago police officers are set into stone there. Three of them, Pat Crowley, Bill Bosak and Marty Darcy, were friends of mine. . . and very good men. There was a primal urge in me to go and see their names in the stone, and once you get there and see the names, the human soul just urges you to run your fingers over the sharp edges of the letters. It's a human urge that's hard to put into words, but everyone who goes there and spots "their"name, does it. I go to honor and remember them; it's as simple as that.

The classic battle of good versus evil still plays out every day in a society we think of as high tech and sophisticated and civilized, and every once in a while the forces of good take a terrible hit. All those names that are chiseled or spoken with reverence at these memorial services make you think of all the plans for the future that were derailed, all the love that was expended. Think of the heroism of these officers who put themselves into that battle of good versus evil. If you watch the people at any of the memorials, you'll notice that this isn't one of those perfunctory events; the reactions seem to come from the very center of the police soul and show reverence and gratitude for these deceased officers. Whatever the color of the uniform and no matter if the department has 30 or 13,000 officers, every copper just knows something no one else does at these memorials. And I wonder how many stand there at attention and wonder what their name would look like chiseled in marble. It's not morbid – it's a real possibility for every working police officer.

Erika Clark

Gold Star Family member Erika Clark discusses the Gold Star Families and her and her family's attendance at the memorials through the years.

In April of 1986, my life was changed forever. My husband, Richard Clark, a tactical officer, was killed in the line of duty. Shortly after my husband's death, some very special people came into my life: Father Tom Nangle of the Police Chaplains Ministry, Ralph Scheu of The Hundred Club, Barbara Klacza, the president of the Gold Star Families, the FOP and many other officers who showed their support.

The Gold Star Families became my support group, someone I could call when my nights and days were unbearable. At times when I didn't think there would be a tomorrow, Barbara and other members of the Gold Star Families were a phone call away.

As time passed, I served as treasurer for the Gold Star Families from 1991 - 1994 and, recently, was re-elected as treasurer for 2001 –2003. In fact, I try to attend the St. Jude's Parade, the Christmas dinner at the Drake Hotel, the outing at Great America and all the other special activities which have been made possible for the Gold Star Families by the Police Chaplains Ministry and the generosity of the officers of the CPD. Because of their concern for all of us, our lives have been blessed and our loved ones have not been forgotten.

Recently, the Gold Star Families attended the dedication of Gold Star Family Memorial Park, which was a dream of Pat Stubig and her son Steve. Again, financial support was made available to remember and honor our loved ones.

I attended my first police memorial in May of 1987 when my husband Rich was honored in Washington, D.C. This dedication was held on the steps of the capital before the memorial wall was built. The support which was made available is indescribable. Seeing our Chicago police officers in their dress uniforms made me feel so proud, because my husband had worn that uniform for 18 years. Many friendships were made that weekend, and many hugs and tears were shared.

I attended the Blue Light ceremony and the dedication of the memorial wall in 1991. My dream is to take my grandchildren there some day to share the honor and experience with them, and let them know how important and proud we are to be part of the law enforcement family.

I attend the Springfield Memorial every year to show my support for the officers and organizers and to make them aware of how much their efforts are appreciated. I also attend to show my support for the most recent members of the Gold Star Families.

My son-in-law even drove my daughter down to the memorial seven years ago to propose marriage because he wanted her dad to be part of this special day. Their son and my grandson calls his deceased grandfather "Grandpa the Star," and, yes, we are very proud that Richard wore his star proudly.

A Great Great Grandson Remembers

Tom Ryan

Tom Ryan is unique as a Gold Star Family member in that he is not an immediate family member of a slain police officer but rather the great great grandson of Casper Lauer, the first police officer killed in the line of duty in Chicago as well as the State of Illinois in 1854.

Remembering the important people in our lives is instinctive. Even when they are gone we can picture them in our minds and hear their voices, but how do we pass on these memories to those who come after us? Most of us recount the stories of these important people to our descendants and pass on treasured bits of evidence of their existence.

From an early age, I remember hearing stories of how my great great grandfather Casper Lauer was a policeman who was killed in Chicago. I remember visiting his grave in St. Boniface cemetery. I remember seeing the chest of drawers that he built. I remember reading the story of his death that was hand-copied from an already old and yellowed newspaper by my great aunt.

These memories were one of the triggers that motivated me to investigate my family genealogy in the late 1970s. I wanted to see if I could find the original story on microfilmed versions of the Chicago Tribune. When I first read the account of his murder on September 18, 1854, I was struck by how similar it was to any story you would read in the paper today, except for some of the old fashioned language. I copied the articles and sent them to relatives, satisfied that I was able to add a bit of new information to Casper's story.

In 1989, my brother Bill called me up and said he saw an article about a new memorial being built in Washington, D. C. - the National Law Enforcement Officers Memorial - that would honor police officers killed in the line of duty. He found out that such officers could only be submitted by the police department in which they served and wanted me to contact the Chicago Police Department to pursue the possibility of having Casper included in this memorial.

I didn't know whether the CPD knew about Casper or not, so I put together a package of information along with copies of the Tribune articles describing his death and forwarded it to them.

Soon after, I received a call from the CPD's Dennis Bingham who related to me that they were researching the archives to put together a list for the memorial in D.C. and that my letter was a pleasant coincidence. He was, in fact, searching for officers killed in the line of duty before 1872 since the Chicago Fire had destroyed many of the Department's records in 1871. On January 8, 1990, I received a letter from the Department stating that they would submit Casper's name to the memorial in Washington. I believe this same list was used to submit officers to the Illinois Police Memorial which was dedicated in 1992.

When I was asked to offer some comments at this dedication in Springfield, I was very nervous but at the same time proud that Casper, my great great grandfather, was finally recognized. In my comments, I noted that I was sure my great great grandfather would be surprised about the recognition given to him, but I believed the decision he made on September 18, 1854 was straightforward and uncomplicated. He got up that morning and decided, "Today, I'm going to do my job." That decision links him to all the other police officers — past and present, whether killed in the line of duty or not — who put their lives on the line for us every day.

Gold Star Family Park

Pat Stubig

Gold Star Family member Pat Stubig and her son Steve came up with the idea of planting a tree for every fallen Chicago police officer.

A few years ago, my son Steve and I were discussing how a city as great as ours could honor their

"There's part of you in these trees of etched into the marble walls at the memorials that you don't realize until you are there." – P.O. Mike Schumacher

Officers help the Make-A-Wish Foundation fulfill a terminally ill youngster's dream come true at the D.C. Memorial.

fallen officers. A tree memorial program offered by the Chicago Park District caught our attention, and voila! an idea was born. This idea was presented to the Gold Star Families at our annual Christmas dinner which was sponsored by the Chicago Police Chaplains Ministry. The vote to adopt this idea was unanimous. With the approval of Mayor Richard Daley, Superintendent Terry Hillard and the Chicago Park District, the idea of the tree park was set into motion.

To honor all 460 officers would be a monumental task and we needed funds! Where to go? We went to the police districts and raised enough funds to purchase three trees for our most recent fallen officers, James Camp, John Knight and Michael Ceriale. With the help of the Chicago Park District, the CPD's Special Services section and many others, theses trees were planted and dedicated at a ceremony at Rainbow Beach Park on the south lakefront.

To plant the other 457 trees, we planned to contact the Chicago business community because this would obviously take considerable funding. To the rescue, however, came Mayor Daley again. Together, he and the Chicago Park District generously provided a beautiful location between Soldier Field and the lakefront and planted 460 trees in commemoration of our fallen officers. Talk about a dream come true, this was it. My son Steve and I, as well as the Gold Star Families, thank Mayor Daley and Superintendent Hillard for honoring our loved ones in such a way.

P.O. Mike Schumacher

Mike Schumacher is a 35 year vet, an FOP Trustee and the Grand Knight in the Knights of Columbus Police Society who attended the Gold Star Family Memorial Park dedication ceremony last November.

It's encouraging to see that we have come to a point where police officers want to learn and reflect on their history, especially those of us who began our careers back in the 1960s and 70s. These were especially trying times for police officers. It not only seemed that we had lost support from much of the public, but there were more of us getting shot every year than ever before.

The Gold Star Family Memorial Park was an important gesture from Mayor Daley and Superintendent Hillard to the Gold Star Families, members of the Department and the citizens of Chicago. Now, in addition to those in Springfield and Washington, D.C., Chicago has a memorial where we can gather, individually or collectively, to remember and pay tribute to those police officers whose lives were taken from them. I emphasize that their lives were "taken," because no one gives their life freely, it is taken from them. Though you really don't like to think about it, what sticks in your mind when you reflect on a lot of the situations and circumstances in which these police officers were killed, is that it could easily have happened to you.

The concept of the Gold Star Family Memorial Park is also especially poignant. 460 young trees, each representing a fallen Chicago police officer, were planted on this special site along our beautiful lakefront. Each lost life has been replaced with a living thing. The symbolism is as unique as it is inspiring. None of the trees has a name attached, for the intention is to remember the collective sacrifice of our fallen comrades.

If a police officer has never been to one of the police memorials, he or she really ought to go. There's a part of you in these trees or etched into the marble walls at these memorials that you don't realize until you are there. It's an awesome feeling, and one that every police officer should experience at least once.

The Chicago Police Star would like to extend its sincere appreciation to John Dineen, Mark Donahue, Carlos Cortes, Tom Nangle, Erika Clark, Tom Ryan, Pat Stubig and Mike Schumacher for their contributions to this article and special thanks to Bill Nolan and Leslie Harris.

CPD members lining up for the Illinois Police Memorial ceremony in Springfield.

May 29, 2002

The Fraternal Order of Police, Chicago Lodge No. 7
hosted a Memorial Service for Chicago Police Officers
who have made the supreme sacrifice.

This year, the following names have been added to our Memorial Wall:

Officer Brian T. Strouse
Officer Eric Lee
Sergeant Hector A. Silva
Officer Donald J. Marquez

They Will Not Be Forgotten

POLICE MEMORIAL MONUMENT
Fraternal Order of Police
CHICAGO LODGE NO. 7

ABBOTT, LOUIS A., Patrolman, Badge 762, Roll 295, March 3, 1947, District 2: Officer Louis Abbott was conducting an extensive investigation into a series of armed robberies and shootings. Officer Abbott apprehended two of the offenders and was searching for the third. As Officer Abbott located the third offender on a street corner and confronted him, the offender fired a shot at Officer Abbott. The courageous officer died from his injury.

ADAMS JR., THOMAS J., Patrolman, Badge 2210, Roll 365, August 26, 1973, Unit 124: Officer Thomas Adams observed a domestic dispute on the street. When he heard gunfire, Officer Adams ran to the scene to investigate. At this point, an individual involved in the dispute pulled out a revolver and fired, striking Officer Adams. The dedicated officer was fatally wounded.

ALFANO JR., JAMES A., Patrolman, Badge 4707, Roll 355, August 16, 1970, Unit 156: Officer James Alfano investigated a report that a gang fight was about to take place. As Officer Alfano patrolled the community, his police vehicle was blocked by an obstruction in an alley. Officer Alfano was suddenly fired upon by a sniper. The brave officer was fatally wounded in the ambush.

ALLISON, WILLIAM J., Patrolman, Badge 304, Roll 159, June 23, 1925, District 21: Officer William Allison was assigned to patrol the city's parks on a motorcycle. While covering his beat, Officer Allison was struck by an automobile. Officer Allison suffered fatal injuries in the tragic accident.

ANDERSON, THEODORE J., Patrolman, Badge 3034, Roll 170, July 22, 1926, District 21: While patrolling on the midnight watch, Officer Theodore Anderson stopped a suspicious man lurking in front of a building. As Officer Anderson searched the man for concealed weapons, the offender produced a revolver. The gunman fired a shot, fatally striking the brave officer.

ANNERINO, CHARLES P., Patrolman, Badge 7936, Roll 309, October 22, 1954, Unit 640: Officer Charles Annerino was conducting a search for an armed robbery offender who had escaped from Cook County Jail. Officer Annerino and his partner located the wanted offender inside a tavern. Upon confronting the offender, a fierce struggle ensued for control of a revolver. During the struggle, the offender fired two shots at the officer. The courageous officer was fatally struck.

BABBINGTON, THOMAS J., Sergeant, Badge 575, Roll 152, January 26, 1925, Unit 640: Sergeant Thomas Babbington, while investigating a wanted man, entered a business establishment after learning that the wanted offender could be found there. While Sergeant Babbington made the arrest, he was attacked by several individuals. A gun battle ensued, during which Sergeant Babbington suffered four gunshot wounds. The brave sergeant died five days later from his injuries.

BAGGOTT, JAMES, Patrolman, Badge 3125, Roll 154, June 7, 1925, District 8: Officer James Baggott was approached by a citizen who identified a man with a gun on the street. As Officer Baggott attempted to place the gunman under arrest, the gunman drew his weapon and fired. Officer Baggott was struck and suffered a fatal wound.

BALDY, LEONARD F., Patrolman, Badge 1451, Roll 322, May 2, 1960, Unit 151: Officer Leonard Baldy, while assigned to the Department's Safety Education Bureau, provided citizens live traffic reports from a helicopter. Officer Baldy was prepared to deliver his traffic report when the helicopter suddenly threw a main rotor blade and crashed in a railroad yard near the expressway. The dedicated officer and his pilot were killed in the accident.

BARKER, GEORGE T., Patrolman, Badge 175, Roll 233, March 13, 1932, District 18: Officer George Barker was on medical leave after being shot in the performance of police duties. A few months later, while still recovering from his injuries, Officer Barker was at a restaurant. At this time, two armed offenders entered and announced a robbery. When Officer Barker confronted the offenders, a gun battle ensued. The brave officer prevented the robbery, but was fatally wounded.

BARRETT, CORNELIUS, Patrolman, Badge 63, Roll 8, May 31, 1885, District 1: Officer Cornelius Barrett was assigned to apprehend an armed offender that had taken control of a train traveling to Chicago. Officer Barrett confronted the offender and was shot. The brave officer died shortly after as a result of the injuries he sustained.

BARRETT, JOHN J., Patrolman, Badge 557, Roll 11, May 6, 1886, District 3: Officer John Barrett was one of the many officers assigned to disperse a protest meeting near Haymarket Square on May 4, 1886. A deadly bomb explosion, followed by an intense gun battle, ensued. Officer Barrett sustained serious injuries. He died two days later from the injuries he received.

BARRON, EDWARD L., Patrolman, Badge 1457, Roll 366, September 28, 1973, District 4: Officer Edward Barron conducted a search for offenders wanted for armed robbery. As Officer Barron located one offender hiding in a gangway, the offender fled. When Officer Barron pursued the offender, he turned and fired a gun. Officer Barron was struck. The dedicated officer died as a result of his injuries.

BEARDSLEY, FLOYD, Sergeant, Badge 881, Roll 173, October 31, 1926, District 4: Sergeant Floyd Beardsley located two auto thieves in a garage. As Sergeant Beardsley attempted to arrest the two offenders, one abruptly drew a revolver and fired a shot. The brave sergeant was seriously wounded and died the next day.

BELL, WILLIAM Y., Patrolman, Badge 3565, Roll 332, February 6, 1967, District 2: Officer William Bell, while off duty, discovered several police officers involved in the pursuit of a robbery offender. Officer Bell immediately assisted in the pursuit. Eventually, the offender hid in a building and began firing at the officers. A fierce gun battle ensued, in which the brave officer was fatally wounded.

BENDER, JAMES A., Patrolman, Badge 2958, Roll 175, February 10, 1927, District 5: Officer Joseph Bender was standing in front of his house when he observed an automobile parked nearby. Two armed offenders exited, approached Officer Bender and announced a robbery. When Officer Bender resisted, one of the gunmen fired. The brave officer was fatally wounded.

BERRY JR., LEROY N., Patrolman, Badge 12789, Roll 345, October 9, 1969, District 5: While on patrol in his squad car, Officer Leroy Berry was murdered, the apparent victim of an armed robbery. Officer Berry was found shortly after the robbery with his service revolver and police star missing.

BIALK, JOHN, Detective Sergeant, Badge 474, Roll 83, September 21, 1916, District 20: Sergeant John Bialk responded to a domestic dispute call. Sergeant Bialk confronted the estranged husband in his home. At this time, the husband shot his own wife as well as Sergeant Bialk as he attempted to intervene. Although wounded, Sergeant Bialk was able to detain his assailant until fellow officers arrived. Sergeant Bialk died three days later as a result of his injuries.

BIRNS, STANLEY J., Detective Sergeant, Badge 322, Roll 70, July 16, 1914, Unit 601: Sergeant Stanley Birns was assigned to lead a team of officers conducting raids on a vice district. At the same time, a group of city inspectors were in the area conducting investigations and raids of their own. The two groups met and, in the confusion, shots were fired. The dedicated sergeant suffered a fatal gunshot wound.

BLACK, SAMUEL, Patrolman, Badge 1121, Roll 286, December 16, 1944, District 2: Officer Samuel Black and his partner responded to a domestic disturbance. As Officer Black entered the building, the offender fired a fatal gunshot at the courageous officer. As the offender fled, he fired several shots at Officer Black's partner, striking him as well. Both Officer Black and his partner, Officer Ezra Caldwell, died as a result of the encounter.

BLACKWELL, PATRICK E., Patrolman, Badge 1235, Roll 51, May 20, 1905, District 7: Officer Patrick Blackwell regulated traffic in a heavily congested business section. At one point, he found himself confined in a narrow passage. While signaling a wagon to pass, the officer fell backwards into an open freight elevator shaft. Officer Blackwell suffered serious injuries. The dedicated officer died ten days later in a hospital.

BLAZEK, FRANK J., Patrolman, Badge 4901, Roll 167, April 29, 1926, District 4: Officer Frank Blazek arrested an offender responsible for more than thirty-five armed robberies. As Officer Blazek transported the offender to the district station, the offender suddenly attacked the officer. Following a struggle, the offender was able to gain control of the officer's revolver and flee. As the offender escaped, he turned back to fire a shot. The brave officer was fatally struck.

BLUMBERG, JOHN B.L., Patrolman, Badge 922, Roll 33, November 7, 1895, District 6: Officer John Blumberg, while on patrol in the historic Pullman community, tragically died from the serious injuries he suffered after being struck by a railroad train.

BLYTH, JOHN J., Patrolman 1395, Badge 1395, Roll 313, June 16, 1956, District 9: While on patrol, Officer John Blyth and his partner heard gunfire. As they responded to the scene, the officers discovered an armed offender had just shot two citizens. The gunman then fired at the officers and fled. As Officer Blyth and his partner courageously pursued, the offender suddenly turned and again fired at the officers. Officer Blyth sustained a fatal gunshot wound.

BOBOSKY, STANLEY L., Patrolman, Badge 1446, Roll 258, July 6, 1934, Unit 151: Officer Stanley Bobosky was assigned to investigate a series of automobile thefts. While conducting the investigation, Officer Bobosky observed three suspicious men in a car. As Officer Bobosky approached, one offender pulled out a revolver and fired two shots, fatally striking the dedicated officer.

BOITANO, DAVID L., Patrolman, Badge 3850, Roll 145, September 25, 1924, District 13: While walking his beat, Officer David Boitano observed a man running directly towards him and carrying an object in his hand. Before Officer Boitano could react, the man fired five gunshots. The dedicated officer was struck and fatally wounded. The murderer continued running down the street.

BONFIELD, JULIAN A., Patrolman, Badge 2310, Roll 174, December 15, 1926, District 21: Officer Julian Bonfield confronted two armed offenders who had just robbed the office of a conservatory. One of the gunmen resisted arrest and opened fire at Officer Bonfield. The courageous officer suffered two fatal gunshot wounds.

BOSAK, WILLIAM P., Police Officer, Badge 3319, Roll 379, District 5: Officer William Bosak and his partner were returning to their police vehicle when a motorist traveling in the opposite direction stopped alongside them. Without any warning, the offender began firing at the officers. Officer Bosak and his partner, Officer Roger Van Schaik, were fatally wounded in the tragic incident.

BRADY, CHARLES H., Patrolman, Badge 6795, Roll 291, September 3, 1945, District 24: While on patrol, Officer Charles Brady and his partner observed a suspicious man standing on a corner. As Officer Brady and his partner approached, the offender drew a revolver and fired several shots. Both Officer Brady and his partner, Officer George Helstern, sustained fatal gunshot wounds in the encounter.

BRANDON, DORELLE C., Police Officer, Badge 2684, Roll 392, January 25, 1984, District 3: Officer Dorelle Brandon was working in an undercover narcotics capacity. A situation presented itself in which Officer Brandon announced her presence and attempted to make an arrest. When assist units arrived, the officers were unable to reach Officer Brandon due to locked burglar bars. Officer Brandon was shot while struggling with the offender. The heroic officer died from her injuries.

BRODERICK, CORNELIUS, Patrolman, Badge 4643, Roll 144, August 25, 1924, District 21: While on patrol, Officer Cornelius Broderick was approached by a citizen who identified a burglary offender. As Officer Broderick approached the suspect to investigate, the offender displayed a revolver and fired. The brave officer suffered a gunshot wound which proved to be fatal.

BRONSON, EDGAR J., Patrolman, Badge 13534, Roll 358, January 30, 1971, District 11: Officer Edgar Bronson was stopped by a citizen. The citizen requested that Officer Bronson resolve a disturbance occurring in a nearby garage. Officer Bronson entered the garage and identified himself as a police officer. Without any warning, one of the offenders produced a revolver and fired three shots. The dedicated officer died from the injuries he sustained.

BROSSEAU, OSCAR, Patrolman, Badge 174, Roll 244, June 20, 1933, District 11: Officer Oscar Brosseau was assigned to preserve order in and around a bakery where a labor demonstration was being held. While performing his duty, Officer Brosseau was attacked by disgruntled demonstrators. The brave officer was severely beaten and died as a result of his injuries.

BROWN, ALBERT H., Patrolman, Badge 2806, Roll 310, July 19, 1955, District 14: Officer Albert Brown, while assigned as the district lockup keeper, became involved in a fierce struggle with an escaped prisoner. During the struggle, the prisoner was able to gain control of Officer Brown's service revolver and shoot Officer Brown. Although wounded, Officer Brown was able to continue to struggle until the revolver was wrestled away from the prisoner. However, the brave officer died soon afterward from the injuries he sustained.

BROWN, JESSIE J., Patrolman, Badge 10329, Roll 373, February 11, 1975, District 4: Officer Jessie Brown responded to a call of "a man with a shotgun." Officer Brown found an offender brandishing a shotgun and a revolver, threatening to kill several people in a domestic dispute. An intense struggle ensued between Officer Brown, the gunman and assisting officers. Officer Brown was shot and fatally wounded during the struggle.

BROWN, MELVIN E., Patrolman, Badge 12360, Roll 351, June 3, 1970, District 3: Officer Melvin Brown observed three armed offenders enter a lounge and announce a robbery. As the offenders ordered the patrons to place their hands on the bar, Officer Brown attempted to subdue one of the gunmen and disarm him. The gunman fired several shots, fatally wounding the brave officer.

BRUNKELLA, JAY F., Police Officer, Badge 3429, Roll 396, October 4, 1986, District 24: Officer Jay Brunkella was assigned to a team actively involved in narcotic investigations. In response to reports from citizens of illegal drug sales, Officer Brunkella and his team stationed themselves around a grammar school. As Officer Brunkella and a fellow officer approached a suspected drug dealer, a struggle ensued. During the struggle a shot went off, and Officer Brunkella was mortally wounded.

BULFIN, PETER R., Patrolman, Badge 1746, Roll 89, July 13, 1917, District 9: Officer Peter Bulfin was shot and killed while escorting two clerks that were transferring bags of money from one bank to another. When the three men entered the transport vehicle, they were approached by four armed offenders. As Officer Bulfin reached for his service revolver, he was shot by one of the robbers. The dedicated officer died instantly.

BUNDA, WILLIAM F., Patrolman, Badge 3848, Roll 140, April 7, 1924, District 8: While on patrol, Officer William Bunda observed three offenders chasing a citizen. Officer Bunda stopped and questioned the three pursuers. As Officer Bunda attempted to search them for concealed weapons, one offender drew a revolver and fired. Officer Bunda was struck and died as a result of his injuries.

BURKE, JOHN C., Patrolman, Badge 1287, Roll 80, December 16, 1915, District 1: While on patrol, Officer John Burke observed a man on the street matching the description of an armed offender that had robbed several delivery trucks. As Officer Burke approached, the offender fired three shots. Officer Burke sustained multiple gunshot wounds. The courageous officer died as the fatal shot struck him just above his police star.

BURKE, RICHARD J., Patrolman, Badge 1236, Roll 104, June 16, 1919, District 7: Officer Richard Burke observed a tavern operating past the legal closing time. When Officer Burke entered and announced that he was closing the tavern, a verbal altercation ensued. During the altercation, a gunman suddenly fired several shots, fatally wounding Officer Burke.

BURKE, THOMAS W., Patrolman, Badge 4986, Roll 125, June 16, 1921, Unit 140: Officer Thomas Burke, while assigned to motorcycle patrol, observed a motorist driving at an excessive speed. Officer Burke immediately pursued the motorist. During the pursuit, the officer's motorcycle overturned. The dedicated officer sustained fatal injuries in the accident.

BURNS, GEORGE C., Detective Sergeant, Badge 207, Roll 107, October 3, 1919, District 8: Sergeant George Burns and Sergeant Bernard Lenehan were conducting a liquor investigation. During their investigation, two masked gunmen entered and announced a robbery. The offenders opened fire upon recognizing the sergeants. Both Sergeant Burns and his partner, Sergeant Lenehan, were fatally wounded.

BUSSE, HARRY J., Patrolman, Badge 289, Roll 110, January 27, 1920, District 21: Officer Harry Busse's assignment was to patrol the city's parks and nearby boulevards. While performing his duties, the dedicated officer became involved in an altercation with a gunman. Tragically, Officer Busse was shot and killed.

BYRNES, JOHN J., Patrolman, Badge 4730, Roll 171, September 30, 1926, District 5: While responding to a "burglary in progress" call, Officer John Byrnes entered a dark alley. Two offenders suddenly emerged and fired at the courageous officer. Officer Byrnes suffered a serious gunshot wound and died later that day.

CALDWELL, EZRA, Patrolman, Badge 2969, Roll 287, December 16, 1944, District 2: Officer Ezra Caldwell and his partner responded to a domestic disturbance. As Officer Caldwell's partner entered the building, he was shot and killed by the offender. Officer Caldwell ran to assist his partner and he was met by the gunman running out the door. The offender fired several shots, fatally wounding Officer Caldwell. Both Officer Caldwell and his partner, Officer Samuel Black, were fatally wounded.

CALI, JOSEPH, Patrolman, Badge 3271, Roll 374, May 20, 1975, District 13: Officer Joseph Cali observed an auto parked illegally in a bus stop. As Officer Cali exited his squad car and began writing the parking ticket, he was struck by a sniper's bullet fired from the third floor of a high-rise building. Officer Cali died the following day.

CALLAHAN, MICHAEL D., Patrolman, Badge 2842, Roll 57, January 4, 1908, District 13: Officer Michael Callahan approached four suspicious men on the street who were planning a holdup. Without warning, one offender fired a shot at Officer Callahan. The wounded officer returned fire, striking his assailant. The courageous officer was transported to a hospital, where he died the following day.

CAMP, JAMES H., Police Officer, Badge 3934, Roll 416, March 9, 1999, District 21: While investigating drug and gang activity in the community, Officer Camp approached and asked a driver to step out of his car. When the driver resisted, a struggle ensued. During the struggle, the offender gained control of Officer Camp's service revolver and fired. The brave officer suffered a serious wound. Officer Camp was immediately transported to the hospital, but the wound proved to be fatal.

CAMPBELL, JAMES W., Patrolman, Badge 15250, Roll 367, February 9, 1974, District 9: Officer James Campbell, while in full uniform, was inside a currency exchange cashing a check. At this time, he was approached from behind. The offender gained possession of Officer Campbell's service revolver. A struggle ensued, during which the dedicated officer was fatally wounded.

CAPLIS, JAMES J., Patrolman, Badge 1511, Roll 230, December 21, 1931, Unit 630: Officer James Caplis observed five offenders enter a nightclub, armed with shotguns, and announce a robbery. As one of the offenders attempted to escape, Officer Caplis pursued him. While pursuing the offender, Officer Caplis was shot in the back by a shotgun blast fired by a second offender. The brave officer died as a result of his injuries.

CAREY, DANIEL J., Patrolman, Badge 116, Roll 138, December 15, 1923, District 21: Officer Daniel Carey was assigned to patrol the city's parks and boulevards. While walking his beat, Officer Carey was tragically struck by an automobile. The impact resulted in Officer Carey suffering fatal injuries.

CARNEY, EDWARD J., Patrolman, Badge 83, Roll 29, December 8, 1893, District 1: Officer Edward Carney and his partner observed and questioned two suspicious men. After the men became confrontational, they were placed under arrest. However, one offender suddenly drew a revolver and shot Officer Carney. The brave officer died during surgery.

CARROLL, JAMES H., Patrolman, Badge 517, Roll 163, November 27, 1925, District 21: Officer James Carroll and his partner were inside a soft drink parlor during their tour of duty. Three armed robbers entered and immediately opened fire. Given little chance to react, the dedicated officers suffered several gunshot wounds. Officer Carroll and his partner, Officer James Henry, died as a result of the injuries they sustained.

CARTON, DANIEL J., Patrolman, Badge 3216, Roll 106, September 18, 1919, District 11: Officer Daniel Carton was assigned to maintain order during a period of civil unrest. After becoming involved in an altercation, the brave officer sustained a fatal gunshot injury.

CASEY, JAMES J., Patrolman, Badge 2807, Roll 227, July 1, 1931, Unit 151: Officer James Casey arrested an offender who had displayed a gun to two citizens during a quarrel. The officer confiscated the weapon and transported the prisoner to the station. While in transit, the offender abruptly drew a second weapon and fired at Officer Casey. The courageous officer sustained multiple gunshot wounds and died the next day.

CASSIDY, ERNEST H., Patrolman, Badge 2692, Roll 129, April 3, 1922: Officer Ernest Cassidy was escorting a savings and loan employee carrying bank deposits. Without warning, five armed offenders pulled up in an automobile and began firing. Officer Cassidy was fatally wounded.

CERIALE, MICHAEL A., Police Officer, Badge 17429, Roll 414, August 21, 1998, District 2: Officer Michael Ceriale was working undercover conducting a narcotics surveillance. During the surveillance, Officer Ceriale was spotted by the offenders. One offender fired a shot, striking Officer Ceriale just below the safety vest. The courageous officer died as a result of the injuries he sustained.

CHAPMAN JR., JOSEPH E., Patrolman, Badge 6239, Roll 323, May 8, 1960, Unit 140: Officer Joseph Chapman observed an armed offender enter a store. The gunman jumped the counter, announced a robbery, and pointed his weapon at the owner and clerk. Officer Chapman courageously entered the store and confronted the offender. During the ensuing gun battle, Officer Chapman suffered five gunshot wounds. Officer Chapman died as a result of his injuries.

CHISKA, JOHN, Sergeant, Badge 888, Roll 187, April 5, 1928, District 25: Sergeant John Chiska, while in civilian dress, was approached by three armed offenders who announced a robbery. Sergeant Chiska then stated he was a police officer, and was able to place two of the offenders under arrest. The third gunman, however, was able to fire his gun, striking Sergeant Chiska. The courageous sergeant was taken to a nearby hospital, where he later died.

CLARK, RICHARD W., Police Officer, Badge 13034, Roll 394, April 3, 1986, District 19: Officer Richard Clark responded to a call of a "man with a gun." An armed offender had murdered his landlord, taken an elderly woman as hostage, and barricaded himself inside his home. Officer Clark took cover near the house. As Officer Clark was crouched down near a squad car, he was struck by a rifle shot fired through the front window. The courageous officer died as a result of his wounds.

CLARK, THOMAS J., Patrolman, Badge 3509, Roll 130, May 10, 1922, District 8: Officer Thomas Clark was assigned to patrol in and around a factory that had recently been bombed. While on patrol, Officer Clark noticed three suspicious men in a parked automobile. As Officer Clark approached to question the men, the men opened fire. The courageous officer was fatally wounded.

CLAUSEN, GEORGE, Patrolman, Badge 3400, Roll 95, April 13, 1918, District 12: Officer George Clausen, while investigating the armed robbery of a drinking establishment, located the wanted offenders. The offenders were committing a second robbery. As Officer Clausen confronted the robbers, a gun battle ensued. Officer Clausen was struck several times during the exchange, and died as a result of his injuries.

CLEARY, EDWARD J., Patrolman, Badge 4220, Roll 149, November 29, 1924, District 8: While on patrol, Officer Edward Cleary was approached by a woman who reported that she had just been assaulted. The woman identified the offender on the street. As Officer Cleary confronted the offender, the man pulled out a revolver and fired. The dedicated officer was struck and fatally wounded.

COLE, JASPER H., Patrolman, Badge 1703, Roll 26, February 10, 1892, District 11: Officer Jasper Cole, while on duty in the police station, was tragically killed by the accidental discharge of a revolver. The revolver was being inventoried as evidence in a homicide investigation.

COLLINS, JOHN S., Patrolman, Badge 11835, Roll 336, December 15, 1967, District 7: Officer John Collins was shot while off duty and Christmas shopping with his wife and young son. As the family returned to the parking lot, Officer Collins observed a thief tampering with his car. After Officer Collins identified himself as a police officer, the offender pulled out a gun and grabbed the officers wife as a shield. When the offender released the officer's wife and fled, Officer Collins gave chase. Officer Collins suffered a gunshot wound to the head and died two days later.

COLLINS, MARTIN, Patrolman, Badge 263, Roll 122, January 4, 1921, District 21: Officer Martin Collins observed an intoxicated motorist driving recklessly down the street. In his attempt to stop the driver, Officer Collins approached the vehicle and ordered the driver to pull over. As the offender pushed Officer Collins away from the car, Officer Collins was tragically crushed between two vehicles. The brave officer died from his injuries.

COLQUITT, THOMAS, Patrolman, Badge 108, Roll 77, February 10, 1915, District 1: Officer Thomas Colquitt, while walking his beat in Lincoln Park, was tragically struck by an automobile near the Ulysses S. Grant Monument. Officer Colquitt died shortly after, as a result of his injuries.

CONLEY, JOHN L., Patrolman, Badge 4636, Roll 200, May 31, 1929, District 13: Officer John Conley and his partner courageously responded to a disturbance call of an intoxicated man armed with a shotgun. The offender had shot his wife and killed a citizen. When confronted, the gunman fired shotgun blasts at the courageous officers. Both Officer Conley and his partner, Officer Herbert Hagberg, were killed in the incident.

CONLON, CHARLES R., Patrolman, Badge 104, Roll 119, December 16, 1920, Unit 151: Officer Charles Conlon, while off duty, was informed by a citizen that a drug store was being robbed. When Officer Conlon rushed to the scene, he observed four armed robbers leaving the store. As Officer Conlon pursued one of the robbers, the offender turned and fired a gun. Officer Conlon was struck and died as a result of his injuries.

COOLEY, JAMES, Patrolman, Badge 792, Roll 177, April 4, 1927, District 21: While on patrol, Officer James Cooley was approached by two robbery victims. When the victims identified the robber on the street, Officer Cooley immediately confronted the offender. The robber drew a gun and fired. The dedicated officer was fatally struck.

CORCORAN, JAMES S., Patrolman, Badge 5044, Roll 219, November 26, 1930, District 12: Officer James Corcoran was killed during an armed robbery. Officer Corcoran resisted the offender and attempted to make an arrest. A struggle ensued in which the offender fired his revolver, striking officer Corcoran.

CORCORAN, MARTIN J., Detective Sergeant, Badge 469, Roll 90, August 13, 1917, Unit 40: Sergeant Martin Corcoran observed two burglars waiting for a street car. They were carrying a basket of jewelry and expensive clothing. When Sergeant Corcoran immediately questioned the offenders, one burglar pulled out a revolver and fired. The dedicated sergeant was fatally wounded in the encounter.

CREED, ANTHONY L., Police Officer, Badge 3245, Roll 390, August 30, 1983, Unit 055: Officer Anthony Creed, assigned to the Mounted Unit, accidentally fell from his horse as he was engaged in the equestrian exercise program. The tragic accident resulted in the death of the officer.

CROWLEY, DANIEL, Patrolman, Badge 296, Roll 5, August 4, 1881, District 3: Officer Daniel Crowley encountered an intoxicated man on the street. The man pointed a revolver at the officer's chest. When Officer Crowley heard the click of the hammer, he deflected the gun the instant it was fired. The bullet entered the officer's leg. Though the bullet was successfully removed, infection spread through the brave officer's body. Tragically, he died nine days later.

CROWLEY, EDWARD T., Patrolman, Badge 929, Roll 300, July 14, 1950, Unit 610: Officer Edward Crowley and his partner, Officer Donald McCormick, attempted to arrest a wanted armed robber at his apartment. Suddenly, the gunman drew a revolver and fired, striking Officer McCormick. During the ensuing struggle, Officer Crowley was shot as well. Both dedicated officers were fatally wounded in the encounter.

CROWLEY, HARRY J., Sergeant, Badge 160, Roll 147, November 8, 1924, District 16: Sergeant Harry Crowley observed two armed robbers enter an establishment and announce a robbery. Sergeant Crowley confronted the offenders and engaged in a gun battle with them. The brave sergeant was fatally wounded.

CROWLEY, PATRICK J., Patrolman, Badge 3614, Roll 375, September 13, 1976, District 6: Following an extensive investigation, Officer Patrick Crowley and other officers conducted a narcotics raid on an apartment. As Officer Crowley reached the porch and announced his office, an armed offender emerged, firing his weapon. The dedicated officer was fatally wounded.

CULLOTTA, LOUIS, Patrolman, Badge 11801, Roll 364, July 26, 1973, District 20: Officer Louis Cullotta was working at a diner. At this time, an offender walked in and, without any warning, pulled out a revolver and fired at Officer Cullotta. The officer sustained a fatal gunshot wound. Later investigation revealed that the offender had been interrogated by Officer Cullotta three years earlier.

CUMMINGS, RICHARD F., Sergeant, Badge 101, Roll 50, May 1, 1905, District 1: Sergeant Richard Cummings commanded a large group of officers assigned to an area experiencing serious labor problems. Verbal conflict flared between strike breakers and strike sympathizers. A horse-drawn wagon driver disobeyed police orders and attempted to force his vehicle into a heavily congested area. The side of the wagon struck Sergeant Cummings, throwing him to the ground. The dedicated sergeant died as a result of the injuries he sustained.

CUNNINGHAM, FRANK J., Patrolman, Badge 60, Roll 237, July 19, 1932, District 12: Officer Frank Cunningham, while investigating suspicious activity in a restaurant, observed four masked offenders committing a robbery. As Officer Cunningham attempted to arrest the robbers, a gun battle ensued. The courageous officer was fatally wounded in the exchange.

CUNNINGHAM, MILES, Patrolman, Badge 1150, Roll 252, September 22, 1933, District 12: While on patrol, Officer Miles Cunningham ran to investigate an automobile accident. Unknown to Officer Cunningham, the five men in one of the cars were attempting an escape after robbing two bank messengers. When Officer Cunningham approached to see if he could assist any injured people, the robbers opened fire with a machine gun. The multiple gunshot wounds sustained by the brave officer were fatal.

DALEY, PATRICK J., Patrolman, Badge 1178, Roll 169, June 27, 1926, District 11: Officer Patrick Daley was found on the street in the early morning hours. Officer Daley had suffered a fatal gunshot wound. The circumstances of his death and the identity of his assailant remain unknown.

DARCY JR., MARTIN E., Police Officer, Badge 6444, Roll 386, September 27, 1982, District 22: Officer Martin Darcy responded to an "armed robbery in progress." The offender had shot a store clerk and later wounded another citizen. Following a search of the area, Officer Darcy confronted the offender. The gunman opened fire. The courageous officer was fatally shot during the encounter.

DAVENPORT JR., RICHARD, Sergeant, Badge 2280, Roll 395, August 4, 1986, District 9: Richard Davenport was alerted to an attempted auto theft and responded immediately. Sergeant Davenport confronted the five offenders and attempted to place them under arrest. One of the offenders resisted arrest, drew a revolver and fired. The brave sergeant was shot and killed.

DAY, JAMES F., Lieutenant, Badge –Lt.-, Roll 261, September 19, 1934, District 6: Lieutenant James Day was attacked from behind in an armed robbery attempt. During the struggle with his assailant, Lieutenant Day sustained a serious head injury. Later, Lieutenant Day suffered a fatal heart attack caused by complications due to the head injury.

DEALY, FRANK, Detective Sergeant, Badge 539, Roll 74, October 5, 1914, District 14: Sergeant Frank Dealy, while walking his beat, observed two suspicious men. When Sergeant Dealy approached them, the two men drew revolvers and began firing. The dedicated sergeant was struck four times. Sergeant Dealy was transported to the hospital by concerned citizens, where he died hours later.

DEAN, EDWARD E., Patrolman, Badge 4480, Roll 155, June 11, 1925, District 16: Officer Edward Dean was detailed to escort an employee of a motor coach company. Four masked men, armed with shotguns, confronted them with the intention of robbing the citizen of the $10,000.00 payroll. The courageous officer prevented the robbery and ensured that no harm came to the citizen, but was fatally shot to death in his confrontation with the masked robbers.

DEAN, STUART N., Patrolman, Badge 72, Roll 82, July 24, 1916, District 13: Officer Stuart Dean was assigned to subdue a distraught man firing a rifle indiscriminately at his neighbors. The man had killed three people and wounded several others before barricading himself in his home. The man continued to fire at people from his window. When Officer Dean courageously entered the building, he was shot and killed.

DEGAN, MATHIAS J., Patrolman, Badge 648, Roll 10, May 4, 1886, District 3: Officer Mathias Degan was among a large group of officers assigned to disperse protesters near Haymarket Square. Suddenly, a bomb was thrown and exploded in the midst of the officers. Officer Degan was the first of eight courageous officers to die in what is known as the historic Haymarket Tragedy.

DELANEY, PATRICK F., Sergeant, Badge 417, Roll 182, October 4, 1927, District 8: While on patrol, Sergeant Patrick Delaney observed three suspicious men in front of a building. As Sergeant Delaney confronted and questioned the men, one offender suddenly drew a revolver and fired, striking Sergeant Delaney. The courageous sergeant died from his injuries.

DEVINE, TIMOTHY, Patrolman, Badge 1814, Roll 42, August 12, 1902, District 15: Officer Timothy Devine and his partner, while following two burglars, were ambushed by a hail of gunshots. Though wounded, Officer Devine was able to return fire, wounding one of the offenders as he fled. Both Officer Devine and his partner, Officer Charles Pennell, were fatally shot in the ambush.

DILLON, HUBERT J., Patrolman, Badge 4957, Roll 218, November 23, 1930, District 12: Officer Hubert Dillon, while responding to a fight between two men, was fatally shot by one of the combatants. The offender produced a revolver and fired as Officer Dillon approached. The courageous officer died as a result of his injuries.

DOFFYN, DANIEL J., Probationary Police Officer, Badge 14030, Roll 408, March 8, 1995, District 15: Officer Daniel Doffyn was just beginning his tour of duty when he responded to a "burglary in progress" across the street from the police station. Officer Doffyn immediately ran to the scene and, as he approached one offender, a second offender pulled out a gun and opened fire. The courageous officer was struck and transported to a nearby hospital, where he died shortly thereafter.

DOHERTY, PATRICK H., Patrolman, Badge 1978, Roll 133, August 10, 1922, District 21: While on patrol, Officer Patrick Doherty observed two men suspected of having committed an armed robbery. As Officer Doherty approached to investigate, the offenders suddenly grabbed the officer and a violent struggle ensued. During the struggle, the men were able to gain control of Officer Doherty's service revolver. The offenders shot Officer Doherty four times. The courageous officer died as a result of his injuries.

DOLL, GERALD E., Sergeant, Badge 477, Roll 333, March 29, 1967, District 15: Sergeant Gerald Doll observed a vehicle traveling at a high rate of speed. Sergeant Doll attempted a traffic stop, but the suspect vehicle fled. Moments later, the speeding vehicle stopped. As Sergeant Doll approached the vehicle, the driver produced a sawed-off shotgun, pointed it, and fired at the unsuspecting sergeant. Sergeant Doll was fatally wounded in the attack.

DONNER, JOHN L., Patrolman, Badge 125, Roll 88, May 7, 1917, District 1: Officer John Donner was assigned to motorcycle patrol in Lincoln Park. While pursuing a motorist, he was struck by another vehicle. Tragically, the accident resulted in fatal injuries to the dedicated officer.

DOYLE, JAMES E., Probationary Police Officer, Badge 9093, Roll 383, February 5, 1982, Unit 124: While on patrol, Officer James Doyle was informed by a citizen that the individual who had robbed him earlier was on a nearby bus. Officer Doyle responded and removed the suspect from the bus. Suddenly, the offender pulled out a revolver and shot Officer Doyle. The courageous officer died as a result of his serious injuries.

DRISCOLL, JOSEPH D., Patrolman, Badge 1774, Roll 46, December 1, 1903, District 24: Officer Joseph Driscoll was investigating the murder of Officer John Quinn. The known offenders were also wanted for numerous armed robberies. When Officer Driscoll located the wanted offenders, an intense gun battle erupted. The heroic officer suffered a fatal gunshot wound.

DUDDLES, EDWARD, Patrolman, Badge 2507, Roll 31, January 3, 1895, District 19: While on patrol, Officer Edward Duddles heard screams. Officer Duddles courageously responded to the scene and discovered two men attacking a woman. Upon being discovered, one of the attackers was able to pull out a gun and shoot Officer Duddles. Officer Duddles perished from his wound.

DUFFY, MICHAEL, Patrolman, Badge 141, Roll 109, November 30, 1919, District 5: Officer Michael Duffy responded to a call of an intoxicated patron displaying a pistol inside a drinking establishment. Upon arrival, Officer Duffy confronted the gunman and attempted to place him under arrest. The gunman fired one shot at the brave officer, fatally striking him.

DUFFY, PATRICK, Patrolman, Badge 1190, Roll 41, May 1, 1902, District 9: Officer Patrick Duffy observed a wanted offender standing in front of a church. While attempting to make the arrest, Officer Duffy was attacked by a second offender. As Officer Duffy turned to face his attacker, the first offender pulled out a gun and fired. The dedicated officer was fatally wounded.

DURKIN, PATRICK, Patrolman, Badge 1549, Roll 223, May 2, 1931, Unit 51: Officer Patrick Durkin located a wanted bank robber at a downtown newsstand. While attempting to make the arrest, the offender drew a pistol and shot, striking the brave officer. Officer Durkin was assisted during the struggle by Officer Anthony Ruthy, who also suffered a gunshot wound during the incident. Both courageous officers died as a result of their injuries.

ECKLES JR., FRED, Police Officer, Badge 13561, Roll 391, January 17, 1984, District 6: Officer Fred Eckles was one of several officers assigned to execute a narcotics search warrant. Officer Eckles and his partner announced their office and stated they had a warrant. When no response was heard, the officers forced entry. A gun battle ensued with three armed offenders. Officer Eckles, suffered multiple gunshot wounds. The courageous officer died a few hours later.

EGAN, THOMAS J., Sergeant, Badge 595, Roll 126, August 25, 1921, District 2: Officer Thomas Egan, while stationed in front of the home of Police Superintendent Charles Fitzmorris, was approached by an armed offender who announced a robbery. In the ensuing gun battle, Officer Egan sustained a serious wound and died six days later. The courageous officer had been promoted just prior to his death.

EICHHORST, CHARLES E., Sergeant, Badge 1364, Roll 329, August 4, 1965, District 20: Sergeant Charles Eichhorst responded to a "robbery in progress" call. Upon arrival, Sergeant Eichhorst observed a robber fleeing the store. Sergeant Eichhorst immediately placed the robber under arrest. While searching the robber, a second robber exited the store. The second robber approached the brave sergeant from behind and shot him several times. Sergeant Eichhorst died from his injuries.

ESAU, ARTHUR F., Patrolman, Badge 4967, Roll 190, April 27, 1928, District 23: Officer Arthur Esau responded to a robbery inside a drug store. As Officer Esau entered the store, he was quickly confronted by armed robbers. The dedicated officer was fatally struck in an exchange of gunfire.

EVANS, DAVID C., Police Officer, Badge 9398, Roll 411, August 25, 1997, District 6: Officer David Evans responded to a call of "police officers requiring assistance." As Officer Evans proceeded to the scene, his police vehicle swerved to avoid striking pedestrians crossing the street. Tragically, his vehicle struck the guardrail and dropped 25 feet onto the expressway below. The dedicated officer sustained serious injuries which resulted in his death.

FAHEY JR., WILLIAM P., Police Officer, Badge 4194, Roll 385, February 10, 1982, Unit 156: Officer William Fahey and his partner stopped a vehicle for a traffic violation. An intense struggle ensued in which one of the offenders was able to gain control of Officer Fahey's gun. The offender shot and killed both Officer Fahey and his partner, Officer Richard O'Brien.

FARLEY, JAMES C., Patrolman, Badge 5269, Roll 180, June 23, 1927, District 16: Officer James Farley and his partner were investigating an armed robbery where the offender had forcibly taken a citizen's automobile. The officers searched the area and confronted the dangerous offender in the stolen car. A fierce gun battle took place in which both Officer Farley and his partner, Sergeant Thomas Kehoe, were fatally wounded.

FENTON, PATRICK, Patrolman, Badge 1169, Roll 34, February 27, 1898, District 9: Officer Patrick Fenton and his partner responded to a disturbance created by a distraught man. The man was armed with a revolver and had threatened to kill his landlady and members of his family. To prevent the gunman from harming himself or others, Officer Fenton forcibly entered the man's apartment. The man fired several times, fatally striking the courageous officer.

FERGUSON, JOSEPH F., Patrolman, Badge 6892, Roll 341, December 27, 1968, District 2: Officer Joseph Ferguson and his partner questioned three suspicious men on the street. Two of the men were placed under arrest and the third was released. Shortly thereafter, the third man returned with a gun. A gun battle ensued, during which Officer Ferguson sustained two serious wounds. The courageous officer died in the hospital.

FINNEGAN, EDWARD C., Patrolman, Badge 3444, Roll 165, March 27, 1926, District 7: Officer Edward Finnegan arrested a motorist for speeding. Officer Finnegan placed the offender in the back seat of his police vehicle in order to transport him to the district station. While en route, the offender suddenly pulled out a revolver and shot the officer. Officer Finnegan was rushed to the hospital, where he died a short time later.

FISCHER, FREDERICK, Sergeant, Badge 36, Roll 272, October 22, 1936, Unit 140: Sergeant Frederick Fischer was assigned to patrol the parks of the city of Chicago. Sergeant Fischer died in the performance of his duties.

FISHER, CLAUDE M., Sergeant, Badge 1570, Roll 330, April 19, 1966, District 21: Sergeant Claude Fisher observed three armed offenders enter a lounge, with one offender carrying a shotgun. Sergeant Fisher drew his service revolver and identified himself as a police officer. An exchange of gunfire ensued, during which the dedicated sergeant was fatally shot.

FITZGERALD, DENNIS, Patrolman, Badge 786, Roll 47, January 20, 1904, District 5: Officer Dennis Fitzgerald observed two men creating a disturbance in the street. As Officer Fitzgerald confronted the offenders, they turned on the officer and began attacking him. During the struggle, the offenders shot Officer Fitzgerald. The heroic officer died the same day from the injuries he sustained.

FITZPATRICK, JOSEPH M., Patrolman, Badge 210, Roll 217, October 25, 1930, Unit 151: As Officer Joseph Fitzpatrick emerged from an automobile, he was approached by five armed men who announced a robbery. Officer Fitzpatrick resisted and attempted to arrest the men. A gun battle ensued and the courageous officer was fatally wounded.

FITZPATRICK, LUKE J., Patrolman, Badge 1084, Roll 53, November 19, 1906, District 5: Officer Luke Fitzpatrick was approached by a train conductor who identified two burglars that were in a train station. As Officer Fitzpatrick approached the burglars in an attempt to make the arrests, he was struck by a barrage of bullets. Officer Fitzpatrick died shortly after identifying one of his assailants.

FLAVIN, TIMOTHY, Patrolman, Badge 691, Roll 13, May 8, 1886, District 3, Officer Timothy Flavin was assigned to Haymarket Square on May 6, 1886, to disperse a protest group. After a bomb exploded, a fierce gun battle ensued in which Officer Flavin suffered several wounds. He later died from those wounds. He was the fourth of eight courageous officers to die in the Haymarket Tragedy.

FLOWERS, WILLIAM A., Patrolman, Badge 1872, Roll 325, October 26, 1960, District 11: Officer William Flowers, while conducting an assault investigation, learned that the offender kept an arsenal of weapons in his apartment. As Officer Flowers stood outside the offender's building, the offender suddenly appeared and opened fire. Officer Flowers sustained fatal wounds in the incident.

FOGARTY, PATRICK, Patrolman, Badge 1352, Roll 65, July 2, 1911, District 4: Officer Patrick Fogarty, while off duty, was attacked by a man on the street. A physical struggle ensued, during which the offender knocked Officer Fogarty's service revolver from his hand. The offender was able to gain possession of the weapon. Subsequently, the gun discharged, resulting in Officer Fogarty being severely wounded. The courageous officer died shortly thereafter.

FOLEY, MATTHEW J., Patrolman, Badge 170, Roll 98, September 12, 1918, District 21: Officer Matthew Foley, assigned to motorcycle patrol in Jackson Park, was tragically killed when he lost control of and crashed his motorcycle. Officer Foley died in the hospital later that day from the severe injuries he sustained in the accident.

FOUNTAIN, DELL O., Police Officer, Badge 18247, Roll 410, March 22, 1996, District 15: Officer Dell Fountain was alerted to a disturbance in an upstairs apartment that was being used for narcotics activity. As Officer Fountain responded to the scene, he was confronted by an offender. A struggle ensued, during which the brave officer was fatally wounded.

FRANCOIS, HARRY, Patrolman, Badge 629, Roll 281, November 20, 1939, Unit 140: Officer Harry Francois encountered a wanted offender while on patrol. As Officer Francois attempted to make the arrest, the offender drew a revolver and fired a shot. The brave officer was struck and killed.

FREDERICK, BRUNO H., Patrolman, Badge 4813, Roll 85, December 3, 1916, District 1: Officer Bruno Frederick was fatally wounded attempting to close a dance hall. Officer Frederick was attacked by an unruly mob when he tried to perform his duty. The dedicated officer was shot and beaten in the incident. Officer Frederick died three days later as a result of his injuries.

FREEMAN, GEORGE T., Patrolman, Badge 2370, Roll 296, April 26, 1947, District 2: Officer George Freeman arrested an offender for disorderly conduct. As Officer Freeman transported the prisoner to the station, the offender became violent and knocked Officer Freeman to the ground. As a concerned citizen came to Officer Freeman's assistance, the offender fled. The dedicated officer died as a result of his severe injuries.

FREICHEL, JOHN J., Patrolman, Badge 3710, Roll 271, August 23, 1936, District 11: Officer John Freichel was confronted and attacked by a gunman he had earlier arrested. The offender pulled out a gun and fired. The courageous officer was struck and fatally wounded.

FRIEDMAN, MORRIS, Patrolman, Badge 2619, Roll 289, June 25, 1945, Unit 620: While on patrol, Officer Morris Friedman observed three suspicious individuals in an automobile. The occupants, who were wanted for several robberies across the Midwest, sped away as Officer Friedman approached. As Officer Friedman curbed the vehicle, one occupant fled on foot. Officer Friedman pursued the offender and a gun battle ensued. The courageous officer was struck and fatally wounded.

FRYER, ADAM W., Patrolman, Badge 752, Roll 22, August 9, 1889, Unit 140: Officer Adam Fryer, while on foot patrol, assisted in the arrest of two known street gang leaders. As the offenders fled, Officer Fryer ordered them to halt. The offenders answered with gunfire, striking and fatally wounding Officer Fryer.

FULLER, WILLIAM A., Patrolman, Badge 3327, Roll 303, April 2, 1953, District 1: Officer William Fuller observed three armed robbers enter a lounge. One of the offenders placed a gun against the back of a patron and announced a robbery. Officer Fuller immediately confronted the offenders and a gun battle ensued. The courageous officer was fatally wounded.

FURST, LOUIS F., Patrolman, Badge 6347, Roll 262, September 22, 1934, District 2: While on patrol, Officer Louis Furst confronted an armed offender attempting to rob a real estate office. In making the arrest, Officer Furst was fired upon several times by the gunman. Officer Furst suffered fatal wounds.

GAGLER, WILLIAM G., Patrolman, Badge 1634, Roll 236, June 19, 1932, District 21: Officer William Gagler was fatally shot while serving an arrest warrant on an offender wanted for theft. While Officer Gagler was in the process of making the arrest, the offender produced a concealed revolver and began shooting. The dedicated officer suffered fatal gunshot wounds.

GALLAGHER, PATRICK J., Patrolman, Badge 4966, Roll 221, April 14, 1931, District 23: Officer Patrick Gallagher, while responding to a disturbance at a hotel, responded to the room that was the source of the disturbance. When the door was opened, one of the individuals inside fired a shot, striking and killing the courageous officer.

GALLAGHER, WILLIAM, Patrolman, Badge 1162, Roll 203, June 25, 1929, District 12: Officer William Gallagher and his partner were assigned to a kidnapping investigation. During the course of the investigation, Officer Gallagher and his partner relocated to a hallway outside an apartment. As they demanded entry, they were met with a burst of gunfire. Both Officer William Gallagher and his partner, Officer Jesse Hults, were killed in the encounter.

GALLOWAY JR., MELVIN A., Patrolman, Badge 13794, Roll 359, March 21, 1971, District 15: Officer Melvin Galloway, while conducting a vice investigation inside a lounge, observed a fight break out. As Officer Galloway interceded, an offender displayed a knife. As Officer Galloway struggled with the offender, other officers came to his aid. During the struggle, the offender gained control of one of the officers' service revolvers. The offender fired one shot, fatally wounding Officer Galloway.

GALLOWITCH, ROBERT L., Patrolman, Badge 15442, Roll 360, May 24, 1972, District 5: Officer Robert Gallowitch responded to a burglar alarm. Upon arrival, Officer Gallowitch discovered three offenders disguised as telephone repair men. The offenders had stolen a telephone truck, taken the driver hostage, and were robbing a jewelry store. As Officer Gallowitch confronted the three offenders in the alley, the offenders began shooting. The brave officer sustained fatal gunshot wounds during the encounter.

GARRISON, BRUCE N., Patrolman, Badge 14775, Roll 368, February 27, 1974, Unit 153: Officer Bruce Garrison and his partner observed a suspicious man emerge from a tavern. The man walked to his car and then, after seeing the officers, re-entered the tavern. As Officer Garrison and his partner investigated, they noticed a sawed-off shotgun near the man's car. As the officers entered the tavern, the offender drew a pistol and fired several shots. Both Officer Garrison and his partner, Officer William Marsek, were fatally wounded.

GARTLEY, ANDREW, Patrolman, Badge 4133, Roll 69, June 1, 1914, District 1: Officer Andrew Gartley, while on patrol, observed a disturbance in a tavern. Several patrons were engaged in a fight. As Officer Gartley attempted to break up the fight, five of the combatants suddenly turned on him. Officer Gartley sustained serious injuries in the struggle. The courageous officer died as a result of his injuries two days later.

GASTER, HARRY, Patrolman, Badge 4913, Roll 143, August 10, 1924, District 9: Officer Harry Gaster was working a second job as a security guard when he noticed suspicious activity under an elevated train platform. When Officer Gaster investigated, he discovered three offenders breaking into an automobile. As Officer Gaster confronted the offenders, one of them fired a gunshot, fatally striking the courageous officer.

GIBBONS, ROBERT, Patrolman, Badge 138, Roll 132, June 26, 1922, District 18: Officer Robert Gibbons was assigned to patrol the city's many parks and nearby boulevards. Officer Gibbons died in the performance of his duties. His star has been enshrined in the Chicago Police Department's Honored Star Case.

GILHOOLY, JOHN J., Patrolman, Badge 3502, Roll 347, November 14, 1969, District 2: Officer John Gilhooly learned that armed offenders had taken refuge in an abandoned building. Officer Gilhooly and assisting units surrounded the building. During the ensuing gun battle, an offender jumped from a window and fired at Officer Gilhooly, striking him. The courageous officer died in the hospital the following morning. Officer Frank Rappaport was also fatally wounded in the incident.

GILMAN, JESSE C., Patrolman, Badge 3953, Roll 63, December 24 1910, District 23: While on patrol, Officer Jesse Gilman observed an individual wanted for attempted murder among a crowd of Christmas shoppers. As Officer Gilman attempted to apprehend him, the offender fired a shot through his overcoat pocket. Officer Gilman was struck. The heroic officer died the following day from the gunshot wound he sustained.

GIOVANNONI, GEORGE F., Patrolman, Badge 1619, Roll 206, October 19, 1929, District 2: Officer George Giovannoni was assigned to locate a gunman who had shot at a police officer and threatened a woman. Officer Giovannoni discovered the offender hiding in a backyard and courageously confronted him. A gunfight ensued, and Officer Giovannoni sustained a fatal gunshot wound.

GOLDEN, ROBERT R., Patrolman, Badge 420, Roll 314, November 14, 1956, Unit 140: Officer Robert Golden observed two armed men robbing a tavern. As Officer Golden attempted to intervene, he was seriously wounded by gunfire from the two gunmen. The wound sustained by the courageous officer was fatal.

GONZALEZ, ORESTE, Patrolman, Badge 6362, Roll 305, October 8, 1953, Unit 640: Officer Oreste Gonzalez and his partner arrested an offender wanted for multiple armed robberies. As Officer Gonzalez transported the prisoner to the police station, the offender drew a concealed pistol and fired a shot. The brave officer was fatally wounded.

GOSSMEYER, MELVIN L., Patrolman, Badge 9775, Roll 324, July 17, 1960, Unit 701: Officer Melvin Gossmeyer was assigned to patrol the neighborhood on a police motorcycle. As Officer Gossmeyer entered the intersection, he was struck by a fleeing hit-and-run offender. Officer Gossmeyer died as a result of the injuries he sustained in the accident.

GRANGER, ROBERT H., Patrolman, Badge 5788, Roll 235, April 9, 1932, District 2: Officer Robert Granger learned from a citizen that an armed robbery was taking place in a nearby building. Officer Granger rushed to the scene and found a gunman robbing the participants of a card game. When Officer Granger ordered the offender to drop his weapon, the gunman opened fire. The dedicated officer was fatally wounded.

GRANT, LEO, Patrolman, Badge 3751, Roll 176, March 12, 1927, District 5: Officer Leo Grant located three offenders who had escaped from Will County Jail. When confronted, one of the escaped prisoners drew a revolver and fired. The bullet struck Officer Grant, resulting in serious injury. The brave officer died in a hospital later that day from his injuries.

GRAY, HARRY J., Sergeant, Badge 886, Roll 160, November 2, 1925, District 4: Sergeant Harry Gray was assigned to lead a team of officers waiting to apprehend a wanted offender. The officers stationed themselves at the offender's apartment and awaited his arrival. As the offender arrived, accompanied by his girlfriend, Sergeant Gray arrested him. However, the girlfriend suddenly produced a revolver and fired. The brave sergeant suffered a fatal gunshot wound.

GUILTANANE, JOHN J., Patrolman, Badge 1325, Roll 213, July 18, 1930, District 22: Officer John Guiltanane arrested two robbery offenders. While in the process of transporting the prisoners to the police station, one of the offenders produced a concealed weapon and fired. The dedicated officer was fatally wounded.

HAGBERG, HERBERT N., Patrolman, Badge 1028, Roll 199, May 31, 1929, District 24: Officer Herbert Hagberg and his partner courageously responded to a call of an intoxicated man armed with a shotgun and causing a disturbance. The offender had shot his wife and killed a citizen. When confronted, the gunman opened fire at the officers. Both Officer Hagberg, and his partner Officer John Conley, suffered fatal injuries.

HALL, SAMUEL P., Patrolman, Badge 5190, Roll 328, October 1, 1962, Unit 156: Officer Samuel Hall and his partner were on patrol in their squad car and heard gunfire. Officer Hall arrived at the scene where a robbery had just occurred. As Officer Hall exited his vehicle, the gunman stepped forward and shot Officer Hall at close range. The courageous officer died as a result of his injuries.

HALLORAN, WILLIAM S., Patrolman, Badge 214, Roll 18, July 17, 1887, District 1: Officer William Halloran was shot by a convicted career burglar whom he had arrested in the past. The offender wanted revenge against Officer Halloran, and vowed that he would kill the officer should Officer Halloran arrest him again. When the courageous officer confronted the burglar, he was shot. The heroic officer died the following day.

HALPERIN, BARNEY, Detective, Badge 7214, Roll 319, December 20, 1957, District 2: Detective Barney Halperin responded to a robbery taking place in a nearby restaurant. Upon arrival at the scene, the courageous detective confronted the armed robber and ordered him to surrender. Instead, the offender fired several times, fatally wounding Detective Halperin.

HANSEN, NELS, Patrolman, Badge 822, Roll 16, June 14, 1886, District 3: Officer Nels Hansen was one of many officers detailed to disperse protesters near Haymarket Square on May 4, 1886. Suddenly, a bomb exploded and a gun battle ensued. Officer Hansen suffered severe wounds. The heroic officer was the seventh of eight officers to die in the historic incident.

HARRIS, ELIJAH, Evidence Technician, Badge 15208, Roll 401, November 16, 1989, District 6: Officer Elijah Harris was informed by citizens that a youth was firing gunshots in the neighborhood. Officer Harris located the suspect and conducted a protective search. As Officer Harris attempted to confiscate a gun tucked in the youth's waistband, the offender grabbed the weapon. A struggle ensued and the youth fired a shot, striking Officer Harris. The brave officer died as a result of his injuries.

HART, PETER M., Patrolman, Badge 1224, Roll 68, January 20, 1913, District 4: The Chicago Police Department received information on the residence of the leader of a notorious gang of armed robbers. Officer Peter Hart was assigned to hide in the offender's apartment and apprehend him. When the offender returned home, Officer Hart attempted to place him under arrest. A fierce struggle ensued, resulting in the dedicated officer sustaining a fatal gunshot wound.

HARTNETT JR., LAWRENCE C., Patrolman, Badge 3044, Roll 137, October 27, 1923, District 14: Officer Lawrence Hartnett was investigating an illegal liquor operation. Officer Hartnett developed information that an entire family was operating a distillery. As Officer Hartnett and fellow officers gathered in an alley in an attempt to make a raid, one of the offenders unexpectedly emerged from the building and began firing. Officer Hartnett was fatally wounded.

HASTINGS, JOSEPH, Patrolman, Badge 6384, Roll 250, August 14, 1933, District 18: While on patrol, Officer Joseph Hastings conducted routine checks of various businesses on his beat. Officer Hastings was confronted by five gunmen committing an armed robbery of an office. This office was being used to issue welfare payments to citizens stricken by the Great Depression. The offenders opened fire. The heroic officer was fatally wounded in the encounter.

HAUSER, GREGORY A., Police Officer, Badge 14680, Roll 402, May 13, 1990, District 25: Officer Gregory Hauser and his partner responded to a domestic disturbance between a woman and her grandson. As they talked to the grandson in a garage, he suddenly grabbed one of the officers' weapons. The offender then fired several shots inflicting fatal wounds on both Officer Hauser and his partner, Officer Raymond Kilroy. The two courageous officers, partners until the end, had joined the Department on the same day twenty years earlier.

HEALY, THOMAS J., Patrolman, Badge 5416, Roll 181, August 7, 1927, Unit 151: Officer Thomas Healy was approached by a citizen who offered to take him to an illegal gambling house. Officer Healy agreed, recognizing an opportunity to raid the house. Upon arrival at a secluded area, the citizen produced a revolver and announced a robbery. As Officer Healy resisted, he was shot twice. The courageous officer died five days later.

HELSTERN, GEORGE H., Patrolman, Badge 1124, Roll 290, September 2, 1945: While on patrol, Officer George Helstern and his partner observed a suspicious man standing on a corner. As Officer Helstern and his partner approached, the offender drew a revolver and began firing. The courageous officers were struck. Both Officer Helstern and his partner, Officer Charles Brady, were killed in the exchange.

HENNESSEY, WILLIAM E., Patrolman, Badge 2461, Roll 115, August 23, 1920, District 21: Officer William Hennessey and his partner were assigned to check on the conduct of patrons in a nightclub. When they arrived, an altercation ensued in which Officer Hennessey's partner was attacked by an offender. When Officer Hennessey rushed to his partner's aid, the offender began to fire a gun. Both Officer Hennessey and his partner, Officer James Mulcahy were fatally wounded.

HENRY, JAMES A., Patrolman, Badge 3275, Roll 164, December 1, 1925, District 21: Officer James Henry and his partner were inside a soft drink parlor during their tour of duty. While there, three armed robbers entered and immediately opened fire. Officer Henry suffered several gunshot wounds which proved to be fatal. His partner, Officer James Carroll, was also killed.

HICKS, WENDELL H., Patrolman, Badge 11561, Roll 363, March 29, 1973, District 5: Officer Wendell Hicks, while off duty, learned that there was an armed robbery taking place in a parking lot. The officer took immediate police action and rushed to the scene. Officer Hicks jumped in his car and pursued the offender who had stolen the victim's automobile. After chasing the offender into an alley, Officer Hicks courageously confronted the gunman. The offender opened fire, fatally striking the dedicated officer.

HOARD, WILLARD E., Patrolman, Badge 223, Roll 251, September 10, 1933, District 21: Officer Willard Hoard, while on motorcycle patrol, pursued a motorist exceeding the speed limit. While in pursuit, Officer Hoard's motorcycle was struck by an automobile that suddenly emerged from a parking lot. Officer Hoard died as a result of the injuries he suffered.

HOBSON, YOUNG C., Detective, Badge 11181, Roll 337, May 3, 1968, Unit 602: Detective Young Hobson observed an individual with a handgun in his waistband. Detective Hobson approached the man and a struggle ensued. The offender fired several shots, striking Detective Hobson. The brave detective died shortly after in a hospital.

HOLMES, WILLIAM, Patrolman, Badge 4042, Roll 151, December 24, 1924, District 21: While walking his beat on Christmas Eve, Officer William Holmes searched for two gunmen who had just robbed a citizen. As officer Holmes spotted the offenders on the street, he attempted to place them under arrest. However, one gunman resisted, displayed a revolver, and fired. The courageous officer was struck and fatally wounded.

HOSNA, JAMES L., Detective Sergeant, Badge 324, Roll 100, February 16, 1919, Unit 610: Detective Sergeant James Hosna, while conducting a robbery investigation, observed the wanted armed robber enter a drinking establishment. As the offender entered, Sergeant Hosna confronted him. The offender fired three shots before the sergeant had time to draw his revolver. Sergeant Hosna was struck and sustained multiple gunshot wounds. He died in a hospital the next day.

HUEBNER, JOHN, Patrolman, Badge 490, Roll 6, February 4, 1882, District 3: While walking his beat, Officer John Huebner responded to a pursuit of two armed burglars. Officer Huebner ran to an intersection and confronted the burglars. As Officer Huebner struggled with one burglar, the other fired several shots at close range. The brave officer died as a result of the multiple wounds he suffered.

HULTS, JESSE D., Patrolman, Badge 3629, Roll 204, September 26, 1929, District 14: Officer Jesse Hults and his partner were conducting an investigation into a reported kidnapping. During the course of their investigation, the officers relocated to a hallway outside an apartment. When they demanded entry, they were met with a burst of gunfire. Both Officer Jesse Hults and his partner, Officer William Gallagher, died as a result of the gunshot wounds they sustained.

ISAACS, JOSEPH V., Patrolman, Badge 5914, Roll 228, October 10, 1931, District 5: Officer Joseph Isaacs observed a disturbance in which three individuals were arguing. As one individual displayed a gun, Officer Isaacs drew his service revolver and intervened. A struggle ensued. During the struggle, one of the offenders gained control of Officer Isaacs' gun and fired. The brave officer was fatally wounded in the encounter.

ISOLA, JOSEPH, Patrolman, Badge 653, Roll 268, November 2, 1935, Unit 140: Officer Joseph Isola encountered an armed robber while on patrol. As Officer Isola attempted to make the arrest, the gunman fired a shot. Officer Isola was wounded in the encounter. The courageous officer died as a result of the injury he sustained.

JACKSON, ERWIN, Patrolman, Badge 12433, Roll 344, April 24, 1969, Unit 156: Officer Erwin Jackson courageously responded to a call of "man with a gun." Upon arrival, Officer Jackson observed the armed offender waving his gun at several citizens. After the gunman refused to drop his weapon, Officer Jackson and fellow officers attempted to disarm him. During the struggle, the gun discharged, striking Officer Jackson. The brave officer died as a result of the injuries he sustained.

JAGLA, LEONARD T., Patrolman, Badge 1151, Roll 193, September 4, 1928, District 23: Officer Leonard Jag, while detailed to the Detective Bureau, responded to a "robbery in progress" of a cigar store. As Officer Jag arrived, the three offenders were attempting to escape by running out the back door and firing their guns. The brave officer sustained multiple gunshot wounds that resulted in his death.

JOHNSON, BROR A., Patrolman, Badge 242, Roll 81, January 21, 1916, District 1: Officer Bror Johnson, while directing traffic near a downtown intersection, was alerted to a robbery taking place in a nearby

business. When the armed robber emerged, the courageous officer was waiting for him. The gunman fired two shots at Officer Johnson, striking and killing him.

JOHNSON, THOMAS J., Patrolman, Badge 387, Roll 226, June 22, 1931, District 21: Officer Thomas Johnson was assigned to patrol the city's parks on a motorcycle. While covering his beat, the officer's motorcycle was struck by an automobile. Officer Johnson was thrown from his motorcycle. The severe injuries suffered by the dedicated officer were fatal.

JOHNSON, WILLIAM R., Detective, Badge 6996, Roll 326, November 18, 1960, Unit 610: Detective William Johnson monitored an emergency call and proceeded to the scene. While en route, Detective Johnson's vehicle was struck broadside by another automobile. The brave detective was thrown from his car, resulting in multiple and fatal injuries.

JOHNSTON, ROSCOE C., Patrolman, Badge 3227, Roll 241, March 21, 1933, District 2: Officer Roscoe Johnston observed three armed robbers enter the office of a bakery. As the offenders attempted to rob the bakery, Officer Johnston emerged. A gun battle ensued, in which the brave officer was fatally wounded by a shotgun blast.

JONES, CHARLES T., Patrolman, Badge 3594, Roll 67, November 10, 1912, District 16: Officer Charles Jones and his partner attempted to arrest offenders wanted for committing several assaults on citizens. The offenders fled and barricaded themselves inside a shed. When the officers made a forced entry, they were brutally attacked. Officer Jones was severely beaten and shot several times. The courageous officer died as a result of the injuries he sustained.

JONES JR., EDDIE N., Police Officer, Badge 11120, Roll 405, January 7, 1991, District 10: Officer Eddie Jones and his partner conducted a narcotics investigation. After making the arrest, the offender stated that he would lead Officer Jones and his partner to his drug source. The informant, in the back seat of the police vehicle, suddenly drew a concealed weapon and fired. Officer Jones and his partner were both wounded. Officer Jones died as a result of his injuries.

KANER, KENNETH G., Patrolman, Badge 2662, Roll 352, June 19, 1970, District 7: Officer Kenneth Kaner sat in his squad car writing a police report. Suddenly, Officer Kaner was attacked by five offenders armed with sawed-off shotguns. The dedicated officer died as a result of his injuries.

KEATING, DAVID F., Patrolman 2259, Roll 298, September 20, 1949, District 9: While on patrol, Officer David Keating observed two youths carrying a suspicious package. As Officer Keating approached to investigate, one of the youths pulled a revolver from the package and fired. The courageous officer was struck and fatally wounded. It was later discovered that the package also contained a shotgun.

KEEFE, JAMES J., Patrolman, Badge 1620, Roll 49, January 5, 1905, District 14: Officer James Keefe, while on patrol, was assigned to apprehend two armed robbers. Officer Keefe and a team of officers relocated to the offenders' apartment to make the arrests. Upon their arrival, an exchange of gunfire ensued. During the exchange, Officer Keefe was fatally wounded.

KEEGAN, EUGENE J., Patrolman, Badge 571, Roll 184, February 9, 1928, District 1: Officer Eugene Keegan and his partner, while conducting an extensive murder investigation, located the offender at an apartment. The courageous officers went to the apartment to arrest the dangerous offender. Upon arrival, the gunman resisted and fired a barrage of bullets. Both Officer Keegan and his partner, Lieutenant Edward Murphy, sustained multiple and fatal wounds.

KEEGAN, JOHN, Patrolman, Badge 768, Roll 20, November 4, 1887, District 2: Officer John Keegan walked his beat, serving and protecting the citizens of the community. Every hour the dedicated officer made his report to the station from a patrol box, confirming that all was well. Abruptly, the calls stopped coming. Hours later, Officer Keegan was found with a fatal gunshot wound. The murder remains a mystery.

KEHOE, THOMAS W., Sergeant, Badge 900, Roll 179, June 23, 1927, District 16: Sergeant Thomas Kehoe and his partner were investigating an armed robbery in which the offender forcibly took a citizen's automobile. The officers canvassed the neighborhood and alertly noticed the gunman in the stolen car. When Sergeant Kehoe and his partner courageously attempted to make an arrest, an intense gun battle ensued in which both Sergeant Kehoe and his partner, Officer James Farley, were fatally wounded.

KELLIHER, LYONS, Patrolman, Badge 6695, Roll 312, January 25, 1956, District 11: Officer Lyons Kelliher, while conducting a narcotics investigation, entered a hotel tavern. During the investigation, Officer Kelliher approached a suspicious man, announced his office, and searched the man for concealed weapons. As Officer Kelliher conducted the search, the offender suddenly drew a revolver from his waistband and fired at the officer. The brave officer sustained a fatal gunshot wound.

KELLY, PHILIP J., Patrolman, Badge 6161, Roll 280, May 10, 1939, District 23: Officer Philip Kelly observed two armed offenders enter a lounge and announce a robbery. Officer Kelly confronted the offenders and an intense gun battle ensued. The heroic officer suffered a serious gunshot wound which later proved to be fatal.

KELLY, RAYMOND C., Patrolman, Badge 5396, Roll 234, April 3, 1932, District 2: Officer Raymond Kelly responded to a disturbance where a man had killed his wife and wounded another citizen. When Officer Kelly arrived, the offender opened fire. Officer Kelly suffered serious wounds. After being rushed to the hospital, the courageous officer died as a result of his injuries.

KELLY, THOMAS J., Patrolman, Badge 12145, Roll 350, March 3, 1970, Unit 53: Officer Thomas Kelly stopped a suspicious automobile. When the courageous officer walked from his squad car to question the two occupants, he was suddenly fired upon by the driver. Officer Kelly was shot and died as a result of his injuries.

KELMA, THOMAS, Patrolman, Badge 427, Roll 265, May 31,1935, District 12: Officer Thomas Kelma observed two armed robbers enter a lounge. As Officer Kelma intervened, a struggle ensued. The gunmen fired at the officer and fled. The brave officer died as a result of his injuries.

KILROY, RAYMOND C., Police Officer, Badge 14686, Roll 403, May 13, 1990, District 25: Officer Raymond Kilroy responded to a domestic disturbance with his partner. The officers entered a garage to talk to a young man who was having a domestic dispute with his grandmother. The offender suddenly grabbed one of the officers' revolvers and began firing. Both Officer Kilroy and his partner, Officer Gregory Hauser, suffered fatal wounds. The two courageous officers, partners until the end, had joined the Department on the same day twenty years earlier.

KING, WAYNE G., Detective, Badge 7413, Roll 393, July 12, 1985, Unit 140: Detective Wayne King, while conducting an investigation of offenders impersonating police officers and city building inspectors, noticed a suspicious man standing nearby. Upon Detective King's approach, the man fled. Detective King apprehended the man after a short chase. A struggle ensued, during which the offender gained possession of the officer's gun and fired. The brave detective was fatally shot.

KING, WILLIAM R., Patrolman, Badge 417, Roll 113, May 25, 1920, District 21: Officer William King responded to a call of a man causing a disturbance on a street car. Upon arriving at the scene, Officer King removed the man from the street car. Shortly thereafter, the offender approached Officer King from behind and fired a fatal shot at the officer.

KLACZA, WAYNE J., Police Officer, Badge 16469, Roll 389, June 28, 1983, Unit 157: Officer Wayne Klacza observed an automobile being driven erratically by an intoxicated motorist. As Officer Klacza attempted to protect a pedestrian from the motorist, the car swerved and struck the courageous officer. Officer Klacza's injuries were fatal.

KLINKE, BERNARD B., Patrolman, Badge 229, Roll 275, February 22, 1937, Unit 140: Officer Bernard Klinke, while patrolling his beat, was tragically struck by an automobile. Officer Klinke sustained severe injuries which resulted in his death.

KLOCEK, JOSEPH, Patrolman, Badge 400, Roll 267, October 8, 1935, Unit 140: Officer Joseph Klocek was assigned to motorcycle patrol. While covering his beat, Officer Klocek was involved in an accident. Officer Klocek sustained serious injuries, which resulted in his death.

KNIGHT, JOHN C., Police Officer, Badge 5119, Roll 415, January 9, 1999, District 22: Officer John Knight observed two suspicious men in a parked car. As Officer Knight approached, the offenders sped away. After crashing into a parked car, the offenders fled on foot in different directions. The courageous officer, still in his squad car, continued in pursuit of one offender. Suddenly, the offender turned, produced a semi-automatic weapon with a laser sight, and fired through the window of Officer Knight's vehicle. The brave officer was fatally wounded.

KNUDSON, MARTIN, Patrolman, Badge 1457, Roll 232, February 5, 1932, District 15: Officer Martin Knudson was detailed to guard cash collections being taken at a newspaper garage. Three armed offenders entered and announced a holdup. In an attempt to foil the robbery, Officer Knudson drew his revolver. A gun battle ensued, in which the courageous officer was fatally wounded.

KOUMOUNDOUROS, JAMES, Police Officer, Badge 4514, Roll 378, September 7, 1977, District 17: Officer James Koumoundouros, while working security at a Chicago bank, observed an armed offender walk in. The offender immediately pointed a gun at Officer Koumoundouros. While discreetly pushing the bank alarm button, Officer Koumoundouros calmly talked to the gunman. The courageous officer then quickly drew his revolver and shot the robber. The gunman, however, returned fire, fatally striking the dedicated officer.

KRAATZ, CHARLES C., Patrolman, Badge 5702, Roll 304, May 8, 1953, District 21: Officer Charles Kraatz responded to a call of "man with a gun." Upon arriving at the scene, Officer Kraatz discovered an armed man threatening a crowd of citizens at an intersection. As Officer Kraatz courageously confronted the gunman, the offender fired three shots at the officer, seriously wounding him. The brave officer died as a result of the injuries he sustained.

KRUM, GEORGE, Patrolman, Badge 1452, Roll 30, November 1, 1894, District 12: Officer George Krum, while on his beat, responded to a disturbance at an apartment building during a Halloween party. While Officer Krum attempted to settle the dispute, a gunman stepped forward and fired a shot at the officer. Despite being shot three times, Officer Krum was able to return fire and kill the gunman. The courageous officer died from his wounds.

KUEBLER, BERNARD A., Patrolman, Badge 238, Roll 35, October 8, 1898, District 2: Officer Bernard Kuebler, while on foot patrol, investigated a burglary that had occurred on his beat. During the course of his investigation, Officer Kuebler observed two suspicious men fitting the description of the burglars. As Officer Kuebler approached, he was shot. The brave officer died as a result of the injuries he sustained.

KURTZ, JOSEPH, Patrolman, Badge 2711, Roll 124, June 7, 1921, District 9: Officer Joseph Kurtz and his partner responded to the scene of a "battery in progress" with two offenders. As Officer Kurtz attempted to subdue one offender, his partner struggled with the other. During the struggle, the second offender gained control of the partner's gun and fired, fatally striking Officer Kurtz. The brave officer died on the way to the hospital.

LANGAN, MICHAEL T., Patrolman, Badge 4860, Roll 207, December 30, 1929, District 19: Officer Michael Langan was inside a soft drink parlor when he observed several men enter. The men then drew revolvers and announced a robbery. As Officer Langan confronted the robbers, they opened fire. Officer Langan was fatally wounded.

LARSEN, CHARLES C.P., Patrolman, Badge 4830, Roll 87, May 13, 1917, District 16: Officer Charles Larsen was walking his beat when he observed two men breaking into the basement of a theater. Officer Larsen confronted the offenders and was immediately shot. Although wounded, the courageous officer continued the pursuit of the offenders. Upon confronting the offenders again, an exchange of gunfire ensued and Officer Larsen sustained additional and fatal wounds.

LAUER, CASPER, Patrolman, Roll A1, September 18, 1854: Officer Casper Lauer had located and detained a man that had been wanted for a domestic abuse case involving the man's elderly parents. While guarding his prisoner until he could be taken to the police station, a struggle ensued and the brave officer was fatally stabbed by the man he had arrested.

LEACH, EDWARD, Patrolman, Badge 2766, Roll 37, February 10, 1899, District 5: Officer Edward Leach was tragically shot during an altercation. The altercation occurred while Officer Leach was off duty. Officer Leach died as a result of the injuries he sustained in the shooting.

LEMONS, OTHA, Sergeant, Badge 1048, Roll 371, August 5, 1974, District 5: Sergeant Otha LeMons observed three armed offenders enter a lounge and announce a robbery. As Sergeant LeMons attempted to prevent the crime, one of the gunmen fired his weapon. Sergeant LeMons was fatally wounded.

LENEHAN, BERNARD J., Detective Sergeant, Badge 536, Roll 108, October 5, 1919, District 8: Sergeant Bernard Lenehan and Sergeant George Burns were conducting a liquor investigation. During their investigation, two armed gunmen entered and announced a robbery. The robbers immediately began shooting once they recognized Sergeant Lenehan and his partner. During an exchange of gunfire, Sergeant Lenehan and Sergeant George Burns were fatally shot.

LEONARD, EARL K., Patrolman, Badge 4558, Roll 201, June 9, 1929, District 11: Officer Earl Leonard, while assigned to motorcycle patrol, arrested a motorist for a traffic violation. While Officer Leonard was conducting the arrest, a friend of the offender approached and shot the officer. The dedicated officer died from his injuries.

LILLY, WALTER E., Patrolman, Badge 5615, Roll 186, February 28, 1928, District 9: Officer Walter Lilly, while off duty and parking in his garage, was accosted by two armed offenders announcing a robbery. As Officer Lilly attempted to draw his service revolver, he was fatally shot by one of the offenders.

LITTLETON, DEWEY L., Detective, Badge 6884, Roll 297, August 14, 1947, Unit 640: Detective Dewey Littleton responded to a call to arrest an offender wanted for shooting his wife. As Detective Littleton and fellow officers ascended the staircase, the offender opened fire. In the exchange of gunfire between the police and the gunman, the brave detective was tragically struck and killed.

LOCASHIO, THOMAS, Patrolman, Badge 184, Roll 214, September 9, 1930, District 18: Officer Thomas Locashio was assigned to motorcycle patrol in Lincoln Park. While covering his beat, Officer Locashio was tragically thrown from his motorcycle in a serious accident. The dedicated officer suffered serious injuries which resulted in his death.

LOFTUS, TERRENCE E., Patrolman, Badge 5701, Roll 376, October 12, 1976, District 14: Officer Terrence Loftus was on his way home when he observed a gang fight. Officer Loftus immediately stopped to take police action. While Officer Loftus was attempting to break up the street disturbance, shots were fired. The dedicated officer was struck and died as a result of his injuries.

LOONEY, JAMES F., Patrolman, Badge 821, Roll 96, May 1, 1918, District 3: Officer James Looney observed two men enter a lounge with drawn revolvers and announce a robbery. Officer Looney took immediate action. The gunmen fired, striking the courageous officer. Officer Looney died as a result of the gunshot wound that he sustained during the incident.

LOVE, ROBERT M., Patrolman, Badge 80, Roll 101, April 9, 1919, Unit 140: Officer Robert Love was investigating a disturbance at a local park. Upon arriving at the scene, a subject fled from Officer Love. Officer Love immediately pursued the subject. During this foot pursuit, the dedicated officer was tragically struck by a passing train. Officer Love died as a result of his injuries.

LUCEY, JEREMIAH C., Patrolman, Badge 1831, Roll 306, February 7, 1954, District 14: Officer Jeremiah Lucey and his partner arrested an offender for assault. During the arrest, the offender grabbed a concealed revolver and fired at Officer Lucey and his partner. Both officers were struck. Officer Lucey and his partner, Officer Roman Steinke, were fatally wounded.

LUKASZEWSKI, MICHAEL, Patrolman, Badge 7165, Roll 317, June 30, 1957, District 18: Officer Michael Lukaszewski and other officers processed four prisoners in the lockup. As Officer Lukaszewski completed the paperwork, one of the prisoners rushed toward him and grabbed his service revolver. As they struggled over the gun, the offender pulled the trigger. The bullet struck the courageous officer. Officer Lukaszewski was rushed to the hospital, where he died of his wounds approximately four hours later.

LUNDY, WILLIAM D., Patrolman, Badge 2179, Roll 239, December 9, 1932, District 9: Officer William Lundy observed two armed robbers enter a grocery store. While Officer Lundy attempted to place the offenders under arrest, both gunmen opened fire. The heroic officer was fatally wounded in the exchange.

LUTKE, STANLEY J., Patrolman, Badge 6510, Roll 243, April 30, 1933, District 20: Officer Stanley Lutke, while on foot patrol, observed a disturbance in a cigar store. As he ran to investigate, an armed robber emerged from the store and began firing his weapon at Officer Lutke. A gun battle ensued. When Officer Lutke pursued the fleeing robber, a second offender emerged and fired at the officer. The courageous officer was struck and died as a result of his injuries.

LYNCH, MICHAEL, Patrolman, Badge 5343, Roll 195, December 8, 1928, District 21: Officer Michael Lynch was detailed to a grocery store. While at the store, two armed offenders entered and announced a robbery. As Officer Lynch confronted the gunmen, one of the robbers turned with a revolver and fired several shots. The dedicated officer was struck and died a short time later.

LYNN, EDWARD J., Patrolman, Badge 132, Roll 279, November 30, 1938, District 11: While on patrol, Officer Edward Lynn responded to a disturbance in a tavern. Upon his arrival, Officer Lynn was informed that a patron was carrying a concealed revolver. As Officer Lynn approached, the patron abruptly pulled out a revolver and began firing. It was later learned that the patron was an escaped convict. The courageous officer suffered fatal gunshot wounds during the encounter.

LYONS, TERRENCE, Sergeant, Badge 11, Roll 131, May 10, 1922, Unit 140: Sergeant Terrence Lyons was assigned to patrol in and around the city's parks. While on patrol, Sergeant Lyons observed three suspicious men in an automobile. As Sergeant Lyons confronted the men, he was shot and fatally wounded. It is believed that the offenders were the same men who had murdered Officer Thomas Clark half an hour earlier.

MADDEN, EDWARD M., Investigator, Badge 7711, Roll 361, October 2, 1972, Unit 630: Investigator Edward Madden searched for an offender who had escaped from custody using a revolver previously stolen from another officer. After receiving a tip, Investigator Madden searched the hallway of an apartment building. As another officer arrived to search the same area, he mistook Investigator Madden for the armed offender and tragically fired his weapon. Investigator Madden was fatally wounded.

MADDEN, PATRICK, Patrolman, Badge 3540, Roll 238, November 20, 1932, District 13: Officer Patrick Madden, while responding to reports of gunfire, was approached by a citizen who identified the shooter on the street. While Officer Madden attempted to make the arrest, the offender suddenly pulled out a weapon and fatally shot the dedicated officer.

MADIGAN, MICHAEL A., Patrolman, Badge 5347, Roll 168, June 18, 1926, District 6: Officer Michael Madigan was conducting a liquor inspection inside a soft drink parlor during the days of Prohibition. As Officer Madigan searched for illegal alcohol in a cupboard behind the bar, the bartender pulled out a revolver and fired. Officer Madigan was seriously wounded and later died in a hospital.

MAHER, JOHN F., Patrolman, Badge 215, Roll 84, October 7, 1916, District 21: Officer John Maher was assigned to motorcycle patrol. The officer's primary responsibility was to enforce traffic rules and regulations. While attempting a traffic stop, Officer Maher pursued a speeding motorist. Tragically, Officer Maher lost control of his motorcycle, crashing it into an automobile at an intersection. The dedicated officer died as a result of his injuries.

MAHONEY, TIMOTHY, Patrolman, Badge 230, Roll 3, June 12, 1881, District 2: Officer Timothy Mahoney was alerted by a citizen that two burglary offenders were standing nearby. Officer Mahoney confronted the two men, but was fatally shot when one of the offenders was able to draw a gun and quickly fire two shots.

MANDLECO, HENRY A., Patrolman, Badge 1403, Roll 102, April 23, 1919, District 5: Officer Henry Mandleco, while on foot patrol, observed two suspicious men in a truck containing stolen cargo. As Officer Mandleco approached to question them, one of the men produced a revolver and fired. Officer Mandleco was struck and died instantly.

MARCUSSON, MAURICE, Patrolman, Badge 1865, Roll 240, January 23, 1933, District 5: Officer Maurice Marcusson was inside a loan office when he was approached by a citizen. The citizen stated that three suspicious men were in the corridor. Officer Marcusson approached the men, announced his office, and questioned them. At this time, the three offenders drew revolvers and began firing. The brave officer returned fire, but suffered fatal wounds in the exchange.

MARPOOL, EDWARD W., Sergeant, Badge 618, Roll 117, October 26, 1920, District 11: Sergeant Edward Marpool responded to a citizen complaint of two men with guns. Upon seeing two suspicious men near an alley, Sergeant Marpool approached to investigate. One of the men suddenly drew a revolver and fired, striking Sergeant Marpool. The courageous sergeant died as a result of his injuries.

MARSEK, WILLIAM C., Patrolman, Badge 14086, Roll 369, February 27, 1974, Unit 153: Officer William Marsek and his partner observed a suspicious man emerge from a tavern. The man walked to his car, observed the officers, and re-entered the tavern. As Officer Marsek and his partner investigated, they noticed a sawed-off shotgun near the man's car. As they entered the tavern, the offender drew a pistol and fired several shots. Both Officer Marsek and his partner, Officer Bruce Garrison, were fatally wounded.

MARTIN, JOHNNY L., Police Officer, Badge 16576, Roll 404, June 28, 1990, District 13: Officer Johnny Martin was approached by a neighbor seeking help in resolving a dispute. As Officer Martin entered an alley, he was confronted by an armed offender. The gunman fired, fatally wounding the dedicated officer.

MARTIN, RAYMOND E., Patrolman, Badge 2313, Roll 197, May 15, 1929, District 25: Officer Raymond Martin volunteered to act as a decoy in a kidnapping plot. Four armed offenders arrived at an intersection to make the arrangements for the kidnapping. Tragically, the offenders realized the police plan and turned on Officer Martin. The courageous officer was shot and killed.

MASHEK, EDWARD F., Patrolman Officer, Badge 3975, Roll 166, April 8, 1926, District 10: Officer Edward Mashek observed three armed offenders attempting to rob a store owner. Officer Mashek confronted the offenders and was able to prevent the robbery. However, Officer Mashek suffered a serious gunshot wound. The brave officer died as a result of his injury.

MATHEWS, JOHN W., Police Officer, Badge 9827, Roll 399, May 21, 1988, District 4: Officer John Mathews was returning home and was confronted by five offenders. All five offenders brutally attacked Officer Mathews. The brave officer died later from his injuries.

MATONICH, JOHN J., Patrolman, Badge 5760, Roll 356, October 16, 1970, Unit 153: Officer John Matonich was assigned to traffic and crowd control. During the course of his duties, Officer Matonich was confronted by an armed robbery offender. During an exchange of gunfire, the brave officer sustained a serious injury and died soon afterward.

MCANENEY, ROBERT, Patrolman, Badge 1412, Roll 55, November 16, 1907, District 5: Officer Robert McAneney was confronted by an armed offender while walking home from work. The gunman fired two shots and Officer McAneney was fatally struck. Investigators believe that Officer McAneney was killed by an ex-convict who had been sent to prison as a result of his police work.

MCCANN, WILLIAM I., Patrolman, Badge 34, Roll 215, September 16, 1930, District 22: Officer William McCann, while responding to a burglary in progress, was tragically shot and killed by a citizen. In the confusion of the burglary, the frightened citizen mistook Officer McCann for the perpetrator and fired a shot, striking and killing him.

MCCAULEY, JEROME J., Patrolman, Badge 6700, Roll 270, May 29, 1936, Unit 151: Officer Jerome McCauley, while on patrol, observed five wanted robbers. A car chase ensued, followed by an intense gun battle. During the exchange, the dedicated officer sustained a fatal gunshot wound.

MCCAW, MARTIN C., Patrolman, Badge 6991, Roll 284, April 27, 1942, District 12: Officer Martin McCaw discovered two intoxicated men creating a disturbance in a vacant lot. When the officer approached, the offenders attacked the officer, resulting in a fierce struggle. Officer McCaw' partner heard the commotion and rushed to assist him. During the struggle, Officer McCaw was tragically shot and killed.

MCCORMICK, DONALD E., Patrolman, Badge 7330, Roll 301, July 14, 1950, Unit 630: Officer Donald McCormick and his partner attempted to arrest a wanted armed robber. During the arrest, the offender was able to retrieve a revolver and fire several shots at the officers. Both Officer McCormick and his partner, Officer Edward Crowley, were shot and killed during the incident.

MCDERMOTT, JOHN F., Patrolman, Badge 1885, Roll 38, April 11, 1900, District 13: Officer John McDermott died as a result of an accidental discharge of his firearm following a tragic accident at his home.

MCDOWELL, HENRY, Patrolman, Badge 1609, Roll 28, September 7, 1892, District 11: Officer Henry McDowell was one of several officers who conducted a raid on an illegal racetrack. The racetrack owner resisted, and while escaping, murdered Officer John Powell. Officer McDowell caught up with the killer and ordered him to drop his weapon. The gunman refused and a gun battle ensued. During the exchange of gunfire, Officer McDowell was able to kill the gunman. However, the brave officer was also fatally wounded.

MCDOWELL, JAMES, Patrolman, Badge 763, Roll 23, October 3, 1889, District 3: Officer James McDowell responded to a tavern to assist a citizen. After talking to the citizen, he suddenly pulled out a revolver and shot Officer McDowell. Though wounded, Officer McDowell was able to assist in subduing the offender. The wound suffered by the courageous officer proved to be fatal.

MCGLYNN, FRANK C., Patrolman, Badge 2229, Roll 142, July 18, 1924, District 6: Officer Frank McGlynn was assigned to escort a messenger carrying a company payroll to an office building. Unknown to Officer McGlynn, three offenders had subdued the office staff and were awaiting the arrival of the payroll. As Officer McGlynn and the messenger entered, the gunmen fired at the officer. The brave officer suffered fatal gunshot wounds.

MCGOUGH, MICHAEL, Patrolman, Badge 2982, Roll 94, December 7, 1917, District 9: While on patrol, Officer Michael McGough apprehended an offender stealing coal from a railroad yard. The thief resisted arrest and fired a revolver at Officer McGough. The wound proved fatal and the dedicated officer died six days later.

MCGOVERN, PATRICK J., Patrolman, Badge 4336, Roll 158, June 22, 1925, District 25: Officer Patrick McGovern was assigned to escort a theater employee carrying cash receipts to a bank. Officer McGovern was unaware that three armed offenders waited in a nearby parked automobile. As Officer McGovern and the citizen passed by, the offenders jumped from the car and opened fire. The brave officer died soon after of multiple gunshot wounds.

MCGUIRE, EDWARD J., Patrolman, Badge 1513, Roll 185, February 24, 1928, District 2: Officer Edward McGuire responded to the scene of an intoxicated man armed with an automatic pistol and threatening citizens. As Officer McGuire confronted the gunman and attempted to place him under arrest, the offender opened fire. During the exchange of gunfire, Officer McGuire was fatally wounded.

MCGURK, FRANK J., Detective Sergeant, Badge 557, Roll 114, august 3, 1920, Unit 610: Sergeant Frank McGurk was assigned to guard a factory payroll. As the payroll was distributed, three masked armed robbers entered. When Sergeant McGurk confronted the offenders, the gunmen fired. Although fatally wounded, the heroic sergeant was able to return fire and cause the gunmen to flee without the payroll.

MCMIKEL JR., HAMP T., Sergeant, Badge 1541, Roll 387, November 20, 1982, District 5: Sergeant Hamp McMikel stopped to make a phone call from a public phone. He was approached by two armed robbers, one of whom was wielding a shotgun. A gun battle ensued, in which Sergeant McMikel was fatally struck.

MEISTER, HARL G., Patrolman, Badge 10054, Roll 372, December 23, 1974, District 10: Officer Harl Meister was shopping with his young son and returned to his car in the parking lot. At this time, Officer Meister was confronted by two armed robbers. As Officer Meister dropped his packages and reached for his gun, one offender fired his weapon. The brave officer was fatally struck.

MELIA, PATRICK, Patrolman, Badge 2243, Roll 61, April 27, 1910, District 8: While patrolling a railroad yard in the early morning hours, Officer Patrick Melia encountered offenders stealing merchandise from the train cars. One of the offenders raised a sawed-off, double-barreled shotgun from under his coat and fired, striking Officer Melia. The courageous officer was fatally wounded.

MELLODY, PETER, Patrolman, Badge 1334, Roll 148, November 27, 1924, District 21: Officer Peter Mellody became involved in a struggle with a man on the street. As Officer Mellody attempted to subdue the man, the man displayed a pistol and fired. Officer Mellody was struck and fatally wounded.

MESSANGER, WILLIAM F., Patrolman, Badge 71, Roll 40, April 25, 1901, District 21: Officer William Messanger, while inside the police station, was approached by an individual whom he had questioned earlier that day. The individual created a disturbance in the station. When Officer Messanger ordered him to leave, the offender drew a revolver and began firing. A gun battle ensued, during which the heroic officer was fatally wounded.

MILLER, GEORGE F., Patrolman, Badge 551, Roll 12, May 6, 1886, District 3: On May 4, 1886, Officer George Miller was assigned to a protest meeting in Haymarket Square. A bomb was thrown by an unknown offender. The explosion was followed by an intense gun battle. Officer Miller was seriously injured and died two days later. He was the third of eight officers killed in the historic Haymarket Tragedy.

MITCHELL, JAMES E., Patrolman, Badge 9840, Roll 316, April 14, 1957, District 22: Officer James Mitchell was engaged in a fierce struggle with an armed offender. During the violent struggle, Officer Mitchell was shot. The brave officer died as a result of the injuries he sustained.

MITCHELL, JAMES F., Probationary Patrolman, Badge 2949, Roll 78, November 17, 1915, District 5: Officer James Mitchell observed four suspicious men on the street. As Officer Mitchell questioned them and began a protective search for possible weapons, one of the men attempted to flee. As he fled, he drew a revolver and fired, striking Officer Mitchell. The heroic officer was transported to a nearby hospital, where he died several hours later.

MONAHAN, JOHN, Patrolman, Badge 3179, Roll 32, January 27, 1895, District 9: Officer John Monahan, while working his regular beat, was tragically killed when he was crushed between a street car and a wall.

MOONEY, WILLIAM R., Patrolman, Badge 2590, Roll 56, January 4, 1908, District 11: Officer William Mooney, while conducting a burglary investigation, observed three suspicious men near a building. As Officer Mooney approached, one offender pulled out a revolver and fired. Officer Mooney was struck as fellow officers engaged in a gun battle with the three offenders. The brave officer was taken to the hospital by concerned citizens, but died two days later.

MORRISON JR., WILLIAM, Police Officer, Badge 9593, Roll 397, September 4, 1987, District 16: While working special employment for Public Housing North, Officer William Morrison learned of a man with a shotgun in the area. Accompanied by other officers, Officer Morrison responded to the scene. Suddenly, his police vehicle was struck broadside by a speeding vehicle. The violent impact resulted in the officers death.

MUDLOFF, FRED, Patrolman, Badge 186, Roll 205, October 6, 1929, District 18: Officer Fred Mudloff was assigned to motorcycle patrol in Lincoln Park. While on his beat, Officer Mudloff lost control of his motorcycle and was involved in an accident. The dedicated officer suffered serious injuries and died as a result of the accident.

MULCAHY, JAMES A., Patrolman, Badge 536, Roll 116, August 23, 1920, District 21: Officer James Mulcahy and his partner were assigned to check on a nightclub. Upon their arrival, an offender approached and attacked Officer Mulcahy. When Officer Mulcahy's partner, Officer William Hennessey ran to his aid, the offender shot and killed both officers.

MULLEN, JOHN J., Patrolman, Badge 4275, Roll 121, January 3, 1921, District 13: Officer John Mullen responded to a disturbance of intoxicated men in a cafe. Officer Mullen placed one offender under arrest for threatening a patron with a gun. The second offender approached Officer Mullen from behind and shot the brave officer. Officer Mullen died two days later.

MULVIHILL, EDWARD J., Patrolman, Badge 2432, Roll 86, December 18, 1916, District 14: Officer Edward Mulvihill was fatally shot attempting to intervene when he observed a man stalking a young woman. Officer Mulvihill observed the man accost the woman on the street. A foot chase ensued, and the offender fired a shot, striking the dedicated officer. The gunman then returned to the fallen officer and fired the fatal shot.

MURPHY, EDWARD T., Lieutenant, Badge -Lt-, Roll 183, February 9, 1928, Unit 650: Lieutenant Edward Murphy and his partner were conducting a search for an offender wanted for two homicides. After learning that the murderer had fled to his brother's apartment, they went there to make the arrest of the dangerous offender. The offender resisted and fired a barrage of bullets. Both Lieutenant Murphy and his partner, Officer Eugene Keegan, sustained multiple and fatal gunshot wounds.

MURPHY, JERRY E., Patrolman, Badge 4447, Roll 208, January 14, 1930, District 11: Officer Jerry Murphy, while on patrol, observed three individuals committing a burglary. When Officer Murphy placed the burglars under arrest, they resisted. The burglars drew revolvers and fired several times. The brave officer was fatally wounded.

MURPHY, THOMAS, Patrolman, Badge 2533, Roll 254, February 1, 1934, District 9: Officer Thomas Murphy was assigned to patrol a coal company in an area experiencing a pattern of robberies. He observed an armed offender enter and announce a robbery. Officer Murphy confronted the robber and engaged in a gun battle. Suddenly, a bullet was fired through the window by another offender standing outside, striking Officer Murphy. The courageous officer died from his wounds.

MURPHY, WILLIAM B., Patrolman, Badge 867, Roll 299, April 25, 1950, District 21: While on his way home after completing his tour of duty, Officer William Murphy observed an armed robbery in progress inside a liquor store. As Officer Murphy entered and attempted to make the arrest, an intense gun battle ensued. Officer Murphy suffered multiple gunshot wounds and was severely beaten. The courageous officer died as a result of his injuries.

MURPHY, WILLIAM J., Patrolman, Badge 7438, Roll 311, August 15, 1955, Unit 610: Officer William Murphy, while assigned to Robbery Detail, searched for a known armed robber. The offender was wanted for a series of grocery store and tavern robberies. Officer Murphy located the offender in a subway station and attempted to place the offender under arrest. However, the robber quickly drew a revolver and fired one shot. The courageous officer was fatally wounded.

MURTAUGH, MICHAEL, Patrolman, Badge 2565, Roll 146, October 11, 1924, District 9: While on patrol, Officer Michael Murtaugh observed a disturbance on the street. Upon further investigation, he discovered that three offenders had just robbed a dry goods store. When Officer Murtaugh confronted the offenders, they attempted to escape in an automobile. As the offenders fled, they began to fire their weapons at the officer, fatally wounding Officer Murtaugh.

MUTTER, ARTHUR D., Patrolman, Badge 1000, Roll 242, April 18, 1933, District 6: Officer Arthur Mutter observed three armed robbers inside a restaurant. One offender was armed with a machine gun. Officer Mutter struggled with the three offenders, attempting to gain control of the machine gun. In the altercation, one of the offenders fired two shots. The courageous officer was struck and killed.

NEIL, GEORGE, Patrolman, Badge 5166, Roll 212, May 22, 1930, District 9: Officer George Neil was having dinner at a local diner. While there, four offenders entered and accosted an African-American patron, demanding that he get off his stool. When Officer Neil confronted the offenders, the four men attacked him. A fight for Officer Neil's service revolver ensued. During the struggle, one of the offenders was able to gain possession of the gun and fire several shots. The courageous officer was fatally wounded and died days later.

O'BRIEN, JAMES J., Patrolman, Badge 1544, Roll 194, September 16, 1928, District 7: While on patrol, Officer James O'Brien observed a wanted auto thief at an intersection. As Officer O'Brien attempted to make the arrest, the thief produced a revolver and fired several shots. The brave officer was fatally wounded.

O'BRIEN, MICHAEL, Patrolman, Badge 216, Roll 17, April 3, 1887, District 2: Officer Michael O'Brien and his partner dispersed a crowd causing a disturbance behind a tavern. During a search for concealed weapons, one of the men resisted and made his escape. Shortly thereafter, Officer O'Brien and his partner observed the offender walking down the alley. After ignoring an order to halt, the gunman fired one shot, striking Officer O'Brien. The dedicated officer died from his injuries.

O'BRIEN, MICHAEL W., Patrolman, Badge 389, Roll 9, November 11, 1885, District 3: Officer Michael O'Brien heard the sound of gunfire and proceeded to the scene to investigate. Officer O'Brien discovered that a distraught businessman had fired the weapon inside of a store. Upon seeing the officer, the offender placed the gun against the officer's chest and fired. The heroic officer died an hour later.

O'BRIEN, PATRICK M., Patrolman, Badge 188, Roll 4, August 3, 1881, District 3: Officer Patrick O'Brien attempted to assist in the arrest of an offender who shot a citizen. The offender had barricaded himself inside his house. After Officer O'Brien demanded entry, the offender fired a revolver through a crack in the door. The brave officer was struck and died two days later.

O'BRIEN, RICHARD J., Police Officer, Badge 5337, Roll 384, February 9, 1982, Unit 156: Officer Richard O'Brien and his partner stopped a vehicle for a traffic violation. A fierce struggle ensued during which one of the offenders, gained control of Officer O'Brien's partner's revolver. The gunman fired, seriously wounding both officers. After shooting Officer O'Brien, the offender stood over the fallen officer and continued to fire. Both Officer O'Brien and his partner, Officer William Fahey, were shot and killed.

O'CONNELL, JEREMIAH E., Patrolman, Badge 1977, Roll 192, July 30, 1928, District 4: Officer Jeremiah O'Connell, while detailed to the Detective Bureau, learned that a gunman had just robbed and murdered a citizen. Officer O'Connell began a search for the dangerous offender and located him near an alley. As Officer O'Connell attempted to place the offender under arrest, the offender resisted and shot the dedicated officer.

O'CONNELL, TIMOTHY S., Sergeant, Badge 266, Roll 39, May 29, 1900, District 5: As Sergeant Timothy O'Connell walked to his car to return home, he was confronted by an armed robber. As Sergeant O'Connell drew his service revolver, the offender fired a shot and fled. The dedicated sergeant died as a result of his injuries.

O'CONNOR, JAMES E., Lieutenant, Badge 434, Roll 349, January 28, 1970, District 5: Lieutenant James O'Connor, in citizen dress, was conducting a robbery investigation at a finance company. While he interviewed the manager, an armed offender entered and announced a robbery. As the robber forced people into a back room, Lieutenant O'Connor attempted to subdue him. The gunman fired a shot, fatally wounding the heroic lieutenant.

O'CONNOR, JAMES M., Police Officer, Badge 4573, Roll 409, September 16, 1995, District 23: Officer James O'Connor observed two offenders committing a robbery. Taking immediate police action, the officer pursued the offender's vehicle. After Officer O'Connor curbed the vehicle, he confronted the robbers. A fierce gun battle ensued, in which the brave officer was fatally wounded.

O'CONNOR, JOSEPH A., Patrolman, Badge 3704, Roll 92, November 4, 1917, District 1: Officer Joseph O'Connor was approached by a man who precipitated an altercation. When Officer O'Connor placed the man under arrest, the offender suddenly pulled out a revolver. An exchange of gunfire ensued. The brave officer suffered fatal wounds during the exchange.

O'CONNOR, TIMOTHY, Patrolman, Badge 2079, Roll 120, December 20, 1920, District 5: Officer Timothy O'Connor, while assigned to guard the garage for delivery trucks of a major department store, observed six armed men enter the garage. After seeing Officer O'Connor, the men began firing their guns. Officer O'Connor suffered a serious wound in the attack and died as a result of his injury.

O'CONNOR, WILLIAM A., Patrolman, Badge 3470, Roll 191, June 4, 1928, District 7: Officer William O'Connor observed armed offenders robbing a soft drink parlor. After preventing the robbery, Officer O'Connor placed the offenders under arrest. Suddenly, one of the offenders drew a revolver and fired. The brave officer was killed instantly.

O'DONNELL, EDWARD M., Patrolman, Badge 3363, Roll 225, June 9, 1931, District 21: Officer Edward O'Donnell was providing security to a businesswoman transporting cash and checks from a bakery to a bank. While en route, they were accosted by two armed robbers. When Officer O'Donnell attempted to arrest one offender, the second offender fired a gun. The dedicated officer was fatally wounded.

O'MALLEY, PATRICK E., Patrolman, Badge 1346, Roll 277, August 30, 1938, District 19: Officer Patrick O'Malley observed four armed offenders enter a lounge and announce a robbery. A gun battle ensued in which Officer O'Malley suffered a serious gunshot wound. The brave officer died as a result of his injuries.

O'MALLEY, WILLIAM J., Probationary Patrolman, Badge 2, Roll 135, December 30, 1922, District 8: Officer William O'Malley was conducting an investigation for a known robbery offender. Officer O'Malley located the offender threatening a citizen on the street. As Officer O'Malley bravely attempted to shield the citizen from danger, the offender drew a gun and shot the citizen. The offender then fired at Officer O'Malley. The bullet dented Officer O'Malley's police star before striking and killing him.

O'MEARA, PATRICK, Patrolman, Badge 94, Roll 1, August 4, 1872, District 1: Officer Patrick O'Meara and his partner were assigned to execute an arrest warrant for an individual who was wanted for battery. While canvassing the taverns in the neighborhood, they were able to locate the offender. Officer O'Meara guarded the front door to prevent the offender's escape, while his partner served the warrant. Suddenly, the offender pulled a revolver from his boot and fired a fatal shot at Officer O'Meara.

O'NEILL, PATRICK J., Detective Sergeant, Badge 2963, Roll 123, March 23, 1921, Unit 620: Sergeant Patrick O'Neill led a squad of detectives to a building to apprehend a murderer. When Sergeant O'Neill and fellow officers surrounded the building, the offender ran out the rear door and opened fire. The brave sergeant died of multiple gunshot wounds.

O'ROURKE, MICHAEL J., Patrolman, Badge 426, Roll 44, October 23, 1903, District 2: Officer Michael O'Rourke provided an escort to a citizen who was a victim of an assault. As they walked, Officer O'Rourke alertly noticed the offender in an alley. The officer pushed the woman into a doorway and confronted the man. The offender fired a gunshot, striking Officer O'Rourke. The courageous officer died two days later.

OAKLEY, MICHAEL W., Patrolman, Badge 5445, Roll 229, December 13, 1931, District 20: Officer Michael Oakley was walking home when he was accosted by an armed robber. A gun battle ensued, during which Officer Oakley was wounded. The brave officer died as a result of his injuries.

OFFICER, JOHN R., Patrolman, Badge 700, Roll 255, April 13, 1934, District 2: While on patrol, Officer John Officer investigated suspicious activity inside a shoe shop. Upon entering the shop, he discovered three armed offenders robbing the patrons and clerks. A gun battle ensued, and the courageous officer was fatally wounded.

OLSEN, HARRY S., Patrolman, Badge 219, Roll 210, February 8, 1930, District 18: Officer Harry Olsen was assigned to motorcycle patrol in Lincoln Park. While covering his beat, Officer Olsen tragically collided with an automobile. Officer Olsen died as a result of the serious injuries he sustained.

OLSON, HAROLD F., Patrolman, Badge 2911, Roll 157, June 13, 1925, District 8: Officer Harold Olson and his partner observed three known criminals in a speeding automobile. The officers pursued the vehicle until the offender's vehicle crashed. The officers immediately pulled up and exited their police vehicle. The criminals staggered out of their vehicle and fired three shotgun blasts. Officer Olson suffered fatal wounds. His partner, Officer Charles Walsh, was also fatally wounded in the incident.

OLSON, JOHN A., Patrolman, Badge 5397, Roll 278, October 20, 1938, District 15: Officer John Olson was assigned to escort a carrier to the bank when an offender approached from behind and struck him with a lead-filled rubber hose. A second offender threatened the cashier with his gun and grabbed the bag of money. As Officer Olson pursued the offender with the money, the other offender fired a shot. The heroic officer was fatally shot.

OMAN, ROBERT E., Patrolman, Badge 188, Roll 294, November 7, 1946, Unit 40: Officer Robert Oman was assigned to motorcycle patrol. While covering his beat, Officer Oman lost control of his motorcycle. Tragically, Officer Oman suffered fatal injuries in the accident.

OSTILLER, PETER H., Patrolman, Badge 3376, Roll 97, June 12, 1918, District 9: While on foot patrol, Officer Peter Ostiller was struck by an automobile at a busy intersection. To avoid colliding with a street car, a motorist made a sharp turn and struck the unfortunate officer. The dedicated officer was immediately rushed to the hospital where he died the same day of his injuries.

OSTLING, ELMER R., Patrolman, Badge 1189, Roll 247, July 22, 1933, District 11: Officer Elmer Ostling and his partner, Officer John Skopek, observed three men in a stolen car. After a short chase, the officers curbed the vehicle. As the dedicated officers exited their vehicle, they were struck by numerous bullets fired by the offenders. Officer Ostling suffered multiple gunshot wounds. Both Officer Ostling and his partner, Officer John Skopek, were fatally wounded in the incident.

PALDINA, CHARLES, Patrolman, Badge 493, Roll 128, January 20, 1922, Unit 610: Officer Charles Paldina entered a drinking establishment to apprehend a wanted felon. As Officer Paldina was making the arrest, the offender produced a revolver and began firing, in his attempt to flee. Officer Paldina was seriously wounded, but continued to pursue the gunman. The courageous officer died as a result of his injuries while en route to the hospital.

PALESE, MICHAEL R., Sergeant, Badge 1514, Roll 377, March 22, 1977, District 17: Sergeant Michael Palese, while participating in an emergency plan to find a missing six-year-old girl, searched the railroad tracks near the child's home. Heavy snow and swirling winds made visibility difficult. While searching near a railroad bridge, Sergeant Palese was too late in noticing an approaching commuter train. Tragically, the dedicated sergeant was struck and killed by the oncoming train.

PEELER, HENRY L., Patrolman, Badge 11174, Roll 338, June 5, 1968, District 7: Officer Henry Peeler and his partner responded to a disturbance on the street. When the officers approached, an offender fled and Officer Peeler took pursuit. The offender suddenly turned into a gangway and opened fire on Officer Peeler. Officer Peeler suffered several fatal wounds. It was later discovered that the offender was wanted in East St. Louis for the attempted murder of a police officer.

PEGUE, RICHARD E., Temporary Patrolman, Badge 371, Roll 293, July 3, 1946, Unit 140: Officer Richard Pegue arrested a criminal sexual assault offender and a woman attempting to obstruct the arrest. As Officer Pegue transported the prisoners to the police station, the female arrestee hit the officer with a bottle. At this point, the male offender gained possession of the officer's revolver and shot Officer Pegue. The brave officer died from his injury.

PENNELL, CHARLES F., Patrolman, Badge 1852, Roll 43, August 12, 1902, District 15: Officers Charles Pennell and his partner were following two suspected burglars. As Officer Pennell and his partner reached an alley, they were ambushed with a barrage of bullets by the suspects. Shots were returned by the courageous policemen, but both Officer Pennell and his partner, Officer Timothy Devine, were mortally wounded in the exchange of gunfire.

PENNEY, WILLIAM F., Patrolman, Badge 5365, Roll 259, July 24, 1934, Unit 640: While conducting an investigation, Officer William Penney was attacked by a group of men. The offenders fled after the attack. When Officer Penney returned later to search for his attackers, he was fatally shot by one of the men.

PERKINS, ROBERT H., Police Officer, Badge 16557, Roll 406, March 7, 1992, District 3: Officer Robert Perkins observed an individual matching the description of a wanted burglary offender. As Officer Perkins questioned the suspect, the man resisted and a fierce struggle ensued. During the altercation, Officer Perkins suffered two gunshot wounds. The dedicated officer died as a result of his injuries.

PERRIN, WILLIAM A., Patrolman, Badge 846, Roll 150, November 30, 1924, District 4: Officer William Perrin was assigned to patrol the community in civilian dress and in an unmarked police vehicle. As Officer Perrin pulled alongside a vehicle, the driver of the other vehicle mistakenly believed that he was about to be robbed, drew a pistol and began firing at Officer Perrin. Officer Perrin suffered multiple and fatal gunshot wounds in the tragic incident.

PIJANOWSKI, JOSEPH L., Patrolman, Badge 1427, Roll 118, November 18, 1920, District 9: Officer Joseph Pijanowski was assigned to escort a former alderman who had recently received threats to his safety. Upon arrival at the politician's home, Officer Pijanowski observed three men hiding beneath the porch. After being ordered to come out, the offenders opened fire. Officer Pijanowski suffered a severe wound and died in a hospital four days later.

POE, BERNIE, Patrolman, Badge 1427, Roll 118, November 18, 1920, District 9: While on patrol, Officer Bernie Poe heard a cry for help and rushed to the scene. He discovered a fellow officer engaged in a violent struggle with an offender. Just as Officer Poe arrived, the offender gained control of the other officer's service revolver. The offender turned and fired, striking Officer Poe. The wound proved to be fatal.

POLLARD, CHARLES, Patrolman, Badge 5540, Roll 335, December 14, 1967, District 10: Officer Charles Pollard was shot and killed behind his home. Officer Pollard was the apparent victim of an armed robbery.

POWELL JR., JOHN, Patrolman, Badge 1168, Roll 27, September 6, 1892, District 14: Officer John Powell, while conducting a raid on an illegal racetrack, pursued a racehorse owner who was brandishing a gun while attempting to escape. Officer Powell was shot twice while apprehending the offender. The brave officer died from his injuries. The same offender also killed a second officer, Henry McDowell.

PRENDERGAST, JOHN J., Detective Sergeant, Badge 375, Roll 73, August 30, 1914, District 18: Detective Sergeant John Prendergast escorted a burglar to the police station. As they waited with several other people at an intersection, an automobile containing five intoxicated men approached at high speed. Sergeant Prendergast shouted a warning to the citizens. The prisoner was pulled to safety, but tragically, the automobile struck Sergeant Prendergast. The heroic sergeant was killed instantly.

QUINN, JOHN, Patrolman, Badge 2797, Roll 45, November 22, 1903: Officer John Quinn was assigned to investigate several armed robberies and murders being perpetrated by known offenders. During the course of the investigation, Officer Quinn located one of the offenders. While attempting to make the arrest, the offender resisted, and Officer Quinn was fatally wounded.

QUINNAN, DANIEL J., Patrolman, Badge 7899, Roll 331, September 19, 1996, District 1: Officer Daniel Quinnan, while working as a vice officer in plain clothes, entered a tavern moments after an armed robbery had occurred. As Officer Quinnan approached the offender in a doorway, the gunman fired a fatal shot.

QUIRK, JOHN W., Patrolman, Badge 9866, Roll 320, January 13, 1958, District 14: Officer John Quirk was sitting in his parked car when two gunmen jumped into the back seat. The offenders announced a robbery and ordered Officer Quirk to start driving. Officer Quirk complied and, in an attempt to thwart the robbery, deliberately crashed his vehicle. At the same time, Officer Quirk drew his service revolver and fired upon the startled robbers. In the ensuing gun battle, Officer Quirk was fatally wounded.

RACE, ALBERT, Patrolman, Badge 7, Roll 2, October 4, 1878, District 1: Officer Albert Race observed a horse-drawn wagon filled with expensive merchandise in front of a pawn shop. Two suspicious men sat in the wagon. When Officer Race approached the men in order to question them, one of the men produced a revolver and fired one shot. The brave officer was struck and died shortly afterward.

RAPPAPORT, FRANK G., Patrolman, Badge 12256, Roll 346, November 13, 1969, District 3: Officer Frank Rappaport responded to a call of a police officer shot. Upon arrival, Officer Rappaport discovered an intense gun battle between officers and offenders. Officer Rappaport observed an officer get shot near a rear porch. As Officer Rappaport attempted to assist the wounded officer, he was struck by gunfire. The brave officer died as a result of his injuries en route to the hospital. Officer John Gilhooly was also fatally wounded in the incident.

REDDEN, THOMAS, Patrolman, Badge 621, Roll 15, May 17, 1886, District 2: Officer Thomas Redden was one of several officers assigned to disperse a protest near Haymarket Square on May 4, 1886. A bomb exploded which was immediately followed by a fierce gun battle. Officer Redden suffered several gunshot wounds during the gun battle, as well as serious injuries from the bomb blast. Officer Redden was the sixth of eight officers to die in what history records as the Haymarket Tragedy.

REDLICH, HARRY J., Patrolman, Badge 5406, Roll 245, July 8, 1933, District 11: Officer Harry Redlich, while directing traffic, was informed that an advertising agency was being robbed. Officer Redlich rushed to the scene and apprehended one of the robbers. While searching the offender for weapons, Officer Redlich was approached from behind by a second armed robber who fired five shots at the officer. The heroic officer died as a result of his injuries.

REDMOND, PATRICK J., Patrolman, Badge 1583, Roll 257, May 8, 1934, District 5: Officer Patrick Redmond was assigned to guard a payroll exchange. At this time, four offenders entered and announced a robbery. Two of the offenders were armed with shotguns. As Officer Redmond confronted the gunmen to place them under arrest, one offender fired. The courageous officer was struck by the shotgun blast and died.

REID, EUGENE L., Patrolman, Badge 5408, Roll 288, May 7, 1945, District 21: Officer Eugene Reid, while on patrol, observed a man attacking a woman on the street. As Officer Reid rushed to the scene, the man displayed a gun and fired a shot. Although wounded, Officer Reid returned fire. The brave officer died as a result of the injuries he sustained.

RILEY, WALTER J., Sergeant, Badge 266, Roll 172, October 26, 1926, District 25: While on patrol, Sergeant Walter Riley's vehicle collided with another automobile. The violent impact resulted in Sergeant Riley sustaining several serious injuries. The dedicated sergeant died at the scene in the tragic accident.

RIORDAN, JAMES J., First Deputy Superintendent, Badge 103, Roll 382, June 6, 1981, Unit 40: First Deputy Superintendent James Riordan was in a restaurant when he took police action to quell a disturbance caused by a patron. As Deputy Riordan was escorting the offender off the premises, the offender drew a revolver and fired several shots. Deputy Riordan was struck and died as a result of his injuries.

RIZZATO, ANTHONY N., Patrolman, Badge 12407, Roll 353, July 17, 1970, Unit 153: Officer Anthony Rizzato and his partner were assigned to foot patrol. While walking their beat in a public housing development, Officer Rizzato and his partner were struck by sniper bullets. The dedicated officer and his partner, Sergeant James Severin, died as a result of the gunshot wounds they sustained.

ROBERTS, WILLIAM A., Patrolman, Badge 3566, Roll 112, May 14, 1920, District 2: Officer William Roberts observed a suspicious man carrying a bag. Unknown to the officer, the man had just robbed a railroad mail car. When Officer Roberts attempted to question the man as to the contents of the bag, the man drew a gun and opened fire. A gun battle ensued, in which Officer Roberts was seriously wounded. The brave officer later died from the injuries he sustained.

ROBINSON, CLAYTON, Detective, Badge 6166, Roll 340, October 26, 1968, Unit 630: Detective Clayton Robinson confronted a man causing a disturbance on the street. After the arrest was made, the offender was able to retrieve a hidden gun and fire a shot at Detective Robinson. The dedicated detective was seriously wounded and died the next day in a hospital.

ROBINSON, PHILIP L., Patrolman, Badge 777, Roll 19, September 5, 1887, District 2: Officer Philip Robinson was informed by two citizens that a man on the street had fired a gun at them. Officer Robinson observed the offender fleeing and immediately took up the pursuit. After ignoring an order to halt, the offender turned and fired three shots at the officer. Officer Robinson returned fire and courageously continued the chase. The gunman fired a final shot, striking the officer. The heroic officer died five days later.

ROSENTRETER, WILLIAM J., Patrolman, Badge 3980, Roll 75, November 6, 1914, District 23: Officer William Rosentreter, while investigating a disturbance at a drinking establishment, observed an intoxicated man smashing a glass door and attempting to enter. As Officer Rosentreter detained him, the offender turned around, placed a revolver to the officer's neck and fired. The courageous officer died shortly thereafter as a result of his injuries.

ROUSHORN, RICHARD, Sergeant, Badge 374, Roll 308, September 11, 1954, Unit 177: Sergeant Richard Roushorn arrested a truck driver who had committed a hit and run. As Sergeant Roushorn effected the arrest, the offender gained possession of the sergeant's service revolver and shot at the sergeant several times. The dedicated sergeant died from the wounds he sustained.

ROWE, JOHN, Patrolman, Badge 3045, Roll 71, August 16, 1914, District 15: Officer John Rowe attempted to apprehend a gang of armed offenders robbing ticket agents in elevated train stations. During their crime spree, they had killed one agent and wounded three other citizens. Officer Rowe assisted fellow officers engaged in a running gun battle with the offenders. When Officer Rowe attempted to stop the gunmen, he was shot. The brave officer died from the injuries he sustained.

RUIZ, IRMA, Police Officer, Badge 16823, Roll 400, September 22, 1988, Unit 074: A heavily armed gunman went on a shooting rampage, killing three people and wounding another. The offender then entered an elementary school filled with children. Already inside the school, Officer Irma Ruiz learned of the situation and confronted the dangerous offender. After wounding one officer, the gunman fired at Officer Ruiz. The courageous officer was fatally wounded.

RUMBLER, WILLIAM P., Patrolman, Badge 2358, Roll 216, October 12, 1930, District 18: Officer William Rumbler, while inside a cafe, observed three armed men enter. At this time, the men announced a robbery. Officer Rumbler stepped forward to stop the robbery and place the offenders under arrest. An intense gun battle ensued, in which the brave officer was fatally wounded.

RUSSELL, WILLIAM J., Detective Sergeant, Badge 85, Roll 58, June 12, 1909, Unit 601: Sergeant William Russell was assigned to maintain order in a union hall. When Sergeant Russell observed a known criminal in the area, he went to investigate. As Sergeant Russell approached, the offender drew a pistol and fired twice. The heroic sergeant was struck and died instantly from his injuries.

RUTHY, ANTHONY L., Patrolman, Badge 4158, Roll 222, April 30, 1931, Unit 151: While directing traffic at a downtown intersection, Officer Anthony Ruthy observed a disturbance on the street involving another police officer. An offender was resisting arrest and was struggling with Officer Patrick Durkin. The offender fired a revolver, striking Officer Durkin. When Officer Ruthy ran to assist, he was shot twice. Both courageous officers were fatally wounded during the incident.

RYAN, JOHN J., Patrolman, Badge 5618, Roll 211, February 24, 1930, District 23: Officer John Ryan was assigned to serve an arrest warrant on a robbery offender. Officer Ryan went to the robbery offender's apartment to make the arrest. In an effort to resist the arrest, the offender produced a revolver and began firing. Courageously, Officer Ryan returned fire, but was fatally wounded in the gun battle.

RYAN, PATRICK J., Patrolman, Badge 4940, Roll 249, August 8, 1933, District 14: Officer Patrick Ryan was approached by a disorderly patron in a drinking establishment. The offender suddenly attacked Officer Ryan and a struggle ensued. The offender fought to gain possession of Officer Ryan's service revolver. The offender fired the weapon, striking and fatally wounding Officer Ryan.

SAUSMAN, JOHN B., Patrolman, Badge 953, Roll 76, January 5, 1915, District 21: While on patrol, Officer John Sausman observed a wanted robbery offender at an intersection. As Officer Sausman attempted to make the arrest, the offender suddenly drew a revolver and fired. The courageous officer was struck and fatally wounded.

SCHAFFER, JAMES R., Sergeant, Badge 824, Roll 324, April 14, 1969, District 4: Sergeant James Schaffer responded to a man shot in an apartment. As Sergeant Schaffer and fellow officers climbed the rear stairs to the apartment porch, they were met with a burst of gunfire. Sergeant Schaffer bravely engaged in a gun battle with the offender. Tragically, the sergeant suffered a fatal gunshot wound. Detective Jerome Stubig was also fatally wounded in the incident.

SCHLINGER, GEORGE, Patrolman, Badge 1671, Roll 24, October 10, 1891, District 10: Officer George Schlinger, while responding to a disturbance, discovered a party being held by two men with extensive criminal records. When Officer Schlinger arrived, one offender jumped from an open window and fled. While Officer Schlinger courageously pursued, he was fatally shot.

SCHMITZ, FREDERICK M., Patrolman, Badge 1253, Roll 161, November 9, 1925, District 1: Officer Frederick Schmitz was tragically killed in a bomb explosion at his home. Subsequent investigation revealed that the bomb was placed in his home by an offender formerly arrested by Officer Schmitz.

SCHNABLE, HENRY, Patrolman, Badge 1062, Roll 59, July 1, 1909, District 2: Officer Henry Schnable encountered a burglar leaving a building with a bundle under his arm. The dedicated officer pursued the fleeing offender, and a gun battle ensued. During the exchange of gunfire, Officer Schnable was fatally wounded.

SCHNELL, WILLIAM H., Patrolman, Badge 2188, Roll 25, January 2, 1892, District 18: Officer William Schnell had served and protected the citizens of Chicago for more than 16 years. Always aware of the importance of firearm maintenance, Officer Schnell became a victim to an unanticipated discharge while cleaning his service revolver. Tragically, Patrolman Schnell died as a result of that unfortunate incident.

SCHOTT, RICHARD R., Police Officer, Badge 12028, Roll 413, December 3, 1997, District 9: While assigned to the lockup in the district station, Officer Richard Schott attempted to subdue a combative prisoner. A violent struggle ensued. Officer Schott, with the assistance of fellow officers, was finally able to restrain and control the offender, and place him in a cell. Officer Schott suddenly collapsed, suffering a fatal heart attack.

SCHUETZ, JOHN F., Patrolman, Badge 4381, Roll 99, January 27, 1919, District 25: Officer John Schuetz arrived at home to discover an armed man in the passageway next to his building. When Officer Schuetz confronted the offender, he fired a shot, striking the dedicated officer. Officer Schuetz died from the injuries he sustained.

SCHUTZ, PAUL E., Patrolman, Badge 4349, Roll 127, October 16, 1921, District 5: Officer Paul Schutz responded to the scene of shots fired. Upon arrival, Officer Schutz placed several offenders under arrest. As Officer Schutz confronted another offender near an alley, he was fired upon and suffered serious injuries. The brave officer perished from his wounds.

SCHWEIG, THOMAS, Patrolman, Badge 3427, Roll 66, July 15, 1911, District 14: Officer Thomas Schweig had just completed his tour of duty and was walking home when he was confronted by an armed offender. The gunman immediately fired a shot, striking Officer Schweig. The brave officer died instantly. Investigators determined that the murder was committed by one of several ex-convicts sentenced to prison as a result of Officer Schweig's police work.

SEVERIN, JAMES L., Sergeant, Badge 1319, Roll 354, July 17, 1970, Unit 153: Sergeant James Severin and his partner were assigned to foot patrol in a public housing development. As they walked their beat, both the dedicated sergeant and his partner, Officer Anthony Rizzato, were fatally ambushed by sniper fire.

SEVICK, JOHN G., Patrolman, Badge 6576, Roll 248, July 24, 1933, District 24: Officer John Sevick, while inside the Criminal Court Building, learned that two prisoners had escaped. Using a gun that had been smuggled to them by a family member, the offenders overtook a Deputy Sheriff, locking him in their cells. Officer Sevick confronted the offenders running through the courthouse hallways. The courageous officer was fatally shot by the escapees.

SEWARD, LEE R., Patrol Specialist, Badge 15906, Roll 398, December 30, 1987, District 23: Patrol Specialist Lee Seward responded to an apartment building to arrest an offender creating a disturbance. When the offender resisted, a struggle ensued. During the struggle, the offender gained possession of Officer Seward's service revolver and fired. The courageous officer was fatally wounded.

SHANLEY, WILLIAM T., Sergeant, Badge 760, Roll 253, December 14, 1933, Unit 610: Sergeant William Shanley was assigned to arrest an individual that picked up a particular car at an auto shop. Detectives had determined the car was owned by a wanted bank robber. As Sergeant Shanley made the arrest, the offender drew a revolver and fired. The brave sergeant suffered a fatal gunshot wound.

SHAUGHNESSY, MICHAEL, Detective, Badge 1475, Roll 48, May 22, 1904, District 14: Detective Michael Shaughnessy stationed himself outside the rear of a tavern, while his partner went inside to arrest a wanted thief. As soon as the partner entered, offenders attacked him. As the partner fired warning shots, Detective Shaughnessy rushed in to assist him. The partner, still being beaten, fired yet another shot, tragically striking Detective Shaughnessy. The wound was fatal.

SHEA, EDWARD G., Patrolman, Badge 3399, Roll 62, August 16, 1910, District 25: Officer Edward Shea was assigned to direct traffic at a railroad crossing. While directing motorists and pedestrians to safety, Officer Shea was tragically struck by a train. The train was traveling eastbound on a track meant to be used only by westbound trains. The dedicated officer died as a result of the injuries he sustained.

SHEEHAN, MICHAEL, Patrolman, Badge 545, Roll 14, May 9, 1886, District 3: Officer Michael Sheehan arrived with several other officers to disperse a protest meeting near Haymarket Square. On May 4, 1886 a bomb was thrown at the officers from an alley. The explosion was followed by an intense gun battle. Officer Sheehan sustained two serious gunshot wounds. He died five days later. Officer Sheehan was the fifth of eight heroic officers to die in the historic Haymarket Tragedy.

SHINE, JOHN P., Sergeant, Badge 44, Roll 52, October 10, 1905, District 9: Sergeant John Shine responded to a call of a gunman terrorizing a neighborhood. The gunman killed one woman, wounded two men and ran through the streets brandishing a pistol. The offender then barricaded himself in his apartment. Sergeant Shine courageously went to the apartment and demanded entry. The gunman fired through the door, striking the sergeant. Sergeant Shine died in the hospital two hours later.

SHOGREN, EMIL, Patrolman, Badge 985, Roll 189, April 18, 1928, District 9: Officer Emil Shogren, while detailed to the Detective Bureau, stopped his squad car to question two suspicious men on the street. As Officer Shogren approached, the offenders drew revolvers and opened fire. During an exchange of gunfire, Officer Shogren sustained fatal gunshot wounds.

SIMPSON, JOHN W., Patrolman, Badge 4774, Roll 105, July 28, 1919, District 21: Officer John W. Simpson was shot and seriously wounded by rioters during a period of civil unrest in the summer of 1919. The brave officer subsequently died from those wounds.

SIMS, OSBOURNE, Patrolman, Badge 4848, Roll 315, December 6, 1956, District 12: Officer Osbourne Sims responded to a burglary in progress. As Officer Sims arrived at the scene, he observed a citizen holding the burglar for the police. Suddenly, the perpetrator broke loose and fled on foot. After an extensive foot pursuit, Officer Sims was able to confront the burglar. At this time, the burglar was able to draw a revolver and fire at Officer Sims. The brave officer was killed in the encounter.

SINGLETON, OLIVER J., Detective, Badge 2131, Roll 348, November 27, 1969, Unit 188: Detective Oliver Singleton, while conducting an investigation, learned that a major armed robbery was about to be committed. Detective Singleton used his vehicle to block the escape route of the offenders. When Detective Singleton confronted the robbers, a gun battle ensued. The courageous detective suffered a serious wound and died several months later.

SKALA, LUDWIG, Patrolman, Badge 11, Row 79, November 21, 1915, District 1: Officer Ludwig Skala was assigned to patrol the city's parks on a police motorcycle. While patrolling his beat, Officer Skala's motorcycle malfunctioned. The officer was thrown from his motorcycle and died as a result of the injuries he suffered in the tragic accident.

SKIBA, VINCENT, Patrolman, Badge 1707, Roll 139, January 7, 1924, District 3: Officer Vincent Skiba was conducting an investigation in search of three armed robbery offenders. Officer Skiba located the offenders and attempted to place them under arrest. As the gunmen resisted, they drew their revolvers and fired. The courageous officer was fatally wounded.

SKOPEK, JOHN J., Patrolman, Badge 6614, Roll 246, July 22, 1933, District 11: Officer John Skopek and his partner, Officer Elmer Ostling, observed three men in a stolen car. After a short chase, the officers curbed the vehicle. As the dedicated officers exited their vehicle, they were struck by numerous bullets fired by the offenders. Officer Skopek was struck several times. Both Officer Skopek and his partner, Officer Elmer Ostling, were fatally wounded in the incident.

SMITH, EDWARD F., Patrolman, Badge 4567, Roll 224, May 30, 1931, District 11: Officer Edward Smith, while on patrol, responded to a disturbance at a local high school. Upon arrival, Officer Smith was confronted by a youth with a gun who turned and fired at the brave officer. Officer Smith was struck and died as a result of the injuries he sustained.

SMITH, EDWARD W., Patrolman, Badge 3002, Roll 54, August 4, 1907, District 25: Officer Edward Smith, while walking to his home, was accosted by an armed offender. The offender fired his gun, striking Officer Smith. Officer Smith, though seriously wounded, managed to arrive home. The murder remains unsolved.

SNEED, JESSE, Patrol Specialist, Badge 5078, Roll 188, April 11, 1928, District 21: Officer Jesse Sneed confronted two suspicious men standing on the corner. As Officer Sneed began to question them, one of the offenders pulled out a revolver and fired a shot. The brave officer sustained a fatal gunshot wound.

SOUNDERS, RALPH S., Probationary Patrolman, Badge 360, Roll 134, December 19, 1922, District 5: Officer Ralph Sounders observed two gunmen in the process of robbing a grocery store. Officer Sounders attempted to arrest the gunmen, and a struggle ensued. As the gunmen attempted to flee, one offender shot and seriously wounded Officer Sounders. The courageous officer died soon afterwards.

SPEAKER, CHARLES J., Patrolman, Badge 357, Roll 282, June 30, 1941, Unit 140: Officer Charles Speaker, while patrolling his beat, was suddenly fired upon from an automobile. The dedicated officer suffered a fatal gunshot wound. It was later learned that the shooter was wanted for three other murders.

SPERAKOS, GEORGE J., Patrolman, Badge 669, Roll 302, April 24, 1952, District 13: Officer George Sperakos observed three armed robbers enter a lounge and shoot at the bartender. As Officer Sperakos responded, an exchange of gunfire ensued. The brave officer suffered a fatal gunshot wound in the encounter.

STALLWORTH, HERMAN, Patrolman, Badge 10965, Roll 334, May 24, 1967, District 3: Officer Herman Stallworth observed a speeding motorist. When Officer Stallworth curbed the vehicle, one of the occupants pointed a gun at him and fired. The brave officer was struck and died as a result of his injuries.

STEINKE, ROMAN C., Patrolman, Badge 4706, Roll 307, February 13, 1954, District 14: Officer Roman Steinke and his partner attempted to arrest an offender wanted for assault. During the course of the arrest, the offender grabbed a revolver and fired three shots, striking both officers and a third person. Though mortally wounded, Officer Steinke was able to return fire, striking the gunman. Officer Jeremiah Lucey was also fatally wounded.

STOKKE, ALFRED M., Patrolman, Badge 2571, Roll 264, January 24, 1935, District 23: Officer Alfred Stokke was assigned to the surveillance of a tire shop in anticipation of a robbery. Officer Stokke observed three armed offenders enter and rob the shop. When the gunmen ordered the employees to the rear of the store, Officer Stokke entered and a gun battle ensued, during which the heroic officer was shot and killed.

STONE, MITCHELL A., Patrolman, Badge 4030, Roll 321, April 29, 1959, District 1: Officer Mitchell Stone learned from a citizen that a man on the street was carrying a concealed gun. Officer Stone followed the offender on foot into a parking lot while his partner in the squad car blocked the other end of the lot. When Officer Stone confronted the offender, the offender drew a weapon and fired. Officer Stone was struck and died as a result of his injuries. It was later learned that the gunman was wanted for several armed robberies.

STORM, WALTER J., Patrolman, Badge 6891, Roll 285, July 6, 1942, District 15: Officer Walter Storm observed an armed robbery in progress inside a liquor store. As Officer Storm entered to prevent the robbery, a gun battle ensued. The robbers fled, and the brave officer suffered fatal injuries as a result of the encounter.

STRINGFELLOW, WILLIAM H., Patrolman, Badge 2272, Roll 266, October 3, 1935, Unit 151: Officer William Stringfellow was assigned to escort a carrier to the bank. En route, Officer Stringfellow was approached by two armed robbers. A gun battle ensued in which the courageous officer suffered fatal gunshot wounds.

STRUGALA, ROBERT J., Patrolman, Badge 10236, Roll 370, June 16, 1974, District 10: While on patrol, Officer Robert Strugala heard gun shots being fired inside a tavern. The courageous officer ran to the scene and observed a man with a gun. As Officer Strugala confronted the man, the offender opened fire. Officer Strugala was struck and fatally wounded.

STUBIG, JEROME A., Detective, Badge 9127, Roll 343, April 14, 1969, Unit 603: Detective Jerome Stubig, while conducting a bomb investigation, observed several fellow officers rushing to apprehend a dangerous gunman. Detective Stubig, in an effort to assist his fellow officers, climbed the rear stairs to the gunman's apartment. Detective Stubig was met by the gunman. Both Detective Stubig and Sergeant James Schaffer were shot and fatally wounded during the encounter.

SUGG, VICTOR H., Patrolman, Badge 3701, Roll 256, April 24, 1934, District 24: While on patrol, Officer Victor Sugg investigated three suspicious men on the street. While conducting the investigation, one of the men attacked Officer Sugg, causing him to fall and strike his head against a brick wall. The brave officer suffered severe injuries and died nine days later.

SULLIVAN, ARTHUR J., Patrolman, Badge 3911, Roll 274, January 14, 1937, District 11: Officer Arthur Sullivan was informed by a citizen that the citizen had just been robbed. The citizen identified the offender. As Officer Sullivan confronted the offender, the man pulled out a revolver and fired. The courageous officer was shot and died as a result of his injuries.

SULLIVAN, JOSEPH J., Patrolman, Badge 5421, Roll 198, May 22, 1929, Unit 620: Officer Joseph Sullivan, while working in civilian dress, was conducting an investigation into the murder of Officer Raymond Martin. Later in the evening, Officer Sullivan was found in his automobile with a fatal gunshot wound. Detectives determined that the courageous officer had been killed in the course of his investigation.

SULLIVAN, LAWRENCE P., Patrolman, Badge 5225, Roll 153, April 16, 1925, District 4: While on patrol, Officer Lawrence Sullivan observed a suspicious man on the street. As Officer Sullivan stopped him for questioning, the offender produced a revolver. The gunman fired several times, striking Officer Sullivan. The brave officer was rushed to the hospital, where he died the following day.

SULLIVAN, TIMOTHY, Patrolman, Badge 811, Roll 21, June 13, 1888, District 13: Officer Timothy Sullivan was one of the courageous men wounded in the protest at Haymarket Square on May 4, 1886. Officer Sullivan sustained a gunshot wound that night which resulted in his death two years later. Officer Sullivan became the eighth and final officer to die as a result of the Haymarket Tragedy.

SUTTON, BLANTON W., Patrolman, Badge 5275, Roll 136, June 4, 1923, District 21: Officer Blanton Sutton observed a suspicious man inside a pool hall. Officer Sutton confronted the man, questioned him, and began to search him for concealed weapons. Suddenly, the offender produced a revolver and fired at the dedicated officer. Officer Sutton was struck and fatally wounded.

SWANSON, ARTHUR M., Patrolman, Badge 547, Roll 269, May 21, 1936, Unit 140: Officer Arthur M. Swanson was assigned to patrol the parks of the City of Chicago. Officer Swanson died in the performance of his duties.

SWEENEY, JOHN J., Patrolman, Badge 411, Roll 202, July 7, 1929, District 13: Officer John Sweeney, while on patrol, observed a gunman robbing a taxi cab-driver. As Officer Sweeney pursued, the offender fled into an alley. Officer Sweeney courageously continued the chase. As Officer Sweeney confronted the gunman, the offender opened fire. Officer Sweeney sustained a fatal gunshot wound during the encounter.

SZEWCZYK, LOUIS C., Patrolman, Badge 2521, Roll 209, January 27, 1930, District 4: While on patrol, Officer Louis Szewczyk observed three suspicious men on the street. As Officer Szewczyk approached to interview the men, one of the offenders suddenly drew a pistol and fired. Officer Szewczyk was struck. The brave officer died shortly thereafter.

THOMAS JR., PAUL G., Patrolman, Badge 5620, Roll 357, November 20, 1970, District 6: Officer Paul Thomas was visiting his father at his father's place of business. While in a rear office, he heard two robbers enter and begin to scuffle with his father. Officer Thomas rushed to his father's aid and struggled with the gunmen. The offenders fired their weapons, striking the officer. The brave officer was rushed to the hospital, but died from his wounds two weeks later.

THOMPSON, GEORGE W., Patrolman, Badge 2009, Roll 162, November 14, 1925, District 21: While on patrol, Officer George Thompson observed two suspicious men on the street. As Officer Thompson stopped the men and began a search for concealed weapons, one of the men produced a revolver and opened fire. Officer Thompson was fatally wounded.

THORNTON JR., SPENCER, Patrolman, Badge 327, Roll 292, September 3, 1945, Unit 140: Officer Spencer Thornton, while on patrol, observed a murder on the street. Officer Thornton courageously confronted the murderer and attempted to place him under arrest. As the offender resisted, he displayed a revolver and fired. The brave officer was fatally wounded.

TIERNAN, JOSEPH P., Patrolman, Badge 3014, Roll 91, August 24, 1917, District 13: While walking his beat, Officer Joseph Tiernan observed suspicious activity behind a dry goods store. As Officer Tiernan investigated, he noticed two burglars breaking into the basement of the store. As Officer Tiernan placed them under arrest, one of the offenders drew a revolver and began firing. The courageous officer was shot three times. Officer Tiernan was taken to a hospital where he died the next day.

TIGHE, THOMAS E., Patrolman, Badge 2700, Roll 64, March 11, 1911, District 10: Officer Thomas Tighe, while on patrol, located a known offender. While making the arrest, Officer Tighe was attacked by a group of the offender's friends. During the struggle, a gunshot was fired, striking Officer Tighe and resulting in a critical wound. Officer Tighe died one month later as a result of the injuries he sustained.

TORPY, THOMAS E., Patrolman, Badge 525, Roll 263, September 22, 1934, District 2: Officer Thomas Torpy and his partner were assigned to apprehend a known murderer and armed robber. The officers waited at the offender's apartment for his return. As the offender arrived, he observed Officer Torpy and opened fire. Officer Torpy was fatally wounded.

TORRES, JOSE M., Police Officer, Badge 13988, Roll 381, August 21, 1979, District 10: Officer Jose Torres was investigating an auto accident at an intersection when he was struck by an intoxicated, hit-and-run driver. The offender was speeding and had disobeyed a stop sign. Officer Torres was critically injured and died of his injuries 15 days after the tragic accident.

TOTH, MICHAEL, Patrolman, Badge 7334, Roll 273, November 8, 1936, District 9: Officer Michael Toth responded to a disturbance call. As Officer Toth searched an offender for concealed weapons, a struggle ensued. During the struggle, the offender drew a revolver and fired. The brave officer was struck several times and died as a result of his injuries.

TRUMBULL, GEORGE H., Patrolman, Badge 899, Roll 72, August 17, 1914, District 21: While on patrol, Officer George Trumbull investigated an assault. While gathering information on the street, Officer Trumbull was confronted by the wanted offender. Officer Trumbull was shot several times while attempting to return fire. The dedicated officer died as a result of his injuries.

TUCKER, JOHN, Patrolman, Badge 9168, Roll 339, October 8, 1968, District 4: Officer John Tucker observed an armed robber enter a bank. Officer Tucker hid behind a pillar as the robber approached a teller's cage. As Officer Tucker approached the gunman from behind, the offender turned around and fired. The courageous officer was fatally wounded in the encounter.

URBAN, JOSEPH H., Detective Sergeant, Badge 518, Roll 93, December 6, 1917, District 18: While investigating burglaries in the community, Sergeant Joseph Urban entered a closed store in the neighborhood. At this time, a nearby patrolman walking his beat observed Sergeant Urban inside the store and mistook him for a burglar. In the confusion, the patrolman fired a shot, tragically striking Sergeant Urban. The dedicated sergeant was taken to a hospital, where he died five days later.

VAN SCHAIK, ROGER, Police Officer, Badge 14299, Roll 380, March 3, 1979, District 5: Officer Roger Van Schaik and his partner were returning to their police vehicle when a motorist traveling in the opposite direction stopped alongside them. Without any warning, the offender began firing at the officers. Officer Van Schaik and his partner, Officer William Bosak, were fatally wounded in the tragic incident.

VINCENT, LARRY, Police Officer, Badge 15161, Roll 388, January 14, 1983, District 2: Officer Larry Vincent responded to a "burglary in progress" call. Officer Vincent and another officer entered the building, while two other officers positioned themselves outside a window. Officer Vincent fired at the offenders as they attempted to escape through a window. The officers stationed outside also fired at the fleeing offenders. Tragically, Officer Vincent was fatally shot in the crossfire.

VOLLMAR, ARTHUR, Sergeant, Badge 886, Roll 196, February 22, 1929, District 23: Sergeant Arthur Vollmar, while on motorcycle patrol, was flagged down by a Citizen who stated that he had just been robbed. The victim identified the offender as he fled the scene. As Sergeant Vollmar pursued, the offender displayed a revolver and fired. The courageous sergeant was struck and died as a result of his injuries.

VONDRUSKA JR., JOHN, Patrolman, Badge 6048, Roll 220, January 1, 1931, District 11: Officer John Vondruska, while protecting the payroll of a taxi cab company, observed five armed robbers enter the company garage. The offenders were armed with a sawed-off shotgun and a machine gun. Officer Vondruska immediately confronted the armed robbers, and a gun battle ensued. The courageous officer was fatally wounded in the exchange.

WALLNER, EDWARD J., Patrolman, Badge 1533, Roll 36, January 5, 1899, District 11: Officer Edward Wallner was in pursuit of six gunmen that had just robbed a store. From a dark alley, the gunmen fired a volley of shots at the courageous officer. Although Officer Wallner was able to return fire, he was fatally struck in the exchange.

WALSH, CHARLES B., Patrolman, Badge 2811, Roll 156, June 13, 1925, District 21: Officer Charles Walsh and his partner observed three known criminals in a vehicle speeding down the street. The officers immediately pursued in their squad car. As the offenders crashed, the officers pulled up behind them. The criminals stumbled out of their vehicle and fired three shotgun blasts. Officer Walsh was struck and died as a result of his injuries. His partner, Officer Harold Olson, was also murdered.

WENZEL, ROBERT F., Patrolman, Badge 7495, Roll 362, January 19, 1973, Unit 151: Officer Robert Wenzel curbed a vehicle for a traffic violation. During the traffic stop, the motorist drew a revolver and fired two shots for no apparent reason. Officer Wenzel, though wounded, was able to return fire. The dedicated officer died as a result of the injuries he sustained.

WHITE, LAVAUGHN, Patrolman, Badge 7473, Roll 327, June 5, 1961, District 7: Officer LaVaughn White was walking past a tavern when he was summoned inside by the tavern owner. Inside, five armed men were committing a robbery. The offenders had seen Officer White through the window and ordered the tavern owner to call him inside. As the officer entered, a heated gun battle ensued. The brave officer wounded one of the robbers, but sustained fatal gunshot wounds during the exchange.

WILLIAMS, CHARLES H., Patrolman, Badge 210, Roll 283, December 10, 1941, Unit 140: Officer Charles Williams observed two armed robbers enter a lounge. As Officer Williams approached, one gunman fired a shot. Although wounded, Officer Williams drew his weapon and fired several shots at the offenders, who fled. The wound suffered by the dedicated officer was fatal.

WILLIAMS, JAMES A., Patrolman, Badge 942, Roll 141, July 16, 1924, District 21: While on patrol, Officer James Williams observed four armed gunmen robbing a citizen in a vacant lot. As Officer Williams attempted to apprehend the armed offenders, one of the offenders fired directly at him. The courageous officer was hit and died two days later from the gunshot injury.

WILSON, CORNELIUS, Patrolman, Badge 2902, Roll 103, May 1, 1919, District 21: While walking home after his tour of duty, Officer Cornelius Wilson observed three men suspected of committing a series of armed robberies. The officer approached them and asked a few questions. Without warning, two of the men produced handguns and began firing. Although Officer Wilson was able to return fire, the courageous officer was killed during the exchange.

WILSON, DENNIS, Patrolman, Badge 3511, Roll 111, April 10, 1920, District 21: Officer Dennis Wilson heard a gunshot while on patrol. The officer immediately rushed to the scene and learned that a gunman had fired at another man during a quarrel. Officer Wilson confronted the gunman and demanded his weapon. The gunman then fired a fatal shot at the brave officer.

WISTERT, KAZIMER, Sergeant, Badge 247, Roll 178, June 7, 1927, District 14: While on duty, Sergeant Kazimer Wistert was approached by a citizen who identified a man on the street who had committed a robbery. Sergeant Wistert followed the suspect into a building. As he entered the hallway, the offender suddenly turned around and fired a revolver. Sergeant Wistert was struck and seriously injured. The dedicated sergeant died from the injuries he sustained.

WITTBRODT, ARTHUR W., Patrolman, Badge 271, Roll 231, January 16, 1932, District 21: While on foot patrol, Officer Arthur Wittbrodt learned of a serious automobile accident. Officer Wittbrodt responded to the scene, riding on the running board of a citizen's vehicle. As they drove to the accident, the citizen lost control and Officer Wittbrodt was thrown from the vehicle. The injuries suffered by the dedicated officer were fatal.

WOLSKI, MARTIN, Patrolman, Badge 559, Roll 276, March 26, 1938, Unit 140: Officer Martin Wolski, while on patrol, noticed two suspicious men in the park. As Officer Wolski approached the men, he was immediately fired upon. The gunshot wound sustained by the dedicated officer was fatal.

WREN, JOHN A., Patrolman, Badge 3987, Roll 60, March 5, 1910, District 23: Officer John Wren investigated three suspicious men walking the streets in the early morning hours. When Officer Wren approached, the three offenders drew guns and fired. Though wounded, Officer Wren was able to return fire. The courageous officer died as a result of his wounds the next day.

WRIGHT, CLARENCE E., Patrolman, Badge 255, Roll 7, November 29, 1882, District 3: Officer Clarence Wright went to the apartment of a dangerous offender who had viciously attacked a citizen. When Officer Wright knocked on the apartment door, it was opened slightly by a woman. Before the officer spoke a word, the offender placed his gun over the woman's shoulder and fired. The courageous officer fell backwards and was killed instantly.

WRIGHT, GERALD L., Police Officer, Badge 3845, Roll 407, August 7, 1993, District 6: Officer Gerald Wright heard gunfire on the street. As Officer Wright responded to the scene, he was struck by a bullet. The wound suffered by the courageous officer proved to be fatal.

YOUNG, GREGORY I., Police Officer, Badge 16148, Roll 412, September 18, 1997, District 15: Officer Gregory Young was parked near a city park when he was approached by an armed robber. When the offender demanded money, Officer Young announced his office. An exchange of gunfire followed. The brave officer was fatally wounded.

ZAPOLSKY, ANTON, Patrolman, Badge 5369, Roll 260, July 30, 1934, District 1: Officer Anton Zapolsky and his partner observed an auto thief being chased by police. Officer Zapolsky and his partner apprehended the fleeing offender. Suddenly, the thief drew a revolver and shot Officer Zapolsky. The courageous officer died three days later.

March 1979, Honors Funeral of Police Officer Bosak, Killed in the Line of Duty.

Index